Enacting the Work
of Language Instruction:

High-Leverage Teaching Practices

Graphic Design by HBP/Ellipse Design

Edited by Robert M. Terry

Graphic in Figure 4.1, **U-Shaped Learning**, reprinted from *Second Language Acquisition* by Susan M. Gass and Larry Selinker with the permission of Taylor and Francis Group LLC Books.

ISBN: 978-1-942544-54-8

© 2017 by The American Council on the Teaching of Foreign Languages
1001 North Fairfax Street, Suite 200
Alexandria, VA 22314

Acknowledgments

The inspiration for this text came from ACTFL's Research Priorities in Foreign Language Education Project, which introduced the concept of high-leverage teaching practices (HLTPs) as a national priority in language education research in 2009, worked to identify these practices during professional meetings in the years that followed, and served as a catalyst for several research projects that were subsequently conducted in this area. These projects have called for further research to identify HLTPs that are specific to language education and that might be used as the focus of teacher education programs (see, for example, Hlas and Hlas, 2012).* The emerging theoretical perspectives and research studies on high-leverage teaching practices carried out by our colleagues, both in language education and in other fields such as mathematics, history, and science, have guided and informed our writing of this text. We believe that HLTPs have the potential to transform the way in which we prepare language teachers and ultimately the classroom experiences of our language learners. It is our hope that this text will be used to mediate initial teacher training and on-going professional development and for continuing the robust dialogue that Research Priorities began.

We recognize the influence of our students, graduates of the teacher preparation programs at our respective institutions, our colleagues, our publisher, and our reviewers on the thinking that enabled this text to materialize. To this end, we are grateful to Marty Abbott, Executive Director of the American Council on the Teaching of Foreign Languages, as well as the ACTFL Board of Directors, for the interest they took in publishing this text and the encouragement that they offered. We thank the production team at ACTFL whose diligent work and commitment to the project made the publication of the text a reality: Lisa Campo, our Production Editor, and Howie Berman, Director of Membership and Administration. We also acknowledge the work of HBP's Ellipse Design team, who are responsible for the cover design and page layout.

The creation of a text is a complex process, and we are extremely thankful for the expert guidance of our Managing Editor, Robert M. Terry (University of Richmond, VA), who provided valuable feedback on the content of each chapter as well as careful copy editing throughout. We appreciate the dedication, enthusiasm, and sense of humor he displayed throughout our months of working together! We are also deeply grateful to Kate Paesani, Director of the Center for Advanced Research on Language Acquisition (CARLA), who enthusiastically agreed to write the introduction to this book. As a former recipient of an ACTFL Research Priorities grant and now the director of CARLA, a nationally recognized research center that focuses on issues of teacher development, she is uniquely positioned to introduce and share her insights on this text.

Additionally, we recognize the contributions of our reviewers, who provided helpful comments and suggestions as well as motivational words to keep us going:

Jesse Carnevali	Franklin Regional School District, Murrysville, PA
Kristin J. Davin	Loyola University, Chicago, IL
Heather Hendry	University of Pittsburgh, PA
Cecilia Weaver	Harford County Public Schools, Bel Air, MD

---

* Hlas, A. C., & Hlas, C. S. (2012). A review of high-leverage teaching practices: Making connections between mathematics and foreign languages. *Foreign Language Annals, 45,* s76–s97.

On a more personal note, Eileen Glisan wishes to thank her institution, Indiana University of Pennsylvania (IUP), for the sabbatical leave she was granted to undertake the writing of this text. Specifically she is grateful for the support of Michael A. Driscoll, President; Timothy S. Moerland, Provost and Vice-President for Academic Affairs; Yaw Asamoah, Dean, College of Humanities and Social Sciences; and Sean McDaniel, Chair, Department of Foreign Languages. Finally, she is grateful for the continued encouragement of her family throughout the writing process: Roy, Nina and Max, Alex; as well as for the inspiration provided by her new granddaughter, Allie Andreya.

Richard Donato would like to thank Dean Alan Lesgold and Associate Dean Anthony Petrosky of the School of Education at the University of Pittsburgh for encouraging him to complete this book during the academic year, and to his graduate students at the University of Pittsburgh in the Department of French and Italian, the Department of Hispanic Languages, and the Department of Instruction and Learning, who piloted these pedagogical tools in their K-16 classes and offered valuable examples and suggestions for their improvement. Finally, he expresses his gratitude and heartfelt thanks to Elisabeth Sauvage-Callaghan, and to his daughter, Claire Donato, for their continued support during the writing of this text (and beyond).

We dedicate this text to the teacher candidates, novice teachers, and teacher educators in the field of language teaching who will use this text as part of their journey as they strive to provide the best possible classroom experience for language learners in the 21st century. It is our hope that this text makes visible what is often invisible and taken for granted during teacher preparation and professional development programs and that it inspires continued conversation about the fundamental practices at the core of what we do as language educators.

Table of Contents

Introduction

In 2015, as I prepared to teach my former department's required foreign language methods course for the first time in thirteen years, I faced a number of challenges. Among these was designing a course for a varied audience representing in-service K-12 teachers, graduate teaching assistants, future collegiate-level instructors, and seven different languages (Arabic, English as a Second Language, French, German, Italian, Latin, and Spanish). Additionally, I grappled with how find adequate time to treat all of the topics typical of a methods course in just fifteen weeks: principles of second language acquisition; an overview of methods and approaches; how to teach grammar, vocabulary, and the modes of communication; lesson planning and classroom management; assessment practices; and so on. Through the process of setting course objectives and designing the curriculum, however, I found that what mattered more to me was not coverage of content or transmission of information, but the opportunity for students to apply what they were learning in practical, yet theoretically grounded ways. As such, I designed the course to allow students time to connect theoretical concepts to the practice of teaching by observing and analyzing classroom practice and applying knowledge through collaborative activities. The result was a course grounded in praxis, or the dialogic relationship between what teachers know and what they know how to do (Lantolf & Poehner, 2014), and a diverse classroom community of practice.

Enacting the Work of Language Instruction: High-Leverage Teaching Practices, with its emphasis on defining, deconstructing, and applying those practices most essential to foreign language teaching, facilitates the kind of praxis orientation that is key to successful teacher learning. Indeed, this book provides a solution to common challenges teacher-educators face in designing and implementing methods courses, and it is a timely contribution to scholarship in teacher development, which has experienced a shift away from an exclusive focus on cognition (i.e., teacher's knowledge base, beliefs, and decision-making related to teaching) toward the behaviors in which effective teachers engage, how those behaviors relate to teacher knowledge, and how teacher-educators can implement professional development experiences that highlight theory-practice relationships (Grossman, Hammerness, & McDonald, 2009; Johnson, 2015; McDonald, Kazemi, & Kavanagh, 2013). In foreign language contexts, this shift was underscored in a recent special issue of the *Modern Language Journal* in which the editors argued that the body of cognitively-oriented research on teacher development has failed to adequately address questions related to how foreign language teachers create effective learning environments for their students or how teacher education programs should best incorporate results from teacher cognition research (Kubanyiova & Feryok, 2015). They further highlighted the need to investigate cognition in action; that is, to create opportunities to study and implement relationships among teacher cognition, teaching practice, and student learning. Likewise, in this same special issue, Johnson (2015) pointed to the importance of approaches to language teacher education that view learning "as a dialogic process of co-constructing knowledge that is situated in and emerges out of participation in particular sociocultural practices and contexts" (p. 516).

High-leverage teaching practices (HLTPs), defined as the "tasks and activities that are essential for skillful beginning teachers to understand, take responsibility for, and be prepared to carry out in order to enact their core instructional responsibilities" (Ball & Forzani, 2009, p. 504), represent one answer to the question of how teacher education programs can apply results from teacher cognition research and assist teachers in creating effective learning environments for their students. Throughout *Enacting the Work of Language Instruction*, the authors illustrate how HLTPs fill this gap in teacher development research by presenting six core practices essential to effective foreign language teaching and connecting them to current research in second language acquisition, language pedagogy, and teacher development. To realize this task, each practice is deconstructed to make it accessible to teachers, put into practice through rehearsal and self-assessment, and contextualized within broader issues related to foreign language teaching and learning. Through this careful work, the authors show that the practice of teaching cannot be reduced to a list of easily replicated behaviors, but rather is principled and purposeful.

As highlighted in this text, HLTPs are not a teaching method or approach; they are core practices that facilitate implementation of a method or approach. A unique feature of *Enacting the Work of Language Instruction*, then, is its complementarity with all types of teaching methods and approaches, such as communicative language teaching, task-based approaches, or literacy- and genre-based approaches. Because the authors do not prescribe a particular method or approach in this text, there is space for teachers and teacher-educators to express their individuality and to decide how HLTPs map onto the approach(es) they use in their classrooms. For example, in applying the model for sequencing tasks related to the practice of guiding learners to interpret authentic texts (HLTP#3, Chapter 3), a teacher adopting a literacy-based approach might incorporate situated practice activities such as predicting into the pre-reading/pre-viewing phase to immerse learners in the text without conscious reflection; overt instruction activities such as information mapping into the interpretive phase to help learners connect language forms to the meanings they convey; critical framing activities such as critical focus questions into the interpretation/ discussion phase to encourage cultural or genre comparisons; and transformed practice activities such as story retelling into the creativity phase to use knowledge gained from the previous phases to communicate in new and creative ways (Kern, 2000; Paesani, Allen, & Dupuy, 2016). Through these varied activity types grounded in literacy-based pedagogy, teachers enact the practice of guiding learners to interpret an authentic text.

In addition to its emphasis on praxis and its adaptability to various teaching methods and approaches, this text is also relevant for a range of teachers and teacher-educators. Although the emphasis is on pre-service K-12 teaching, as the authors point out, the practices, concepts, activities, and discussions herein are applicable across K-16 contexts and to novice and experienced teachers alike. As such, HLTPs may help bridge the divide that often exists between researchers and practitioners and between secondary and post-secondary teaching contexts; they can serve as a mediating tool to unite those who share the common goal of effective foreign language teaching. Moreover, because the six practices presented in this text build on well-established and empirically tested research in areas such as mathematics, history, and science education, *Enacting the Work of Language Instruction* exemplifies what we share in common with other disciplines. This work is essential given the prioritization of STEM fields and the less prominent role of the humanities in 21st century educational contexts. Scholarship on HLTPs in foreign language contexts of the type presented in this text shows that there is a shared language for talking about teaching and teacher development across disciplines and that the humanities have a relevant and vital role to play in determining that shared language.

At the Center for Advanced Research on Language Acquisition (CARLA) at the University of Minnesota, part of our mission is to advance the quality of foreign language teaching and learning by conducting research and sharing the knowledge gained from that research across disciplines and educational contexts. We therefore cultivate a unified view of the enterprise of teaching and apply the very principles that underlie work on HLTPs: the dialogic relationship between research and practice and the importance of developing skillful language teachers who impact upon student learning. *Enacting the Work of*

Language Instruction will therefore serve as a useful reference as we develop future research projects, workshops, summer institutes, and other activities that promote foreign language teaching and learning. In addition, through the principled presentation of six practices essential for effective foreign language teaching, the authors provide a solid foundation for future research on HLTPs in areas such as determining additional core practices; exploring practices in which experienced teachers engage and how those practices inform education of novice teachers; investigating how teachers appropriate HLTPs into their classroom practice; mapping HLTPs onto specific methods or approaches; or connecting HLTPs in foreign languages to other disciplines. Lastly, *Enacting the Work of Language Instruction* is a valuable tool for teacher-educators facing the challenges of designing and implementing a foreign language methods course and for novice and experienced instructors facing the challenges of teaching effectively and promoting student learning. Both audiences have much to gain from the praxis orientation of this text, the definition, deconstruction, and application of each core practice presented within it, the cycle of enactment presented in the final chapter, and the ways in which HLTPs are situated in relation to broader issues in foreign language teaching and learning.

Kate Paesani
Director, Center for Advanced Research on Language Acquisition (CARLA)
University of Minnesota

References

Ball, D. L., & Forzani, F. M. (2009). The work of teaching and the challenge of teacher education. *Journal of Teacher Education, 60*, 497–511.

Grossman, P., Hammerness, K., & McDonald, M. (2009). Redefining teaching, re-imagining teacher education. *Teachers and Teaching: Theory and Practice, 15*(2), 273–289.

Johnson, K. E. (2015). Reclaiming the relevance of L2 teacher education. *Modern Language Journal, 99*(3), 515–528.

Kern, R. (2000). *Literacy and language teaching.* Oxford, England: Oxford University Press.

Kubanyiova, M. & Feryok, A. (2015). Language teacher cognition in applied linguistics research: Revisiting the territory, redrawing the boundaries, reclaiming the relevance. *Modern Language Journal, 99*(3), 435–449.

Lantolf, J. P., & Poehner, M. E. (2014). *Sociocultural theory and the pedagogical imperative in L2 education: Vygotskian praxis and the research/practice divide.* New York, NY: Routledge.

McDonald, M., Kazemi, E., & Kavanagh, S. S. (2013). Core practices and pedagogies of teacher education: A call for a common language and collective activity. *Journal of Teacher Education, 64*(5), 378–386.

Paesani, K., Allen, H. W., & Dupuy, B. (2016). *A multiliteracies framework for collegiate foreign language teaching.* Upper Saddle River, NJ: Pearson.

PRELIMINARY CHAPTER

Introducing High-Leverage Teaching Practices (HLTPs)

"Great teachers aren't born—they're taught."
—Teacher Works, 2016

The purpose of this text is to present a set of **high-leverage teaching practices** that are essential for novice teachers to enact in their classrooms to support second language learning and development. High-leverage teaching practices (HLTPs) are the "tasks and activities that are essential for skillful beginning teachers to understand, take responsibility for, and be prepared to carry out in order to enact their core instructional responsibilities" (Ball & Forzani, 2009, p. 504). The focus of this text, therefore, is not on a body of knowledge that teachers should possess or standards that they must attain nor is its focus on a long list of "best practices" that teachers should intuitively be able to orchestrate in their classrooms. Rather, this text is designed to assist teachers in learning *how* to enact specific practices deemed essential to foreign language teaching by deconstructing them into various **instructional moves.** Deconstruction of the practice is essential given that the instructional moves of these practices are complex, often impossible to perceive through observation, and difficult to envision and enact based only on theoretical descriptions and discussions. Thus, this text is focused on "practicing" the practices as a way to acquire skill in enacting them through the use of a set of tools to plan and self-assess performance when carrying them out. In other words, this text seeks to make *visible* complex teaching moves that are often *invisible* through observations of classroom teaching.

Further, the text seeks to enable novice teachers to understand how the selected practices can address specific teaching challenges and to think strategically about how their actions within a given practice serve a larger educational and instructional purpose. The goals of the text will be accomplished by means of a purposeful discussion of the practices, including the teaching challenges they address, their deconstruction into smaller parts, and suggestions for ways to rehearse them in a guided fashion as well as to self-assess teaching performance.

This text is intended to complement a methodology textbook by providing the "practice" elements of teacher preparation. The text presupposes a professional knowledge base regarding the fundamental principles of language acquisition and teaching, such as those found in a methodology text for novice teachers. Although a brief theoretical foundation is provided as the basis for each HLTP, users of this text will need to consult a methodology text for more detailed information about concepts that are either new or not thoroughly understood.[1]

---

[1] One such methodology text with a comprehensive theoretical foundation regarding language acquisition and language teaching is *Teacher's Handbook: Contextualized Language Instruction*, 5th edition, by Shrum and Glisan (2016).

The text is designed to serve multiple audiences. First, it can be implemented as a tool by faculty in foreign language teacher preparation programs as they guide their teacher candidates to do the work of teaching in field experiences, i.e., to enact the selected high-leverage teaching practices. Pre-service teachers who are enrolled in a practicum course or peer-teaching laboratory course can use this text as they engage in practicing these HLTPs in anticipation of enacting them in their student teaching or practicum experiences. Additionally, more experienced in-service teachers can benefit from the text to deepen their understanding of current research-based practices and how to enact them in their classes. In a similar vein, the text can be a tool to mediate the professional development of in-service teachers and teacher educators, who might use the text for purposes of lesson study and collaboration with peers within a practice-oriented approach to teacher preparation. In essence, this text is a valuable resource for foreign language professionals at all levels of instruction and at any point in the career continuum. Further, it is the authors' hope that this text will spark much dialogue in the profession about HLTPs in foreign language education as well as promote further research in practice-oriented teacher preparation.

Practiced-Based Teacher Preparation—Doing the "Work of Teaching"

In recent years a strand of research in teacher education receiving increasing attention has suggested that professional training be focused on the "practices" of teaching (Ball & Forzani, 2009; Forzani, 2014). This recent emphasis on **practice-based teacher education** emphasizes the inclusion of carefully designed and purposeful early field experiences in K-12 classrooms that are closely linked to coursework in pedagogy (Grossman & McDonald, 2008). Current research and professional dialogue are calling for teacher preparation programs to engage prospective teachers in *doing* teaching rather than simply talking *about* it (Hlas & Hlas, 2012; Sleep, 2009). Central to this discussion has been the identification of specific teaching practices across disciplines and levels of instruction "that are essential for novices to become capable at before they are permitted to assume independent responsibility for a classroom" (Forzani, 2014, p. 357). This movement has occurred in part in response to the perceived shortcomings of the contemporary teacher education curriculum that tends to focus only on a professional knowledge base and belief system at the expense of developing the ability to perform the core tasks that teachers must be prepared to carry out to motivate and engage learners and to support their learning. According to Ball and Forzani (2009), most initiatives to improve teacher quality have centered on teacher recruitment and retention and on creating new pathways to learning such as through technology, collaborative work, and problem-based curricula. As an alternative, this new line of research situates *practice* at the center of teacher education, which involves detailed attention to training teachers to enact the work of teaching so that their students are motivated and engaged in learning and make progress. Placing practice at the center of teacher education does not mean that novice teachers do not need the professional knowledge base (e.g., history of language education, national standards, current research findings) and theoretical understandings that inform instruction, curriculum design, assessment, etc. It is through practice that theory can be exemplified, examined, critiqued, and understood. As the knowledge of theory deepens and is experienced in action, teaching practice is refined and transformed and professional expertise develops.

What is meant by the "work of teaching"? Teaching is unique from other endeavors in at least three ways. First, teaching is *unnatural* work that requires carefully designed lessons for novices to learn the practices that constitute this work. Professional classroom teaching is very different from informally showing or helping someone perform some action or solve a problem. It involves knowing a great deal of information about learners and the learning process that, in turn, enables teachers to intervene and guide learners so that what they can do today with assistance, they can do in the future on their own in related contexts of activity. For instance, in language teaching, teachers do not just simply point learners to a textbook and expect language acquisition to occur. Teaching is a unique form of professional activity and goes beyond informal helping or "lending a hand." The uniqueness of formal instruction requiring professional expertise and differentiating it from informal assistance includes, for example,

- asking questions to which teachers might know part of the answer, or can predict how students might respond

- probing learners' ideas; i.e., pushing students to provide more details, think more critically

- not presuming shared identity; learning others' perspectives and experiences, so that background knowledge, interests, learning styles, etc., can be used as the springboard for learning

- seeing people more descriptively—knowing what learners bring to the learning task, how they learn, what challenges them, among other characteristics

- being in a professional role (adapted from Ball & Forzani, 2009, p. 500).

A second way in which teaching is unique is that teachers must not only know their content areas but they must be skilled in perceiving how others envision and understand it and how it can be explained. That is, they must be skilled at

1. identifying the ways in which a learner thinks about a particular topic, problem, or task;

2. designing the steps to guide the learner's development; and

3. monitoring and assessing the learner's progress to effect learning and continued development (Ball & Forzani, 2007, 2009).

A third characteristic that sets teaching apart from other helping behaviors is that it is *intricate and complex* work (Ball & Forzani, 2009). That is, each episode of teaching consists of many tasks and moves not always visible to an observer (Lewis, 2007). These pedagogical moves are the individual steps that the teacher takes to enact a particular practice. For example, in the foreign language practice "leading a discussion about a news article" in a newspaper from the target language country, the teacher makes many moves, including providing culturally relevant information, activating prior knowledge about the topic, developing interpretive questions to guide the discussion, grouping students to provide greater opportunities for participation, motivating students to share their ideas and opinions, providing expressive reactions and assisting questions to move the discussion forward, and informally assessing students' contributions to the discussion. These individual moves and the sequence in which they occur may not be readily visible to an observer, especially a novice teacher.

The unique work of teaching, as explored above, involves the "core tasks that teachers must execute to help pupils learn" (Ball & Forzani, 2009, p. 497). In the educational literature these core tasks are referred to as **core practices** or **high-leverage teaching practices (HLTPs)** given that they provide the greatest "leverage" for new teachers in bringing about effective student learning. As defined in the opening of this chapter,

HLTPs (which is the term used in this text) refer to "tasks and activities that are essential for skillful beginning teachers to understand, take responsibility for, and be prepared to carry out in order to enact their core instructional responsibilities" (Ball & Forzani, 2009, p. 504). The skillful enactment of HLTPs is likely to result not only in large advancements in student learning but also in teaching skill (Teaching Works, 2016). In fact, given that these practices are central to teaching, "if teachers cannot enact them competently, they are unlikely to be able to engage students with content" (TEI Curriculum Group, 2008, p. 4). In other words, without the enactment of these practices, learning is unlikely to occur.

Characteristics of High-Leverage Teaching Practices

The professional dialogue surrounding HLTPs was initiated by the University of Michigan School of Education, and more specifically by its Teacher Education Initiative (TEI), an endeavor begun in 2004 to introduce into teacher education the kind of hands-on practical training and that occurs routinely in all other professional communities, for example, in medicine, architecture, and counseling, to name a few, by increasing time spent unpacking the complexity of instruction, "practicing" teaching, and supervising teacher candidates (Thomas, 2010). Initial research by this group revealed the following characteristics of high-leverage teaching practices from two standpoints, one related to teaching and the other related to the challenges of teacher education:

Considerations related to high quality teaching:

1. They are effective/powerful in advancing pupils' learning both distally (i.e., as a result of a respectful learning community) and proximally (i.e., as a result of giving clear and usable explanations). In the case of foreign languages, many are key for language acquisition to occur and to move students' language ability along the proficiency continuum.

2. They are specifically effective in using and managing differences among students, and in confronting inequities.

3. They are useful in many contexts and across content areas, although some practices are unique or especially important to a particular subject area.

Considerations related to high quality professional education:

4. They can be assessed. Teachers' performance in enacting these practices can be assessed in terms of each instructional move and in whether the enactment of the HLTP results in student learning.

5. They serve usefully as building blocks for learning practice. They are complex instructional practices inasmuch as each practice requires multiple instructional moves and an understanding of the relationship among these moves.

6. They can be unpacked and taught to beginners and learned by them. That is, each practice needs to be teased apart so that teachers understand each instructional move that must be taken to enact the practice. Teachers learn how to enact these practices by rehearsing them and receiving coaching by an experienced mentor, which is analogous to an apprentice learning on the job. Apprentices practice the task as the mentor watches and coaches them. Sometimes there are false starts or even unsuccessful moves, requiring the apprentice to begin again

or redo a part of the task, using the immediate feedback and coaching from the mentor. Through coaching, teachers learn to perform the HLTPs in special instructional activities and for specific purposes.

7. They can be justified and made convincing to teacher candidates (and others) as being meaningful and useful for becoming skilled practitioners, both now and later. Because these practices are based on current pedagogical theory, research, and student learning, they are deemed essential in the language classroom.

8. They are unlikely to be learned well only through experience or modeling/observation. Simply observing these practices will not enable a teacher to enact them successfully because they require practice and coaching (adapted from TEI Curriculum Group, 2008).

The TEI, which has served as a reform initiative for teacher training at the University of Michigan, was the catalyst for the launching of Teaching Works, the mission of which is to "ensure that all students have skillful teachers who are committed to and able to support their growth" (Teaching Works, 2016). Promoting its belief that "great teachers aren't born—they're taught," Teaching Works advocates preparing entry-level teachers to enact a set of HLTPs with different content, students, and contexts to respond to three key questions: (a) What is worth learning? (b) How does learning take place? (c) What kind of teaching can support that learning? More specifically, the high-leverage practices are based on 5 main ideas:

1. The goal of classroom teaching is to help students learn worthwhile knowledge and skills and develop the ability to use what they learn for their own purposes.

2. All students deserve the opportunity to learn at high levels.

3. Learning is an active sense-making process.

4. Teaching is interactive with and constructed together with students.

5. The contexts of classroom teaching matter, and teachers must manage and use these contexts well (Teaching Works, 2016).

The Teaching Works initiative identified nineteen high-leverage teaching practices that "are the fundamentals of teaching, ...are used constantly...and are critical to helping students learn important content" (2016). As depicted in Figure P.1, these HLTPs are used across subject areas, grade levels, and contexts.[2]

Teaching Works, under the directorship of Deborah Ball at the University of Michigan, defines these 19 practices as high-leverage because they are the basic fundamental capabilities necessary for responsible teaching:

> These practices are used constantly and are critical to helping students learn important content. The high-leverage practices are also central to supporting students' social and emotional development. These high-leverage practices are used across subject areas, grade levels, and contexts. They are "high-leverage" not only because they matter to student learning but because they are basic for advancing skill in teaching. (http://www.teachingworks.org/work-of-teaching/high-leverage-practices)

Discipline-specific HLTPs. While the HLTPs listed in Figure P.1 are generic in that they are relevant to all subject areas, grade levels, and contexts, work in teacher education has

---

[2] For a detailed discussion of each of these HLTPs, see http://www.teachingworks.org/work-of-teaching/high-leverage-practices.

1.	Leading a group discussion
2.	Explaining and modeling content, practices, and strategies
3.	Eliciting and interpreting individual students' thinking
4.	Diagnosing particular common patterns of student thinking and development in a subject-matter domain
5.	Implementing norms and routines for classroom discourse and work
6.	Coordinating and adjusting instruction during a lesson
7.	Specifying and reinforcing productive student behavior
8.	Implementing organizational routines
9.	Setting up and managing small group work
10.	Building respectful relationships with students
11.	Talking about a student with parents or other caregivers
12.	Learning about students' cultural, religious, family, intellectual, and personal experiences and resources for use in instruction
13.	Setting long- and short-term learning goals for students
14.	Designing single lessons and sequences of lessons
15.	Checking student understanding during and at the conclusion of lessons
16.	Selecting and designing formal assessments of student learning
17.	Interpreting the results of student work, including routine assignments, quizzes, tests, projects, and standardized assessments
18.	Providing oral and written feedback to students
19.	Analyzing instruction for the purpose of improving it

Figure P.1. **HLTPs identified by Teaching Works (2016)**

also emphasized the importance of a teacher's pedagogical content knowledge (Shulman, 1986). According to Shulman, **pedagogical content knowledge** "goes beyond knowledge of subject matter per se to the dimension of subject matter knowledge for teaching" (1986, p. 9). From this perspective, knowing only the content area is not sufficient for teaching. In addition to content area knowledge, teachers need to understand how learners can be best supported in learning the content, the types of misunderstandings they might have, and the types of instructional strategies that make the content accessible to them. Hence, educators are faced with the challenge of identifying *which* teaching practices are high leverage in their respective content areas. Indeed several fields have already undertaken this endeavor. Mathematics was one of the first disciplines to identify specific HLTPs; examples that have appeared in the literature include

- "unpacking" mathematical ideas and... scaffolding them for pupils' learning
- figuring out what pupils are doing mathematically and how it makes sense to them
- engaging learners in a whole-class mathematics discussion (Ball, Sleep, Boerst, & Bass, 2009, pp. 461, 468).

History educators have also identified HLTPs such as the following for their field:

- employing historical evidence

- assessing student thinking about history

- facilitating discussion on historical concepts (Fogo, 2012; as cited in Kennedy, 2016, pp. 8–9).

HLTPs that have been proposed by science educators include:

- helping students make sense of material activity

- pressing students for evidence-based explanations (Windschitl, Thompson, Braaten, & Stroup, 2012).

One of the challenges in identifying HLTPs in a given discipline is what has been termed **grain size** (Ball & Forzani, 2009, 2011). Some practices, such as *leading a discussion* (see Figure P.1 above), have a **large grain size** and entail a set of **smaller grain-size practices** such as situating the discussion topic within a meaningful context, motivating learners to participate, providing scaffolding such as vocabulary that learners might use, asking assisting questions to promote thinking and move the conversation forward, and offering incentives for participation. In turn, these smaller grain-size practices can be broken down to specific steps or *instructional moves*. Often these smaller grain-size practices are not visible to a novice teacher and must be overtly broken down into micro-practices that are explicitly taught, coached, and practiced. The point is that whenever we discuss a practice, we always view it from a particular perspective. What must be remembered is that teaching is a complex activity and the instructional moves that contribute to an HLTP cannot be easily captured in a single generic label (see section on "best practices" below).

HLTPs ≠ Best Practices. In further defining and identifying HLTPs, it should be noted that high-leverage practices are *not* synonymous with the concept of "best practices." As explained by Hlas and Hlas (2012), although ***best practice*** "seeks to identify effective teaching strategies," the term *best* has been interpreted in various ways and is yet to be clearly defined in the field (p. S77). Figure P.2 compares the notion of best practice with the detailed definition of high-leverage teaching practices found in the practice-based teacher education literature. Another way to conceptualize HLTPs is to think of them as practices that an accomplished novice must be able to enact in order to be offered a teaching position; conversely, if an applicant could not perform these practices, he or she would likely not be a viable candidate for the position.

The Larger Picture of HLTPs. On first glance, it may be easy to fall into the trap of thinking that HLTPs simply provide a prescribed list of moves that teachers must make to enact them. To fully understand the concept of HLTPs, it is essential that these practices be viewed as "decision-making" practices and *not* as "imitative practices" reproduced in a procedural manner (Kennedy, 2016). In this vein, novice teachers must recognize *why* teachers use HLTPs—that is, for different instructional purposes within the overall lesson depending upon their students and contextual factors such as lesson objectives, learner needs, and available time. Kennedy (2016) warns that clarity regarding purposes of HLTP use is critical because novices have many misconceptions about what teachers do and why. Further, she suggests that HLTPs be characterized in terms of teaching challenges that they address, which may include

- portraying the curriculum content in ways that make it comprehensible to learners

- enlisting student participation and motivating and engaging students in learning

Best Practices...	High-leverage Teaching Practices...
are defined as "what works" based on experience and anecdotal evidence.	are based on theory, research on student learning, accumulated wisdom of practice.
explain WHAT to do but not HOW to do it.	can be deconstructed into instructional moves that explain HOW to enact the practice.
are thought to be learnable through modeling and observation.	cannot be learned through observation alone and require explicit instruction and practice.
are reduced to general statements of practice or labels such as "use authentic materials," "model activities."	are complex and are not reduced to a single label or professional slogan.
consist of long lists of general statements that do not consider teacher experience, foundational pedagogical skills, or the relationship of one practice with another.	are not as extensive in number but are selective, mutually supporting, and considered fundamental to teaching, especially for the beginning teacher.
are sometimes associated with personality issues, intuition, common sense, rather than being learned; e.g., Don't correct every error a student makes so as to lower the anxiety filter.	can be explained, taught, and coached.
reflect good practice but are not used as a basis for a teacher education curriculum.	are considered developmentally appropriate for novice teachers, what they need to know to be prepared for the foreign language classroom, and useful and essential for teacher education purposes. A teacher education curriculum could be based on HLTPs.

Figure P.2. **Comparison of HLTPs and Best Practices**

- making student thinking visible so that teachers are certain of what their students understand and don't understand
- managing student behavior in the classroom
- addressing instructional challenges in a way that is consistent with teachers' own personalities and personal needs (based on Kennedy, 2016).

An interesting way to view how HLTPs may serve these instructional challenges, then, is to conceive of what teachers *do* in terms of the following 5-part definition:

- They portray curriculum content in a way that renders it comprehensible to naïve minds;

- For students who are not necessarily interested in learning;
- And whose grasp of the content is not readily visible to the teacher;
- And who are restless and easily distracted;
- In a way that satisfies the teachers' personal needs (Kennedy, 2016, p. 13).

In sum, a focus on the challenges that HLTPs address will guide novices to think strategically about how their practices address a larger purpose (Kennedy, 2016).

High-Leverage Teaching Practices in Foreign Language Education

Foreign language teacher education turned its attention to practiced-based preparation in 2012 in response to the Research Priorities in Foreign Language Education initiative developed by the American Council on the Teaching of Foreign Languages (ACTFL), which identified HLTPs as an area worthy of research given its potential to improve classroom instruction. As a part of this project in 2012, Hlas and Hlas conducted a review of the literature on practice-based teacher preparation and adapted four HLTPs from mathematics education to the context of language pedagogy based on "their historical nature, their empirical evidence provided in previous studies, their continued importance in teacher training, their emphasis on the development of student understanding..." (p. S80). Each large grain-size practice, as applied to foreign language, was exemplified through several teaching moves (called *micropractices* in their review), although each could be further deconstructed into additional moves or smaller grain-size practices that illustrate how a novice would enact the larger practice:

1. Anticipating Student Errors and Misconceptions during Planning
   Example of Micropractice: Designing four-column lesson plans

2. Making Connections Between Multiple Representations

   Example of Micropractice: Using external and material representations (e.g., pictures, technological resources, charts, manipulatives) to help students develop, externalize, and elaborate on their internal representations (e.g., conceptual knowledge)

3. Leading a Classroom Discussion

   Example of Micropractice: Eliciting and reacting to student contributions during discussions

4. Teaching Through Problem Solving
   Example of micropractice: Targeted scaffolding through routine questioning
   (Hlas & Hlas, 2012, pp. s80–s89).

Subsequent to this initial Research Priorities project, several studies have emerged in the last several years that have examined the use of specific HLTPs by foreign language teachers. Four HLTPs specific to foreign language teaching emanated from these studies and were selected because they are grounded in research and theory and are viewed as pivotal to student learning:

1. Using the target language comprehensibly during instruction (Davin & Troyan, 2015; Troyan, Davin, & Donato, 2013)

2. Questioning for building and assessing student understanding (Davin & Troyan, 2015; Troyan, Davin, & Donato, 2013)

3. Teaching grammar using a dialogic approach to understanding form-function relationships (Troyan, Davin, & Donato, 2013)

4. Leading an open-ended group discussion (Kearney, 2015).

As this early research on prospective foreign language practices had begun to be disseminated, in March 2015, ACTFL assembled a group of individuals who comprised the ACTFL Research and Assessment Committee and the ACTFL Research Priorities in Foreign Language Education Task Force to launch the dialogue about HLTPs and to begin to identify them for foreign language instruction. After extensive discussion and deliberation, the following six practices were selected and they became the basis for ACTFL's inaugural summer institute of its Leadership Initiative for Language Learning (LILL), as well as a series of ACTFL webinars available online to language educators:

1. Use the target language as the vehicle and content of instruction.

2. Design and carry out interpersonal communication tasks for pairs, small groups, and whole-class instruction.

3. Design lessons and tasks that have functional goals and objectives, to include specifying clearly the language and activities needed to support and meet the communicative objective.

4. Teach grammar as concept and use in context. Understand the various approaches to grammar instruction and how to select one over the other.

5. Design and carry out interactive reading and listening comprehension tasks using authentic cultural texts of various kinds with appropriate scaffolding and follow-up tasks that promote interpretation.

6. Provide appropriate feedback in speech and writing on various learning tasks (ACTFL, 2015a, 2015b).

As discussed previously, these six HLTPs are at a rather large grain size and require further refinement and definition to be useful to as a guide to what (beginning) teachers should know and be able to do. For this reason, and for the purposes of this text, the major themes of the committee's deliberations were recast into six specific and recognizable HLTPs that should be familiar to any language teaching professional as part of initial teacher training and certification. In some cases, only a slice of the original larger grain-size practice is presented so that it can be deconstructed in a manageable practice suitable for rehearsal, practice, and coaching. Although not identical to the original committee selections in scope, all of the six practices presented in this text reflect the decision of the committee, entail aspects of the above practices, and qualify as HLTPs due to their complexity and need for skillful execution for ambitious teaching. The literature on HLTPs defines **ambitious teaching** as "instructional experiences that support students in carrying out cognitively demanding tasks" (Troyan, Davin, & Donato, 2013, p. 174). Additionally, the six practices included in this text have a theoretical basis and research support for their inclusion, which is presented as introductory material in each chapter (see next section below). Finally, experienced teachers and teacher educators will most likely recognize the usefulness of these HLPTs for teaching and learning and the detailed understanding and explicit instruction that is needed to enact these practices with professional expertise. The scope of this text will present the following six HLTPs, which are all based on the initial identification of high-leverage teaching practices in foreign language education. The relationship of the following six HLTPs is keyed below to the work of the ACTFL Research and Assessment Committee, the ACTFL Research Priorities in Foreign Language

Education Project, and the 2015 Leadership Initiative for Language Learning (LILL) Summer Institute.

HLTP#1: Facilitating Target Language Comprehensibility (#1, #3)

HLTP#2: Building a Classroom Discourse Community (#1, #2)

HLTP#3: Guiding Learners to Interpret and Discuss Authentic Texts (#3, #5)

HLTP#4: Focusing on Form in a Dialogic Context Through PACE (#4)

HLTP#5: Focusing on Cultural Products, Practices, and Perspectives in a Dialogic Context (#3, #4)

HLTP#6: Providing Oral Corrective Feedback to Improve Learner Performance (#6)

There are three important caveats to keep in mind about these six practices:

1. These practices are not the only HLTPs that novice teachers should know, and there are others. However, these were selected because they are learnable in initial teacher preparation programs, have been shown to be developmentally appropriate for novices, represent fundamental skills of language teaching, are inter-connected and mutually support each other (i.e., one builds on the other), and are key to supporting students' language learning;

2. These HLTPs do not represent the maximum expectations for novices, or for all language teachers for that matter, but rather the minimum practices that all novices should be able to demonstrate when they enter the language classroom; and

3. These HLTPs represent what *novice* teachers should know and be able to enact and the expectation that more accomplished teachers already know how to perform these practices. Nonetheless, more accomplished teachers may find it helpful to review these practices as a refresher or study those that they had not explored in their earlier teacher preparation.

Organization of the Text

Each of the following 6 chapters presents one HLTP; in some cases, a large grain-size practice is broken into a few smaller grain-size practices to be deconstructed. Throughout all chapters, each key term that is used for the first time appears in boldface along with its definition. Users should remember important terms in the text, and some may be cross-referenced with a methods book for further explanation and elaboration. The 6 chapters are organized in the following manner:

Research and Theory Supporting the Practice: The chapter begins with a justification for selection of the practice as high-leverage and situates it within research and theory. As this section is only a thumbnail overview, only the most relevant research findings and theoretical frameworks are presented. The reader is encouraged to read more in-depth treatments of this research by consulting *Teacher's Handbook: Contextualized Language Instruction*, 5th edition, by Shrum and Glisan (2016). References for further reading appear at the end of each chapter.

Considerations about the Practice: This section features a discussion about the key points, including caveats regarding the practice, discussed from the standpoint of a series of questions that novice teachers typically ask. Teachers will find that this part is constructed as if it were an informal dialogue with the teacher.

Deconstructing the Practice: Next the practice is **deconstructed** into a series of detailed steps that the teacher can follow in rehearsal, practice, and enactment. It should be noted that (1) this careful deconstruction is the hallmark of an HLTP and until now has not been done in foreign language education; and (2) the steps suggested must be carried out while simultaneously keeping in mind the unique instructional context of each teacher—that is, the level of learners, lesson goals, how learners are motivated, etc. To this end, there is always flexibility with the specific steps, content, and level of challenge of each practice. In this way, the practices can be adapted to address the realities of each teacher's instructional context. Therefore, the authors opted not to include entire sample lessons that illustrate each HLTP so as not to create a misunderstanding that there is only one way for the practices to be enacted within lessons. Teachers may also find it helpful to consult the rubrics that accompany each HLTP as they deconstruct the practice.

Rehearsing the Practice: This section enables teachers to put to practice and rehearse the deconstructed steps that they just learned. These activities can be done in collaboration with classmates, in the case of pre-service teachers, or colleagues, in the case of in-service teachers. Some chapters feature multiple activities that are sequenced to enable teachers to focus on specific aspects of the practice before rehearsing the whole practice (referred to as approximations of practice). It should be noted that answers are not provided for these activities because they are designed to prompt reflection, analysis, and discussion, and because specific responses do not necessarily apply to all instructional contexts. It is important to note that the rehearsal of an HLTP must be placed in some instructional activity with a clear purpose and goal (Teaching Works, 2016). HLTPs cannot be rehearsed and practiced in a void and are always used at the service of some larger instructional goal. Teachers will find it helpful to consult the External Mediational Tools (EMTs) (see later explanation) and rubrics that accompany each HLTP before beginning the rehearsal stage.

Assessing the Practice: Teachers may use the rubrics that accompany each HLTP in self-assessing their own performance and/or to assist a peer or colleague in assessing performance. It should be noted that **rubrics** are a tool for assessing performance based on specific criteria and detailed performance descriptions for each point or level of performance (Wiggins & McTighe, 2005). The rubrics developed for the HLTPs in this text have the following characteristics:

- They describe the criteria by which teachers' performance in enacting the practices can be assessed; i.e., these 3 to 5 criteria address the instructional moves that were deconstructed and rehearsed within each chapter; and

- They use a range of 4 performance levels to rate teachers' performance according to the degree to which the criteria have been met: Exceeds expectations, Meets expectations, Developing, Unacceptable. It should be noted that the "Exceeds expectations" category describes performance that is far beyond what most novice teachers are able to do, and thus, a small percentage of teachers are likely to demonstrate performance at this level. Nonetheless, as is the case with all useful rubrics, the HLTP rubrics include this level of performance to define how teachers may go beyond the minimal expectations and to encourage a higher level of performance.

The HLTP rubrics serve two purposes:

1. To define expectations for enacting the practices before teachers rehearse them—that is, to describe what effective performance looks like even before the practices are enacted; and

2. To rate teachers' performance and provide feedback so that they can reflect on and improve their ability to enact the practices.

A set of rubrics for each HLTP appears at the end of the chapter and can be easily duplicated for use. For information regarding how to assign grades or scores based on performance ratings using a rubric, see Shrum and Glisan (2016, pp. 384-387).

Putting the Practice into a Larger Context: Addressing Instructional Goals and Challenges. Each of these 6 chapters concludes by prompting teachers to think about the practice (1) within the larger context of their teaching and (2) as an avenue for addressing common teaching challenges that they confront in today's classrooms. Thus, the teaching practice is placed into the wider context of educational issues and priorities and teachers' classroom experiences. Further, this discussion provides additional support to help novice teachers understand the HLTPs through the lens of "decision-making" practices and *not* "imitative practices" mindlessly reproduced in a procedural manner (Kennedy, 2016).

Other Features of the Text

The final chapter presents a model for how teachers might practice enacting these HLTPs, how they might collaborate with others in this practice, and how they might reflect on and assess/self-assess their progress along the way. This enactment model can be adopted by teachers who immerse themselves in practice and by teacher educators who guide their teacher candidates in rehearsing and enacting the HLTPs.

In addition to a helpful list of references and rubrics for each HLTP, the end of each chapter features **"External Mediational Tools (EMTs)"** to assist teachers in enacting the practices. These EMTs are resources that list the key instructional moves for each HLTP (i.e., a "cheat sheet" of sorts), many which appear in the form of checklists and may be photocopied for use by the teacher.

Finally, another unique feature of this text is that it can be used to assist college faculty as they prepare their teacher preparation programs to undergo national recognition review by ACTFL and the Council for Accreditation of Educator Preparation (CAEP), the agency that accredits colleges and universities and "recognizes" their teacher preparation programs. To this end, each HLTP is cross-referenced with the pertinent ***ACTFL/CAEP Program Standards for the Preparation of Foreign Language Teachers*** (ACTFL, 2013) to assist faculty in collecting evidence needed for an ACTFL/CAEP national recognition program review. Teacher preparation faculty will find this cross reference helpful inasmuch as the standards represent national expectations for what beginning language teachers should know and be able to do in the classroom. A summary of the standards appears in this chapter's Appendix A, and the full description of the standards can be found at https://www.actfl.org/assessment-professional-development/program-review-services.

For Further Reading

American Council on the Teaching of Foreign Languages (2013). *ACTFL/CAEP program standards for the preparation of foreign language teachers.* Alexandria, VA: Author. Retrieved from https://www.actfl.org/assessment-professional-development/program-review-services

American Council on the Teaching of Foreign Languages (ACTFL). (2015a). Leadership Initiative for Language Learning Summer Institute, July 21-23, 2015, The Ohio State University, Columbus, OH.

American Council on the Teaching of Foreign Languages (ACTFL). (2015b). Webinar Series: Core practices for effective language learning.

Ball, D. L., & Forzani, F. M. (2007). What makes education research "educational"? *Educational Researcher, 36*(9), 529–540.

Ball, D. L., & Forzani, F. M. (2009). The work of teaching and the challenge for teacher education. *Journal of Teacher Education, 60*(5), 497–511.

Ball, D. L., & Forzani, F. M. (2011). Building a common core for learning to teach and connecting professional learning to practice. *American Educator, 35,* 17–21, 38–39. Retrieved from: http://files.eric.ed.gov/fulltext/EJ931211.pdf

Ball, D. L., Sleep, L., Boerst, T. A., & Bass, H. (2009). Combining the development of practice and the practice of development in teacher education. *The Elementary School Journal, 109,* 458–474. doi:10.1086/596996

Davin, K. J., & Troyan, F. J. (2015). The implementation of high-leverage teaching practices: From the university classroom to the field site. *Foreign Language Annals, 48,* 124–142.

Fogo, B. (2012). Round 3: Summary and demographic data. In *Core teaching practices Delphi panel.* Retrieved from https://cset.stanford.edu/sites/default/files/History-Round%203%20Summary%20and%20Demographic%20Data.pdf

Forzani, F. M. (2014). Understanding "core practices" and "practice-based" teacher education: Learning from the past. *Journal of Teacher Education, 65*(4), 357–368.

Grossman, P., & McDonald, M. (2008). Back to the future: Directions for research in teaching and teacher education. *American Educational Research Journal, 45,* 184–205.

Hlas, A. C., & Hlas, C. S. (2012). A review of high-leverage teaching practices: Making connections between mathematics and foreign languages. *Foreign Language Annals, 45,* s76–s97.

Kearney, E. (2015). A high-leverage language teaching practice: Leading an open-ended group discussion. *Foreign Language Annals, 48,* 100–123.

Kennedy, M. (2016). Parsing the practice of teaching. *Journal of Teacher Education, 67*(1), 6–17.

Lewis, J. M. (2007). *Teaching as invisible work.* Unpublished dissertation. University of Michigan, Ann Arbor.

Shrum, J. L., & Glisan, E. W. (2016). *Teacher's handbook: Contextualized language instruction.* 5th edition. Boston, MA: Cengage Learning.

Shulman, L.S. (1986). Those who understand: Knowledge growth in teaching. *Educational Researcher, 15,* 4–14.

Sleep, L. (2009). *Teaching to the mathematical point: Knowing and using mathematics in teaching*. Unpublished doctoral dissertation. University of Michigan, Ann Arbor.

Teacher Education Initiative (TEI) Curriculum Group. (2008). *High-leverage teaching practices*. University of Michigan School of Education. Unpublished manuscript.

Teaching Works. (2016). *High-leverage practices*. Retrieved from http://www.teachingworks.org/work-of-teaching/high-leverage-practices

Thomas, A. G. (2010, January 21). School of Education to revamp curriculum. *The Michigan Daily*. Retrieved from https://www.michigandaily.com/content/school-education-revamp-teaching-norms

Troyan, F. J., Davin, K. J., & Donato, R. (2013). Exploring a practice-based approach to foreign language teacher preparation: A work in progress. *Canadian Modern Language Review/La revue canadienne des langues vivantes, 69,* 154–180.

Wiggins, G., & McTighe, J. (2005). *Understanding by design*. Alexandria, VA: Association for Supervision and Curriculum Development.

Windschitl, M., Thompson, J., Braaten, M., & Stroupe, D. (2012). Proposing a core set of instructional practices and tools for teachers of science. *Science Education, 96,* 878–903. doi: 10.1002/sce.21027

Appendix A

ACTFL/CAEP Program Standards for the Preparation of Foreign Language Teachers

Standard 1: Language Proficiency: Interpersonal, Interpretive, and Presentational
Pre-service teachers will:

1a. Speak in the interpersonal mode of communication at a minimum level of "Advanced Low" or "Intermediate High" (for Arabic, Chinese, Japanese and Korean) on the ACTFL Oral Proficiency Interview (OPI) according to the target language being taught.
1b. Interpret oral, printed, and video texts by demonstrating both literal and figurative or symbolic comprehension.
1c. Present oral and written information to audiences of listeners or readers, using language at a minimum level of "Advanced Low" or "Intermediate High" according to the target language being taught.

Standard 2: Cultures, Linguistics, Literatures, and Concepts from Other Disciplines
Pre-service teachers will:

2a. Demonstrate target cultural understandings and compare cultures through perspectives, products, and practices of those cultures.
2b. Demonstrate understanding of linguistics and the changing nature of language, and compare language systems.
2c. Demonstrate understanding of texts on literary and cultural themes as well as interdisciplinary topics.

Standard 3: Language Acquisition Theories and Knowledge of Students and Their Needs
Pre-service teachers will:

3a. Demonstrate an understanding of key principles of language acquisition and create linguistically and culturally rich learning environments.
3b. Demonstrate an understanding of child and adolescent development to create a supportive learning environment for each student.

Standard 4: Integration of Standards in Planning and Instruction
Pre-service teachers will:

4a. Demonstrate an understanding of the Standards for Foreign Language Learning in the 21st Century or their recently refreshed version *World-Readiness Standards for Learning Languages* (2015) and their state standards and use them as the basis for instructional planning.
4b. Integrate the goal areas of the *Standards for Foreign Language Learning in the 21st Century* or their recently refreshed version *World-Readiness Standards for Learning Languages* (2015) and their state standards in their classroom practice.
4c. Use the *Standards for Foreign Language Learning in the 21st Century* or their recently refreshed version *World-Readiness Standards for Learning Languages* (2015) and their state standards to select and integrate authentic texts, use technology, and adapt and create instructional materials for use in communication.

Standard 5: Assessment of Languages and Cultures—Impact on Student Learning
Pre-service teachers will:

5a. Design and use ongoing authentic performance assessments using a variety of assessment models for all learners, including diverse students.

5b. Reflect on and analyze the results of student assessments, adjust instruction accordingly, and use data to inform and strengthen subsequent instruction.

5c. Interpret and report the results of student performances to all stakeholders in the community, with particular emphasis on building student responsibility for their own learning.

Standard 6: Professional Development, Advocacy, and Ethics
Pre-service teachers will:

6a. Engage in ongoing professional development opportunities that strengthen their own linguistic, cultural and pedagogical competence and promote reflection on practice.

6b. Articulate the role and value of languages and cultures in preparing all students to interact in the global community of the 21st century through collaboration and advocacy with all stakeholders.

6c. Use inquiry and reflection to understand and explain the opportunities and responsibilities inherent in being a professional language educator and demonstrate a commitment to equitable and ethical interactions with all students, colleagues and other stakeholders.

Source: American Council on the Teaching of Foreign Languages (2013). *ACTFL/CAEP program standards for the preparation of foreign language teachers.* Alexandria, VA: Author. Retrieved from https://www.actfl.org/assessment-professional-development/program-review-services

CHAPTER 1

HLTP #1: Facilitating Target Language Comprehensibility

*Learning how to engage learners in comprehensible
talk-in-interaction is fundamental to all language instruction
and at all levels.*

Research and theory indicate that effective language instruction must provide significant amounts of comprehensible, meaningful, and interesting talk and text in the target language for learners to develop language and cultural proficiency. Further, according to brain-based investigations, learners constantly ask themselves two questions in the face of new ideas or information: "Does this make *sense*?" and "Does this have *meaning*?" (Sousa, 2011, p. 52). Learning experiences that are comprehensible (i.e., make sense to learners) lead to improved retention (Maquire, Frith, & Morris, 1999). In this regard, meaning is an essential criterion for bringing about understanding and learning (Sousa, 2011). Therefore, it should come as no surprise that one high-leverage teaching practice that is essential for *all* foreign language teachers is the use of the target language during instruction in ways that make meaning clear and do not frustrate or de-motivate learners. This chapter will focus on the issue of **target language (TL) comprehensibility**, that is, ways in which teachers can make the target language comprehensible to students, create contexts that support target language comprehensibility, and engage learners in comprehensible interactions.

ACTFL/CAEP Standards addressed: #1a, 1c; #3a, 3b; #4a, 4b

Research and Theory Supporting the Practice

The use of quality target language in sufficient quantity can be supported from three perspectives. First, research has shown that language learning can occur when learners are exposed to language that is made comprehensible to them. The concept of providing comprehensible and meaningful language to learners to promote language learning is referred to as the **Input Hypothesis** (Krashen, 1981, 1982). The hypothesis claims that to acquire a new language, learners need a large quantity of **comprehensible input** that is interesting, a little beyond their current level of TL competence, but understandable. However, Swain (1985) challenged Krashen's position and claimed that input is *necessary* but *insufficient* for language learning. Swain argued that using the target language, or what is referred to as **comprehensible output**, is equally important because it allows learners to notice where gaps exist in their language knowledge, hypothesize about different ways to express ideas, and focus on how language constructs meaning. What both input and output theories point to is the importance of teachers and learners speaking *in* the target language rather than just speaking *about* the target language, which is typical of grammar-based approaches to language teaching. For learners to progress in their proficiency, they need to experience the target language in action and use the TL for expressing their own meanings. What is more, this view of comprehensible language use in the classroom can never be equated to fill-in-the-blank exercises or language drills.

A second perspective is based on research that confirms that opportunities for learners to engage in conversational interactions in which they work to make themselves understood and to understand their conversational partners are also necessary for language learning (Long, 1983; Long & Porter, 1985; Pica, 1994; Pica, Young, & Doughty, 1987). According to the theory of **modified interaction**, conversational partners modify their target language as necessary to increase comprehensibility, thereby clarifying the input to be processed. Donato (1994) and Swain (1998, 2000) contest this rather narrow view of interaction in second language acquisition and re-conceptualize interaction as dialogic collaboration. During **collaborative interactions** in the target language, learners mediate their own **metalinguistic awareness** by focusing conscious attention on their own language use and meaning-making abilities. As learners interact using the target language, they can be observed to talk about the language that they produce, question their language use, ask for assistance when needed, and other- or self-correct. Through collaborative and supportive interactions with teachers (and with each other), learners make considerable gains in their ability to function in meaningful ways in the target language.

What these two important considerations (input and collaborative interactions) mean for beginning teachers is that learning how to engage learners in comprehensible **talk-in-interaction** is fundamental to all language instruction and at all levels. Accomplished language instructors know how to help students learn *through* the language and not just *about* the language.

A third perspective is based on **sociocultural theory** (Vygotsky, 1986) and the role of language as a **mediational tool** for language learning. A major tenet of sociocultural theory is that using language as a cultural meaning-making tool is the result of mediation in a social context. **Mediation**, as the term suggests, refers to the types of support that learners use to make meaning and sense out of the target language they hear. In this way, the use of the target language for instruction becomes a tool to mediate language learning and development and not just a way to provide input to learners' brains for internal processing. The way we speak to and interact with learners develops a supportive relationship that enables learners to perform with assistance and go beyond what they cannot do on their own. Sociocultural theory claims that the use of language as a mediational tool, or more specifically how we speak to learners, is essential for learning and the quality of this mediation can determine what learners learn and what they do not learn.

This pivotal role of target-language interaction in language learning is emphasized in the K-16 *World Readiness Standards for Learning Languages*, which cite language and communication as being "at the heart of the human experience" (National Standards in Foreign Language Education Project, 2015, p. 7). The foundation on which these standards exist is the belief that learners must be exposed to language and culture study infused within the whole educational experience. In this regard, the standards envision a future "...in which ALL learners will develop and maintain proficiency in English and at least one other language..." (p. 7).

Use of the target language has become so central to our professional vision regarding foreign language study that in 2010 the American Council on the Teaching of Foreign Languages (ACTFL) released a special position statement that addresses it. As shown in Figure 1.1, ACTFL "recommends that language educators and their learners use the target language as exclusively as possible (90% plus) at all levels of instruction during instructional time and, when feasible, beyond the classroom."

Research indicates that effective language instruction must provide significant levels of meaningful communication* and interactive feedback in the target language in order for learners to develop language and cultural proficiency. The pivotal role of target-language interaction in language learning is emphasized in the K-16 Standards for Foreign Language Learning in the 21ˢᵗ Century. ACTFL therefore recommends that language educators and their learners use the target language as exclusively as possible (90% or more of the time) at all levels of instruction during instructional time and, when feasible, beyond the classroom. In classrooms that feature maximum target-language use, instructors use a variety of strategies to facilitate comprehension and support meaning making. For example, they:

1. provide comprehensible input that is directed toward communicative goals;

2. make meaning clear through body language, gestures, and visual support;

3. conduct comprehension checks to ensure understanding;

4. negotiate meaning with learners and encourage negotiation among learners;

5. elicit talk that increases in fluency, accuracy, and complexity over time;

6. encourage self-expression and spontaneous use of language;

7. teach learners strategies for requesting clarification and assistance when faced with comprehension difficulties; and

8. offer feedback to assist and improve learners' ability to interact orally in the target language.

*Communication for a classical language refers to an emphasis on reading ability and for American Sign Language (ASL) to signed communicative ability.

Figure 1.1. **ACTFL Position Statement on Use of the Target Language in the Classroom**

Source: American Council on the Teaching of Foreign Languages. (2010). Retrieved from http://www.actfl. org/news/position-statements/use-the-target-language-the-classroom

In classrooms that feature maximum target-language use for input and interaction, teachers use a variety of strategies to facilitate comprehension and support meaning-making in interaction. For the novice teacher, often these features of target language use are subtle and difficult to learn through observation of skilled teachers conducting classes in the target language. This chapter deconstructs and makes explicit how new teachers can use the target language as a vehicle of instruction, how speech modifications can be made to increase comprehensibility, and how target language interactions with learners can promote target language use. Although the theories and research supporting interaction and the teachers' comprehensible use of the target language are based mainly on focusing learner attention on the grammatical and syntactic features of the target language, it should be noted that perhaps more importantly, using the target language for meaningful communication with learners creates a **discourse community** in the classroom (see Chapter 2). In classrooms in which teachers' language use promotes comprehension rather than leads to confusion, learners can interact and freely use language creatively without fear of excessive error correction or reproach. Learning to conduct a language class in the target language necessitates both considerable practice and the ability to tailor one's language use for learners at different levels of instruction. In classrooms that feature comprehensible use of the target language, learners will not make demands on the teacher for translation or voice frustrations when classes are conducted in the TL. Further, they will experience a classroom discourse community in which using target language becomes the rule rather than the exception.

Considerations about Using the Target Language During Instruction

Several important considerations need to be understood about target language use in the classroom.

(1) *What do I talk about?* The target language must always occur in **meaningful contexts**. Effective TL is always used within the context of an overarching **communicative goal** and **purposeful activity**. For example, an overarching goal and purpose of communication is to engage learners in comparing and contrasting a particular cultural perspective after hearing or reading about certain cultural practices and products. Learners can learn to provide autobiographical information in the context of applying for a job or a study abroad program. To increase comprehensibility, the TL needs to be connected to learners' background knowledge and interests, needs to motivate sustained listening and meaning-making interaction, and needs to focus on meaning over form. Using the TL when completing mechanical textbook exercises rarely qualifies as the type of language that is useful for language learning or for developing learners who are willing to take risks to express themselves.

(2) *Can't I just translate what they don't understand?* Continually translating what is said in the TL into the learners' first language needs to be avoided. If the teacher's TL utterances are always followed by a translation, learners quickly realize that they need not focus on the target language message and that, if they just wait long enough, a translation of the target language will be provided.

(3) *What is most important is that I talk in the TL, right?* Using the TL alone in the absence of knowing how to make the target language comprehensible to learners is not sufficient. Further, using the TL for instruction does not mean giving a teacher-fronted lecture to the class. Mediating TL comprehension means interacting with learners through frequent and reliable **comprehension checking**, e.g., engaging in question and answer exchanges, cueing learner responses, or asking them to demonstrate actively their comprehension of what they heard through gesture, dramatization, or by manipulating objects or images.

(4) *Can't I just use pictures and gestures to make my learners understand me?* Using the TL in ways that foster comprehension requires more than showing pictures or making gestures to illustrate what is said. Relying on these ways alone to increase comprehension actually works against developing learners' ability to make meaning from what they hear. It is said that a picture is worth a thousand words. However, language learning is precisely about language and meaning; an overreliance on using pictures and gestures could prevent learners from engaging cognitively with the TL. Pictures and gestures certainly support comprehension and are frequently used by teachers, but they should never entirely replace learners' attention to the meanings and functions that language forms convey.

(5) *What do I do if learners complain about my using the TL to the maximum extent in class?* Learners need incentives to engage in sustained listening and use of the TL. While some are motivated by assessing their own progress in language use, others may need external motivations such as recognition for their achievement or the earning of special awards and privileges for their attempts to use the TL during class. Creating a classroom discourse community in which the target language is used for instruction takes time and patience (see Chapter 2). Teachers may need to provide motivation for target language use beyond simply the threat of a bad grade.

(6) *What are learners supposed to comprehend?* Learners need clear goals that indicate what they are expected to understand (Crouse, 2014). Using the TL in class does not mean that learners are required to understand every word that is said or every idea that is expressed. If the teacher believes that learners need to understand every word, target language use will become nothing more than repetitions of isolated words and phrases. Using the TL means modifying one's language and adjusting it to the level of the learners in much the same way that a native speaker speaks to a non-native speaker. What is comprehensible to a third- or fourth-year learner will not be comprehensible to a first-year learner. Using the TL for instruction means constantly adjusting how teachers speak in relation to what learners know, are able to do, and are in the process of learning to do.

Deconstructing the Practice

The tool depicted in Figure 1.2 has been developed as a way to understand how the TL can be made comprehensible to learners through the teacher's language modifications, the context of instruction, and interactions with learners. The purpose of the tool is to provide guidance for observing, monitoring, and practicing classroom TL use. Although the tool is in the form of a checklist, as such, this does not imply that all boxes need to be checked off or that the items on the list need to be enacted in a linear fashion. Checklists are used by many professionals such as pilots, doctors, and business owners, to overcome failure and to ensure success by taking advantage of what they know but inevitably may forget. As Gawande (2009, p. 13) points out, using a checklist seems almost ridiculous in its simplicity but is a powerful tool to manage the volume and complexity of professional know-how. In the case of this high-leverage teaching practice, our professional know-how includes how the TL can be used for the majority of the time to mediate learning and stimulate target language interaction in language classrooms.

The Interaction and Target Language Comprehensibility (I-TLC) Tool is divided into three main parts, each further subdivided into some of the most important pedagogical moves that enact the practice of interactive and comprehensible TL use during instruction. Each of these parts will be deconstructed below.

I: Creating Comprehensible Language

II: Creating Contexts for Comprehension

III: Creating Comprehensible Interactions

Interaction and Target Language Comprehensibility Tool

Name of teacher: _____

Date of observation: _____

This observation tool will help you *monitor the comprehensibility* of your target language use or of other teachers whom you observe. By completing the checklist, the teacher will understand areas of strength and in which improvement is needed.

Category I: Creating Comprehensible **LANGUAGE**
- ❏ The teacher paraphrases new words and expressions.
- ❏ The teacher defines new words with examples rather than translation.
- ❏ The teacher slows down the rate of speech according to the level of the learners.
- ❏ The teacher uses vocabulary and structures that learners know and builds on them over time.
- ❏ The teacher uses new words and expressions more than once or twice and enters and re-enters these language elements frequently in the input.
- ❏ The teacher signals new words and structures with tone of voice.
- ❏ The teacher uses connected discourse rather than presenting isolated words for drill and repetition.

Category II: Creating **CONTEXTS** for comprehension
- ❏ The teacher uses gestures to make new language clear.
- ❏ The teacher uses visuals and concrete objects to support comprehension.
- ❏ The teacher focuses learner attention on the topic and objective of the lesson in advance of presentations and discussions.
- ❏ The teacher creates a lesson with a purpose relevant to learners' lives.

Category III: Creating comprehensible **INTERACTIONS** with learners
- ❏ The teacher interacts with learners using active comprehension checking strategies (e.g., signaling).
- ❏ The teacher interacts with students and checks how well they are following what is said by cuing for recurrent words and phrases in the discourse.
- ❏ The teacher uses question sequences that begin with yes/no questions, move to forced-choice questions, and end with open-ended, WH-questions.
- ❏ The teacher provides useful expressions and phrases to help learners negotiate meaning, such as asking for repetition, asking for clarification (Can you say more?), checking their comprehension (Do you mean...?), and confirming their understanding (I think you are saying... Am I right?).

Figure 1.2. **Interaction and Target Language Comprehensibility Tool**

Source: Donato, original material, 2011, modified 2016

Creating Comprehensible Language

Comprehensibility is a relative concept based on what learners know, where they are in their language development, and how familiar they are with the topic. What this fact means is that teachers need to constantly monitor how they are speaking to learners to ensure that their talk-in-interaction is neither too difficult for them to understand and therefore over the heads of the learners, nor too simple and therefore not challenging enough to maintain learner engagement with meaning-making. To make language comprehensible, teachers need to understand and practice the following discourse features.

(1) **Paraphrase** new words and expressions to ensure that learners focus on them and understand their meaning. To paraphrase means explaining new vocabulary or phrases in a simpler way using familiar language that learners might recognize. The following are examples in English of paraphrases. The word in italics is considered new vocabulary for learners and the focus of the paraphrase. The paraphrase is underlined. Note how the target word is introduced and then re-introduced after the paraphrase so learners have multiple opportunities to experience the word in context.

    a. That actor is *bald*. He has no hair on his head. He's *bald*. Who are other actors or singers who are *bald*?
    b. Pizza is a *popular* food in the United States. Many Americans like to eat pizza. Pizza is a very *popular* meal. Where else in the world do you think pizza is *popular*?
    c. Lady Gaga is a *famous* singer. She is known all over the world. Her songs are very *famous* in many countries. Who are some *famous* singers whom you listen to?

(2) Defining new words and expressions by example is a way to increase the comprehensibility of classroom talk and a way to maintain learner engagement with the language. For example, if the word *transportation* causes difficulty, it can easily be defined by providing examples of different types of transportation, such as bus, taxi, car, train, plane. These definitions can be easily inserted into discussions and presentations and thus prevent the need to break up the discourse by translating key vocabulary and expressions that are critical to the topic of discussion. Defining by example also provides learners with a model of what they may do when they wish to express an idea in which a particular word in the target language may not be known to them.

(3) Slowing down the **rate of speech** is necessary especially when expressing complex ideas cast in new language for the learners. Language learners can become extremely frustrated when trying to understand what is said if the rate of speech is so fast that they do not have the time to grasp and process the words and meanings that they hear. This frustration can make learners abandon attempts to understand, lose attention, and decrease their motivation to participate in a classroom discourse community. Some teachers may think that slowing down the rate of speech implies that they are "talking down" to learners as if they were speaking to a small child. From the learner's perspective, however, the rate of speech supports comprehension and connection with the flow of the class and is therefore a necessary component of target language use in the classroom. Slowing down the speed of what is said occurs in much the same way that a native speaker would naturally tailor the speed of talk when the non-native speaker shows a lack of understanding. However, there are two important caveats to keep in mind. First, slowing down speech should be used only when there is a need to help learners focus on and process complex language. If the teacher speaks slowly and in an unnatural manner on a regular basis, learners will have serious difficulty processing language that is spoken at a more natural rate. Secondly, the teacher should monitor the rate of speech that he or she uses across language levels to

match learners' language ability so that over time they are able to understand the language at a relatively normal rate of delivery. The rate of speech in a first-year language class will be different from how the language is spoken in advanced classes. Determining how quickly or slowly to speak the target language will depend on the teacher's ability to monitor learner comprehension and attention across levels of instruction and according to learners' abilities.

(4) <u>Use vocabulary and structures that learners know and build on them over time</u>. Although language learners can often understand more than they can say, this fact does not mean that what is said to them can contain a high density of new vocabulary, expressions, complex grammatical structures, or obscure cultural references. Teachers are often well aware of what their learners know and do not know at certain points during a course. Supporting comprehension of new words and expressions by introducing them in the context of what learners already have learned is one important way that learners learn *through* the language. Flooding learners with a large quantity of new language elements that they will struggle to understand will frustrate them and create class confusion. New words and expressions need to be added gradually to what learners already know within a meaningful and interesting context that makes meaning visible and that encourages listening and a willingness to make the effort to understand. This requires careful attention to teacher talk by monitoring what is said relative to the learners and where they are in terms of what they know and can do with the language.

(5) <u>Use new words and expressions in context more than once or twice</u> and re-enter these words and expressions frequently in talk. It is commonplace for beginning teachers to present too few occasions for listening to and comprehending new elements of the language. Language is learned and comprehension is achieved by giving learners multiple opportunities to hear new language in natural ways that go beyond repeating the word several times for learners or asking them to repeat after the teacher. In fact, asking learners to repeat words and expressions in a rote fashion leads to boredom and lack of learner engagement. Learners need multiple opportunities to process and assign meaning to the new language within various meaningful contexts. Learning how to enter and re-enter new vocabulary in a natural way takes practice and for the beginning teacher may also require scripting (in writing) how new language will be introduced in context. A pitfall of beginning teachers is that often when they introduce a new TL word, they use pronouns (e.g., it, they, them) instead of re-entering the word as they continue the lesson. For example, if novice learners are presented with pictures to identify popular foods in target language countries, the teacher's use of "it" or "they" to refer to this new vocabulary will not help novices to learn these new words and may create confusion. Re-entering the vocabulary naturally in context is a way to help learners process the new language, make meaning of what is said, and retain new language elements from the presentation. Beyond beginning levels of language instruction, however, the goal may be for learners to produce TL that is increasingly more natural and coherent. In this case, the teacher would want to call attention to the use of pronoun referents to avoid unnatural repetitions of the noun.

(6) <u>Signaling new words and structures with tone of voice</u> focuses learners on key elements of what is being said and supports attention. For example, key elements of the message can be signaled by adding stress to a word or expression, using a slightly louder tone of voice, or pausing before the word. In the course of schooling, learners become quite adept at interpreting how teachers talk to them and what the teacher's tone of voice conveys. They come to realize by tone of voice alone what pleases or displeases the teacher, when answers are correct or incorrect, or when the teacher expects them to say more about a topic.

Consider a teacher who repeats a learner utterance with rising intonation and how the learner correctly interprets this response as a signal that what was said may not have been entirely accurate or comprehensible (*You are 3 years old?*). Consider also how challenging it is in our everyday lives to process information and pay attention to a message that is delivered in a monotone voice. Tone of voice is a powerful tool for establishing and focusing attention when using the target language in the classroom.

(7) <u>Using connected discourse makes language easier to understand</u> rather than presenting isolated words for drill and repetition. In elementary language classes, beginning teachers often follow a linear discourse pattern of teacher presentation-learner repetition when presenting new vocabulary. This discourse pattern is difficult for learners to understand because it lacks a context (see *creating contexts* below) and presents learners with unnatural acts of communication that have little resemblance to the ways language is used in life. As Hall (1995) illustrates in one of her classroom-based studies, using language in unnatural ways in the classroom creates communicative incompetence rather than communicatively competent users of the language.

To create comprehensible language means using language at appropriate levels in a discourse context in which the teacher becomes a conversational partner rather than a mechanical provider of isolated vocabulary words. For example, in presenting the parts of a house to a class of young learners, the teacher situates new language elements in a well-developed discourse that directs learners to complete a drawing task in which he or she can visually monitor learners' levels of comprehension. Compare Presentation A with Presentation B and decide in which context it would be easier for learners to grasp the meaning of new vocabulary and to retain it and why.

Presentation A

T: Now we will draw a *house* together. Watch me as I draw the *house* on the paper. The *house* has two *floors*. Now you draw the *house* with two *floors* on your paper. The *house* also has a *door*. Draw the *door* on your *house*. It can be a big *door* or a small *door*. There are *windows* too. The *house* has two *windows* on the first *floor* and two *windows* on the second *floor*. I am drawing two *windows*. You draw *windows* now on your *house*. Everyone, show me your *house* now. Now point to the *windows*, please. Point to the *door*, please (teacher checks comprehension). Thank you. Your drawings look beautiful! Now, let's draw a tree next to our (teacher pauses, points to house, and learners chime in).

Ss: *House.*

Presentation B

T: *House* (shows a colorful laminated picture of house from a children's book). Repeat *house*.

Ss: *House*

T: Very good. (Points to door on picture) *Door*. Repeat *door*.

Ss: *Door*

> **T:** Again, repeat *door*.
>
> **Ss:** *Door*
>
> **T:** Very good. (Points to window) *Window*, repeat after me, *window*.
>
> **Ss:** *Window*
>
> **T:** Very good. What is this (points to house)?
>
> **Ss:** (no answer; learner forgets the word)
>
> **T:** *House*, repeat *house*
>
> **Ss:** *House*

As the two presentations illustrate, Presentation A is more memorable for learners because of the natural way the new vocabulary is introduced in the task and the numerous times that vocabulary is entered and re-entered (see #5) into the discourse. For example, in Presentation A, the teacher uses the word *house* 10 times in the drawing activity, an appropriate context for young learners, compared to the use of the word *house* 2 times in the teacher presentation-learner repetition activity. Despite the attractive visual used in Presentation B, learners are clearly not given sufficient opportunity to see the language in action or hear the target vocabulary to establish its form and meaning in memory. In Presentation B, forgetting is inevitable and can be anticipated. The teacher's question in Presentation B is a test of learners' memory. Conversely, the teacher's statements and requests for checking comprehension (e.g., point to the *window*) in Presentation A assist learners in learning new vocabulary in the context of a drawing task that introduces new words, provides an authentic model of how language is used for directing action, and teaches language through the teacher's developmentally purposeful activity.

The following is an example of the same theme of the house/housing but for novices at the secondary or post-secondary level. In this example, the teacher decides upon a context that appeals to adolescents and older learners who live in a particular geographical area. Her purpose for introducing this context is to provide a basis for comparison of housing in some parts of the US with various types of housing in the target language country, setting the stage for a later discussion on housing from the perspective of social justice issues in the global arena. Note how the TL is introduced within a natural discussion that reflects the type of exchange that is heard in an academic subject area class, e.g., social studies or world cultures.

> **Teacher:** Class, today we begin to talk about housing and to compare housing in the US with housing in many (insert Latin American, Francophone, East Asian) cultures. I found a house ad from a local newspaper, so let's see how we would describe to our peers who live in X country what a typical house might look like in our geographical area. Later on we'll look at typical types of housing in their country and make some comparisons and discuss why there are differences. [Teacher projects house visual onto screen for class to see.] It looks like this house has 3 *floors* including a *basement*. The *basement* is on the *lower level*, or under the *first floor* of the house. Can you tell how many *rooms* are on each *floor*? Is this typical of most houses around here?
>
> **S1:** There are 3 *rooms* on the first *floor* and 4 *rooms* on the second *floor*.

T: This *house* looks big, doesn't it? So let's look at the first *floor*. This is the *kitchen*, where the family prepares meals and most of the time eats there also. This *kitchen* has an *island* with *chairs*, but not every *kitchen* has an *island*. Does your family spend a lot of time in the *kitchen*?

S2: Yes, we eat in the *kitchen* every day and talk while we cook.

T: Same for my family. Some houses in the US have big *kitchens* and some houses have small *kitchens*. In the *kitchen*, there are *appliances*. Can you guess which is the *refrigerator*? *Stove*? *Microwave*? *Dishwasher*? Which *appliances* do you all use the most? .... [In some languages such as Spanish some of these words are cognates and students will recognize them because of their similarity to English.]

Note that the focus in this presentation is to engage learners from the beginning of the lesson to talk about the house in the TL through a focus on meaning and within an interesting context. Instead of being asked to repeat new vocabulary in a rote fashion, learners experience natural repetition as they hear the teacher's input, look at the accompanying visual, and relate what is being said to their own worlds.

Creating Contexts for Comprehension

Casting the target language in an interesting, meaningful, and familiar context is a powerful way to support comprehension in the classroom. As in life, information out of context is difficult to understand and can be easily misinterpreted (e.g., "*That's not what he meant. What he said was taken entirely out of context!*"). **Context** implies the concrete circumstances for social and cultural discourse practices. For example, context requires knowing who are the participants of an activity or event, how they are described, what actions they take, where and how they act, what they are trying to achieve, and how these actions are appraised and evaluated. When what is said is framed in a familiar and interesting context, the language and its functions are made understandable and memorable. In foreign language classes, teachers are faced continually with creating contexts for language use that support comprehension and invite participation. Many textbooks are organized around contexts for instruction in the form of themes (leisure time activities, school, family and relationships, holidays and seasons). However, these themes in and of themselves do not create comprehensible contexts for using the target language for instruction and creating a class conducted the majority of the time in the target language. In this section, creating contexts for comprehension is deconstructed into four techniques that support a thematic focus of a lesson.

(1) <u>Using gestures to make new language clear</u>, e.g., outlining a circle in the air to refer to an object with that shape or using mime to act out the meaning of actions, e.g., acting out moves that are associated with certain sports that learners play or watch regularly. What must be kept in mind is that gestures and mime contribute to building comprehension but should never be the only channel through which learners understand what is said. The goal of increasing comprehension through gesture and mime is for learners to connect what they hear (forms) to meanings and to be able to use these forms to express themselves during the course of the lesson.

(2) <u>Using visuals and concrete objects to support comprehension</u>. Photos, drawings, videos, and various concrete objects may help learners create visual images of the language rather than associate it with an English translation. Additionally, images and objects should

reflect target language cultures and will support teaching language in a cultural context (see Chapter 5). Creating contexts with visuals and objects does not have to be in the margins of the lesson simply to illustrate the meaning of what is said. These contextual supports to comprehension can also be the focus of a discussion about cultural products, practices, and perspectives (National Standards in Foreign Language Education Project, 2015). For example, in a thematic lesson on food in an advanced class, learners might compare images of breakfast in the US with images of breakfast in a target language country and discuss why certain foods are eaten for breakfast in certain areas of the world, their health benefits, and give their reactions to differences in these mealtime eating habits (Barnes-Karol & Broner, 2010).

(3) <u>Focusing learner attention on the topic and objective of the lesson in advance of presentations and discussions</u> creates a framework and purpose that support comprehension of target language use in the classroom. Prior knowledge of a topic of conversation or of a presentation alleviates confusion and allows learners to navigate classroom discourse. When we drop into a conversation, begin to watch a TV program already in progress, or listen to a talk without knowing the overarching topic, we struggle to comprehend what is said and can easily lose motivation to continue listening to make meaning of utterances. Explicit explanation by the teacher about the topic and objective of the lesson is required for learners to engage with the language and for sustained target language use in the classroom. This explicit attention involves initially stating the objective of the lesson (i.e., perhaps also displaying it visually such as writing it on the board) and indicating what learners will be able to do at the end of the lesson, e.g., learning how to extend an invitation, learning how to agree or disagree with a statement, or learning how to provide personal information. The objective and topic of the lesson also need to relate to the learners' lives and their interests (see #4 below). In this way, comparisons may be made with how they perform certain language functions in their first language with how they are performed in the language they are learning, thus helping learners become conscious of what they are saying in the target language, how they are saying it, and why (see Comparison Goal Area, National Standards in Foreign Language Education Project, 2015)

(4) <u>Creating a lesson with a purpose relevant to learners' lives</u> is a significant factor in assisting learners with comprehending and using the target language in the class. The more relevant the purpose and its relationship to the learners' interests, the more learners will be willing to accept target language use for instruction. In the same way that the objective and topic of the lesson need to be made explicit, so too does the purpose of the lesson. *Topic*, *objective*, and *purpose* are three vital pieces of information that learners need to make meaning of the target language during instruction. With this preliminary knowledge, learner comprehension is supported and confusion and complaints about classroom target language use may diminish. Additionally, the purpose for a lesson cannot be developed without intimate knowledge of learners, their backgrounds, social environment, and life circumstances. Not all purposes are created equal. For example, learners who do not engage in skiing as a routine pastime activity or who live in an area where skiing is not common or possible given the climate, may not find learning how to buy a lift ticket meaningful or relevant to their lives. Conversely, learners who work in part-time jobs while in high school may find learning how to apply for a part-time job or discussing the qualities of a good part-time job as immediately relevant to their daily lives. In summary, to increase comprehension through purposeful target language use requires knowledge of learner-lived experiences. Relying on the textbook for purposes of communication is seldom the best way to create learner-relevant contexts that increase comprehension in the

classroom. Here the teacher must exert professional judgment and decide if the purpose of the textbook lesson is connected to the lives of learners and to the experiences that they bring to the classroom. If the textbook lesson falls short in this regard, the teacher must make the necessary adaptations or create a new lesson that is relevant to learners.

Creating Comprehensible Interactions

In addition to meaningful contexts and language modifications, talk-in-interaction with learners transforms passive listening into active meaning-making processes. Conducting a class the majority of the time in the target language is not delivering a lecture to learners who sit passively in seats ostensibly listening and understanding what the teacher says. Interaction involves the learners in target language use and assists them with comprehending what may be incomprehensible to them. Interaction may be verbal or non-verbal. With beginners, interaction can be created with initial non-verbal forms of interactive comprehension checking, moving gradually to more verbal forms of participation. In this way, teachers monitor the comprehensibility of what they say as they say it rather than at the end of a long segment of teacher talk, when it may be too late to repair discourse missteps and refocus the attention of learners.

In this section, creating comprehensible interactions is deconstructed into four steps.

(1) <u>Signaling is an effective comprehension checking strategy</u>. Signaling involves the use of non-verbal actions that indicate comprehension of the ongoing discourse. There are many non-verbal and creative ways for learners to signal their understanding and to keep them connected to what is being said and the topic of the lesson. Learners may agree or disagree with thumbs-up or thumbs-down; point, touch, or move objects as the objects are being talked about; draw pictures of what they hear; stand up if they hear a description that relates to them; act out parts of a story; or hold up small pictures of characters, places, or objects at appropriate times when listening to a story told by the teacher.

(2) <u>Cueing a learner for a verbal response</u> is a way to develop an interaction during target language use. As learners demonstrate comprehension of what is said, recurrent patterns in the discourse can be used to invite learner participation. Cueing involves making an incomplete statement (not asking a question, see (3) below) and then pausing for learners to complete it. For example, in telling the well-known fairy tale of the *Three Little Pigs*, learners might be cued with "I'll huff and I'll puff and I'll blow _____." In discussing TV shows learners might be asked to complete the phrase "The Big Bang_____" or names of other TV shows that are frequently viewed by the learners. The point is that once meaning is established and learners have enough practice with the content of the spoken text, they can participate in what is being said and can collaborate with the teachers to construct meaning. Cueing is not having a conversation. It can be used, however, to keep learners connected to the target language in the classroom and as a way to show them they indeed can follow, understand, and remember key points in what is being talked about. Finally, a teacher should never try to use cueing before learners have had a sufficient amount of exposure to the expected response. Premature cueing can result in silence, frustration, and confusion.

(3) <u>Using question sequences</u> is a useful strategy for engaging learners in target language interaction in the classroom. Learners are quite used to answering teacher questions. Using questions to create interaction in the target language and to maintain maximum target language use needs to be go beyond simply assessing what learners have learned to discovering and assessing what they know to help them build on this knowledge and

continue to learn. In this way, assessment and instruction go hand in hand. A good way to think about *questioning to support learning* vs. *questioning to test what is learned* is to think about questions as a form of scaffolding that move from less demanding to more complex responses. This type of question sequences moves from (a) yes-no answers to (b) forced-choice answers in which the answer to the question is one of the two choices, to (c) open-ended questions asking for opinions, feelings, and ideas or for learners to retrieve from memory a particular piece of information. Using a story discussion as the context, an example of these three levels of questions is presented below:

Yes-no:	Was the setting of the story in a city?
	Was the setting of the story in another country?
Forced-choice:	Was the setting of the story in a city or in the country?
	Was the setting of the story in the Unites States or in Latin America?
Open-ended:	Where was the setting of the story?
	In what way did the setting of the story affect how you reacted to the actions of the main character?

The sequence is not fixed and will depend on the level of the class and on the teacher's assessment of what learners know and can do in the interaction. If working with beginners who are being introduced to new material, such as learning new vocabulary or expressions, it is likely that beginning with open-ended questions will result in a struggle for learners to respond. In this case, beginning with yes-no questions is a better way to create interaction in the target language. Assessing the level of understanding of the class is essential before moving to more demanding questions, such as forced-choice and open-ended. In more advanced classes, learners can more easily express ideas and opinions about different kinds of texts and topics and respond to open-ended questions. If these more advanced learners struggle, teachers can adjust the level of questioning to the abilities of the learners.

(4) Providing useful expressions and phrases to help learners negotiate meaning and increase comprehension promotes interaction and prevents the teacher from lecturing. Learners can be explicitly taught the ways to manage conversations through the use of formulaic expressions that serve to ask for clarification, check the comprehension of others, and to confirm that they have indeed understood the contents of the talk that is taking place (see Figure 1.2). Learners can be given a list of these expressions or they can be posted in the classroom large enough for everyone to see so that they can be used for reference during presentations of new material or discussions. These expressions can vary depending on the level of the class. As learners progress in their language proficiency more complex and sophisticated away of managing a conversational interaction can be taught (e.g., *Repeat, please* vs. *Sorry, I didn't understand your point. Could you tell me more?*). If age-appropriate videos of target language interactions are available, learners could analyze how a conversation unfolds and how speakers signal their comprehension or lack of it, request clarification, and confirm that they have understood intended meanings. Teaching learners how to manage conversations and how to become full participants in interactions is often not addressed in language classes or in commercially prepared materials, yet it is precisely this kind of language that fuels conversation, comprehension, and meaning-making.

Rehearsing the Practice

The following tasks are provided to practice and rehearse ways to use the target language in the classroom to increase comprehensibility and interaction. Complete the tasks and then practice the particular discourse features with your peers. You may find it helpful to use External Mediational Tools #1a, 1b, and 1c in this chapter's Appendix A as you engage in this rehearsal.

(1) Select three words from a textbook that you anticipate will be difficult for learners to understand. Find a visual or several visuals for these words and describe the word using a paraphrase following the model described in this chapter.

(2) Think of a vocabulary item (or select one from a textbook) that a student would learn in a first-year or first-semester language course. In round robin fashion, say the word to the class and ask classmates for suggestions on how to define the vocabulary word using target language examples to make its meaning clear.

(3) Alone or working with a classmate, write a script for a micro-lesson in context in which you make instructional decisions based on the features of the checklist (a-g below and in no specific order). Specific steps for scripting the micro-lesson are provided after the features. After scripting your lesson, rehearse it with classmates or friends outside of class. After rehearsal, come prepared to present the micro-lesson to the class.

Discourse Features

   (a) Using frequent non-verbal (e.g., signaling) and verbal comprehension checks in proper sequence

   (b) Using questions in a sequence from simple to complex to support language production

   (c) Creating a meaningful and interesting context that is relevant to learners

   (d) Entering and re-entering the new words in a natural and purposeful way

   (e) Cueing responses

   (f) Providing the topic, objective, and purpose of the lesson

   (g) Using of objects, visuals, and/or gestures

Steps to Follow When Scripting

   (1) Select a topic and six thematically related vocabulary words to introduce in the micro-lesson.

   (2) Identify the context for presenting these words. Ask your instructor to approve the context.

   (3) Identify the lines of discourse with (T:) for teacher, with (Ss:) for whole class responses, or (S:) for individual learner responses.

   (4) Write exactly what you anticipate saying and doing and what you anticipate learners should say and do, realizing that you cannot totally predict what learners will say. New words need to be used in sufficient quantity so that learners can establish meaning and to facilitate memory. Underline target vocabulary and

count the number of times the vocabulary word is used. Provide the word count for each word at the end of the script.

(5) Provide descriptive information for teacher actions in parentheses next to where it occurs in the discourse. For example, (teacher shows a picture of a city map to the class), (teacher asks learners to point to XYZ), (teacher asks learners to stand up), (teacher asks learners to point to XYZ).

(6) Identify the discourse and interactive features (a-g above) that are used next to each utterance. You should make a column or margin large enough next to the lines of the script for identifying these features.

(7) By at least the fifth line of interaction, active comprehension checking should take place. Later in the script, learners should move from comprehension to production through the use of questions.

(8) Never use the phrase "Repeat after me." Create an interaction in which learners need to speak rather than being forced or coerced to speak.

Assessing the Practice

1. Use Rubric #1 in this chapter's Appendix B to assess classmates' presentations of the micro-lesson (task 3). After the presentation, discuss the ratings in terms of where agreement or disagreement is found among observers. Observers should provide concrete evidence from the micro-lesson to justify and explain reasons for specific ratings.

2. If you are currently teaching in a school, ask your cooperating teacher or a colleague to use the rubric to assess how you create comprehensible language, contexts, and interactions. Explain the categories of the rubric to the person observing you so the observer has a clear idea of what each category means and describe what each category may look like in practice. Give specific examples. After the class, discuss the ratings that your observer gave and the reasons why. Be an active listener rather than trying to defend your pedagogical actions.

3. After a class you have taught, use the checklist in Figure 1.2 to review the features of each category to determine which of the features you recall using and those you did not use and why. Based on your assessment of how the class performed, try to identify the feature or features of the checklist that deserve more attention in future classes or that need to be modified.

Putting the Practice into a Larger Context: Instructional Goals and Challenges

This chapter has illustrated that interactive and comprehensible target language use in the language classroom to build discourse communities and to focus learner attention on language is a complex undertaking that requires practice, patience, and the ability to adjust talk-in-interaction to particular levels, whole classes, and individual learners. Considering the larger context, this HLTP is the foundation upon which all language instruction occurs and sets the stage for the types of experiences learners will have and the degree to which they may be motivated in the classroom. With experience, teachers often can predict and plan the kind of language to use with their classes and learners, the types of questions that are needed, and the types of language modifications they need to make.

Beginning teachers often need to "test the waters" to see if they provide enough support for comprehension or if the complexity of their target language and lack of sufficient attention to learners' comprehension is a source of learner resistance, irritation and frustration.

The discourse features, contextual elements of a lesson, and interactive moves to involve the class work together to shape a community in which target language use is a regular feature of the foreign language class and simultaneously the vehicle and content of instruction. Teachers must be aware that making meaning clear and focusing attention on language, providing a context for instruction, and creating interactions with learners are essential features of any lesson and flexible tools to be used with *all* learners at *all* levels of instruction. Hence, creating a classroom community in which learners experience target language use in various modes of communication and at appropriate levels of challenge is truly an HLTP. Significant learning outcomes can only occur if teachers are willing to invest the time to analyze, plan, and reflect on the various ways that classroom discourse is made accessible and comprehensible to learners.

Beyond the immediate purposes of this high-leverage teaching practice, Kennedy (2016) highlights the importance of understanding how HLTPs address larger teaching challenges. One of these challenges for all teachers regardless of the level of language they teach is helping learners get beyond their reluctance, and at times hostility, toward classroom target language use. Worse yet, teachers can unconsciously view learners as being incapable of understanding and participating. Supporting target language comprehension through the ways that language and context are used, checking frequently that learners are following the thread of discourse, and eliciting learner participation in a language class is key to discovering how learners are making sense of the language to which they are exposed and, given the right kind of support and mediation, orienting ourselves to them as capable language learners.

A related challenge that this HLTP addresses is teachers' ability to manage the classroom. A well-designed class that addresses learners' interests and engages them actively in the lesson is also a well-managed class. Being in an environment in which language is spoken too quickly to be understood, contains too many unknown language elements or complexities that the learners cannot process, or uses cultural references unknown to the learners can result in disruptive behavior in learners or boredom in the class. Conversely, classes in which learners are challenged and provided with support to meet these challenges and in which progress is recognized and acknowledged can transform disruption and boredom into dynamic cooperative learning experiences.

Finally, teaching is a personal endeavor involving teachers' individual personalities and creativity (Kennedy, 2016). Deconstructing these practices, as we have done in this chapter, is not to be understood as an inflexible prescription for teaching practice, but as a way for teachers to make instructional decisions that are appropriate for their classes and infuse their teaching with their own creativity and personal characteristics and qualities that make every teacher unique.

For Further Reading

American Council on the Teaching of Foreign Languages (ACTFL). (2010). ACTFL Position Statement on Use of the Target Language in the Classroom. Arlington, VA: Author. Retrieved from http://www.actfl.org/news/position-statements/use-the-target-language-the-classroom

Barnes-Karol, G., & Broner, M. A. (2010). Using images as springboards to teach cultural perspectives in light of the ideals of the MLA Report. *Foreign Language Annals, 43*(3), 422–445.

Crouse, D. (Oct/Nov 2014). What counts as comprehensible? Allowing ambiguity in the learning process. *The Language Educator, 9*(5), 27–29.

Donato, R. (1994). Collective scaffolding in second language learning. In J. P. Lantolf & G. Appel (Eds.), *Vygotskian approaches to second language research* (pp. 33–56). Norwood, NJ: Ablex.

Gawande, A. (2009). *The checklist manifesto: How to get things right.* New York: Metropolitan Books.

Hall, J.K. (1995b). 'Aw, man, where we goin?': Classroom interaction and the development of L2 interactional competence. *Issues in Applied Linguistics, 6*(2), 37–62.

Kennedy, M. (2016). Parsing the practice of teaching. *Journal of Teacher Education, 67*(1), 6–17.

Krashen, S. D. (1981). *Second language acquisition and second language learning.* Oxford, UK: Pergamon Press Inc.

Krashen, S. D. (1982). *Principles and practice in second language acquisition.* Oxford, UK: Pergamon Press Inc.

Long, M. (1983). Native speaker/non-native speaker conversation and the negotiation of comprehensible input. *Applied Linguistics, 4*(2), 126–141.

Long, M. & Porter, P. (1985). Group work, interlanguage talk, and second language acquisition. *TESOL Quarterly 19*(2) 207–228.

Maquire, E. A., Frith, C. D., & Morris, R. G. M. (1999). The functional neuroanatomy of comprehension and memory: The importance of prior knowledge. *Brain, 122,* 1839–1850.

National Standards in Foreign Language Education Project (NSFLEP). (2015). *World-Readiness standards for learning languages.* Alexandria, VA: Author.

Pica, T. (1994). Research on negotiation: What does it reveal about second language acquisition? Conditions, processes, and outcomes. *Language Learning 44*(3), 493–527.

Pica, T., Young, R. & Doughty, C. (1987). The impact of interaction on comprehension. *TESOL Quarterly 21*(4), 737–758.

Sousa, D. A. (2011). *How the brain learns* (4th ed.). Thousand Oaks, CA: Corwin Press.

Swain, M. (1985). Communicative competence: Some roles of comprehensible input and comprehensible output in its development. In S. Gass & C. Madden (Eds.), *Input in second language acquisition* (pp. 235–257). Rowley, MA: Newbury House.

Swain, M. (2000). The output hypothesis and beyond: Mediating acquisition through collaborative dialogue. In J. P. Lantolf (Ed.), *Sociocultural theory and second language learning* (97–114). Oxford: Oxford University press.

Vygotsky, L. (1986). *Thought and language.* Cambridge, MA: MIT Press.

Appendix A

External Mediational Tool #1A: Facilitating TL Comprehensibility: Category I: Creating Comprehensible LANGUAGE

❑ The teacher paraphrases new words and expressions.
❑ The teacher defines new words with examples rather than translation.
❑ The teacher slows down the rate of speech according to the level of the learners.
❑ The teacher uses vocabulary and structures that learners know and builds on them over time.
❑ The teacher uses new words and expressions more than once or twice and enters and re-enters these language elements frequently in the input.
❑ The teacher signals new words and structures with tone of voice.
❑ The teacher uses connected discourse rather than presenting isolated words for drill and repetition.

External Mediational Tool #1B: Facilitating TL Comprehensibility: Category II: Creating CONTEXTS for Comprehension

❑ The teacher uses gestures to make new language clear.
❑ The teacher uses visuals and concrete objects to support comprehension.
❑ The teacher focuses learner attention on the topic and objective of the lesson in advance of presentations and discussions.
❑ The teacher creates a lesson with a purpose relevant to learners' lives.

External Mediational Tool #1C: Facilitating TL Comprehensibility: Category III: Creating Comprehensible INTERACTIONS with Learners

❑ The teacher interacts with learners using active comprehension checking strategies (e.g., signaling).
❑ The teacher interacts with students and checks how well they are following what is said by cuing for recurrent words and phrases in the discourse.
❑ The teacher uses question sequences that begin with yes/no questions, move to forced-choice questions, and end with open-ended, WH-questions.
❑ The teacher provides useful expressions and phrases to help learners negotiate meaning, such as asking for repetition, asking for clarification (Can you say more?), checking their comprehension (Do you mean…?), and confirming their understanding (I think you are saying… Am I right?).

Appendix B

RUBRIC: HLTP #1: Using the Target Language for Instruction*

	EXCEEDS EXPECTATIONS	MEETS EXPECTATIONS	DEVELOPING	UNACCEPTABLE
Amount of Target Language Used	Target language is used all of the time.	Target language is used 3/4 of class time.	Target language is used 1/2 of class time.	Target language is used less than 1/2 of class time.
Comprehensible Language	Teacher paraphrases and adjusts rate of speech; defines new words with examples and re-enters new words frequently in input; signals new words and structures with tone of voice; uses familiar vocabulary and structures and builds on them over time.	Teacher paraphrases and adjusts rate of speech; defines new words with examples; uses familiar vocabulary and structures and builds on them over time.	Teacher paraphrases but may not adjust rate of speech; tends not to define new words with examples and may resort to English at times; uses familiar vocabulary.	Virtually no strategies are used to make language comprehensible other than translation to English.
Comprehensible Contexts	Meaningful and purposeful context drives lesson. Students know topic and objective of lesson in advance. Teacher uses gestures, visuals, and objects in creative ways to support comprehension.	Lesson has a meaningful context. Students know topic and objective of lesson in advance. Teacher uses gestures, visuals, and/ or objects to support comprehension.	Lesson has a meaningful context. Students tend to know either topic or objective of lesson in advance but not both. Sporadic use of gestures, visuals, or objects to support comprehension.	Context may not be meaningful or purposeful. Students do not know topic and objective of lesson in advance. Little use of gestures, visuals, objects to support comprehension.

	EXCEEDS EXPECTATIONS	MEETS EXPECTATIONS	DEVELOPING	UNACCEPTABLE
Comprehensible Interactions	Teacher engages all students in presentation of new material. Teacher sequences questions from yes/no to forced-choice to open-ended format. Teacher provides phrases for students to negotiate meaning, ask for clarification, check their comprehension, and confirm their understanding.	Teacher involves most of the class in presentation of new material. Teacher sequences questions from yes/no to forced-choice to open-ended format. Teacher provides phrases for students to negotiate meaning and ask for clarification.	Teacher involves a few students in presentation of new material. And/or teacher asks a variety of question types but not in a sequence from yes/no to open-ended. Teacher provides a few phrases for students to negotiate meaning and ask for clarification.	Students are passive as teacher presents new material. No sequencing of questions from yes/no to open-ended. And/or teacher does not provide phrases for students to negotiate meaning and ask for clarification.

*All communication referred to in rubric is carried out in the target language.

Chapter 2

HLTP #2: Building a Classroom Discourse Community

PART 1: Engaging Learners in Oral Classroom Communication
PART 2: Designing and Conducting Oral Interpersonal Pair and Group Tasks

What students ultimately learn about language and communication is closely connected to the types of the interactional practices that teachers provide in their classrooms.

The discussion in Chapter 1 highlighted the pivotal role of conversational interactions in enabling students to make sense of the target language they hear to mediate their language learning. The quantity and quality of these interactions depends to a large degree on the type of discourse community developed by the teacher over time. The term ***discourse*** refers to communicative exchanges between individuals by means of a connected group of utterances, the context of which is shared through social interaction and a bank of common experiences (Wells, 1999). According to Wells (1999), discourse builds on understanding that develops over time and occurs in a variety of situations in which both students and the teacher actively participate as speakers and listeners. A high-leverage teaching practice that is intricately linked to use of the target language is building a **classroom discourse community** in which communicative discourse can be nurtured. Within this larger grain-size HLTP are two smaller grain-size practices critical to developing and maintaining a positive classroom discourse community that supports a meaningful exchange of ideas and language learning:

1. Engaging learners in oral classroom communication (between teacher-student); and

2. Designing and conducting oral interpersonal pair and group tasks (between student-student).

It should be noted that, while the HLTP presented in Chapter 1 dealt with how teachers can make their target language use comprehensible to learners (i.e., through comprehensible interactions), the practices presented in this chapter focus on how to engage learners in becoming active participants in meaningful conversations and exchanges.

ACTFL/CAEP Standards addressed: #1a, 1b; #3a, 3b; #4a, 4b; #5a, 5b

Research and Theory Supporting the Practice

The overarching HLTP of building a classroom discourse community is supported by research in two areas: (1) classroom discourse patterns between the teacher and students, and (2) the role of social interaction in developing oral interpersonal communication.

A large body of research examining discourse patterns between the teacher and learners in language classrooms over the past several decades has revealed that teacher talk often lacks the development of a clear and meaningful topic and provides little foundation upon which students can participate and extend their talk in meaningful ways (Hall, 1995, 1999, 2004, 2010, 2012). Further, teachers' questions frequently reveal their own grammatical agendas, for example, to elicit a particular grammatical form such as a specific verb tense or to practice some aspect of syntax (Toth, 1997, 2004, 2011). For this reason, a commonly observed structure of classroom talk that is pervasive between the teacher and learners is referred to as **IRE**:

- The teacher INITIATES an assertion or asks a question.

- The learner RESPONDS.

- The teacher EVALUATES, by giving an evaluative statement such as "excellent" or by asking similar questions of another learner (Mehan, 1979).

This type of questioning is motivated by the teacher's desire to check whether the student has learned a particular grammatical structure or vocabulary item and then to inform the student whether his or her response was accurate or not. In this regard, the teacher asks **assessing questions**, which usually have one correct answer or answers that can be anticipated (Tharp & Gallimore, 1991). For example, the teacher may ask learners "What's today's date?" Afterwards, the teacher then provides feedback such as "Yes, correct!" or "You're missing a word." IRE, although perhaps useful to some degree in assessing how well learners have achieved control of the specific material taught or grammatical objective of the lesson, is mechanical, repetitious, and evaluative and impedes the development of classroom discourse that expresses meaningful ideas, opinions, and feelings and fails to nurture learner involvement in the communicative exchange (Hall, 1999; Shrum & Glisan, 2016). The following is an example of IRE in an English as a Foreign Language (EFL) class:

Teacher: What time is it?

Student: It's ten o'clock.

Teacher: Right! Very good. *It's* ten o'clock (Johnson, 1995, p. 4).

Clearly the teacher's purpose in this exchange is to check the learner's ability to tell time, and the evaluative response confirms the learner's correct use of the verb *it's* in giving the time. It should be noted that the exchange ends abruptly since the focus on meaning is now lost given the teacher's focus on use of the correct English contraction '*It's*' vs. on a genuine need to know the time, i.e., there is no motivation for the learner to engage further in a meaningful exchange of information.

The pervasive use of IRE also promotes the teacher's use of what Hall calls **lexical chaining**, the connecting of utterances by using the same or similar words that have "no connection to any larger topically related goal" (1995, p. 34). The following example is indicative of the type of meaningless exchanges that feature lexical chaining and unfortunately are common in many language classrooms:

Teacher: Susie, what color are Jasmine's jeans?

Susie: Jasmine's jeans are blue.

Teacher: Yes, they are blue. Ricardo, what color is Jason's backpack?

Ricardo: Jason's backpack is green.

Teacher: Right, it's green. Shijuan, what color is Rafael's hair?....

As seen in this example, lexical chaining takes place within the IRE structure, prompts the use of known information, has no clear topical focus, and thwarts sharing of new information within a larger communicative goal. Lexical chaining in the above example also makes visible the teacher's instructional objective, that is to assess if learners have mastered color vocabulary rather than to use color words in a meaningful discussion, e.g., a survey of the class' favorite colors, the relationship of color to feelings, the color of flags from various countries, a comparison of the signature colors of athletic teams in the US and in target language countries.

Given the fact that IRE does not promote a type of interpersonal communication that occurs in the world outside the classroom, an alternative classroom strategy to promote **talk-in-interaction** (Hall, 2010) is the use of **IRF**, which focuses on developing meaningful topics in discourse rather than on assessing the accuracy of learner responses:

- The teacher INITIATES an assertion or asks a question.

- The learner RESPONDS.

- The teacher gives FEEDBACK, by moving the conversation forward and encouraging learners to perform at higher levels—e.g., "Tell me more!" "Then what happened?" (Wells, 1993).

The type of feedback offered by the teacher can take the form of expressive reactions (e.g., "That's unbelievable!") or **assisting questions** that "encourage learners to think, push learners to perform at higher levels, and integrate content and topics" (e.g., "Could you give more details?") (Tharp & Gallimore, 1991, c.f. Shrum & Glisan, 2016, p. 82). Even in the earlier example of asking students for the time, the teacher can provide a more natural response such as, "Already? I guess it's time to begin class. At what time do you all have lunch today?" to illustrate how people typically respond to questions concerning the time of day or to inquire about the time of upcoming events. In sum, the IRF type of conversational sequences holds much promise for building a discourse community in the language classroom in which the norm should be meaningful communication between teacher and learners within larger topical contexts. The point is that a steady diet of IRE discourse patterns will never produce learners who are communicatively competent and who can initiate, participate in, and sustain interactions in the target language.

Sociocultural theory, as discussed in Chapter 1, offers additional research-based support for this HLTP, inasmuch as social interaction among learners is consequential to developing their ability to communicate within the interpersonal mode of communication, i.e., through two-way communication and sharing of ideas and opinions. Work in the area of **interactional competence** confirms the importance of learners' abilities to manage and participate in discussions in meaningful and relevant ways (Celce-Murcia, 2007; Hall, 1995; Mehan, 1979; Walsh, 2011). Interactional competence involves knowing how to perform speech acts within conversational exchanges such as expressing and defending opinions, complaining; managing a conversation by opening/closing conversations, taking turns, interrupting, changing topics; and using non-linguistic communication such as gestures and body language to support meaning-making (Celce-Murcia, 2007). A key strategy employed in interacting with others is **negotiation of meaning**, which has been defined as "exchanges between learners and their interlocutors as they attempt to resolve communication breakdown and to work toward mutual comprehension" (Pica, Holliday, Lewis, & Morgenthaler, 1989, p. 65). In the classroom, both speakers in an exchange "must seek clarification, check comprehension, and request confirmation that they have understood or are being understood by the other" (Shrum & Glisan, 2016, p. 22). These types of exchanges in which meanings are negotiated and created do not occur through mastery of grammar rules or through IRE patterns of discourse. They must be explicitly taught in the context of having meaningful exchanges in which the focus is on meaning and not form.

Hall (1995) proposes the use of "real" conversations in the classroom featuring topics that students develop through a shared purpose for how they unfold in interactions through turn-taking, inference making, and participation that contributes to and moves the topic or issue forward. She argues that for learners to become communicatively competent, as opposed to communicatively incompetent, classroom discourse should reflect the interactive features of conversation that learners experience outside the classroom for various purposeful social practices. The following features can guide the teacher in monitoring and assessing classroom conversations:

- Opening utterances establish the topic: "Hey, what's new with you?" In the classroom, the teacher might propose a topic by saying: "How many of you watched the Super Bowl commercials last night? I thought we might discuss which ones were our favorites."

- *Ellipsis* refers to not repeating information that is already known, and providing new information. For example, in the question "Did you see the movie last night?" both conversational partners enter into a communication that presupposes that they are talking about a movie and that the only new information required is a "yes" or "no." If known (i.e., shared) information is re-stated, it could be considered redundant or could change the intended meaning of what is said. This type of response contrasts with the routine practice in most classrooms that requires learners to respond in complete sentences (Teacher: "Use a complete sentence, please") when an elliptical answer would be more appropriate and typically provided. Compare the following and note how in Exchange 1, the full sentence response without the contraction *didn't* actually has an aggressive and angry tone compared to Exchange 2 that sounds more like an exchange between friends who simply want to share experiences and bond socially.

Exchange 1:

- **Teacher:** Did you see the movie last night?
- **Student:** No, I did not see the movie last night.

Exchange 2:

- **Teacher:** Did you see the movie last night?
- **Student:** No, I went to bed early. OR No, I didn't.

- Related lexical items occur in exchanges that have a topical goal and are connected by virtue of the topic being discussed. For example, in a discussion about sports, related lexical items could include *game/match, score, teams, ball park/stadium, scoreboard, referees, uniforms, penalties, time out*.

- Expressive reactions to what is said such as "Wow, I can't believe that!"; questions that move the topic forward such as "Could you explain that a little more?"; and, when needed, explicit transitions to a new topic, as in "Well, changing the subject slightly, ..." (adapted from Hall, 1995).

In her research examining the nature of classroom interactive practices, Hall (1995) found that typical exchanges did not reflect these characteristics of everyday conversations described above. A key implication of this research is that what students ultimately learn about language and communication (or lack thereof) is closely connected to the types of the interactional practices that teachers provide in their classrooms. If the only interactive practice that a learner experiences in the classroom is hearing a teacher's request (I) for a response (R) that is in turn evaluated for accuracy (E), the discourse that students will learn will be impoverished and unusable for communicative interactions in the world out of the classroom.

Considerations about Developing a Classroom Discourse Community

(1) *What makes oral communication "interpersonal"?* **Interpersonal communication** occurs between two or more individuals who interact to clarify and negotiate meaning. Oral interpersonal communication involves both speaking and listening in an interactive way. Examples of oral interpersonal communication include face-to-face or phone conversations as well as exchanges that occur by means of media such as Skype and FaceTime. Interpersonal communication has the following characteristics:

- It is spontaneous—it is not scripted and read aloud or memorized.

- It can feature an **information gap** in which one speaker seeks information that another speaker has. Interpersonal communication can also occur for social reasons, such as showing approval, being considerate, asking about feelings, demonstrating support for another. This kind of communication is called *phatic communication.*

- It occurs within a meaningful context in which a message is being shared. Working in pairs to complete fill-in-the-blank text exercises focusing on providing one-word answers with no regard for meaning is *not* an example of interpersonal communication.

- It requires conversational partners to listen to one another to obtain the necessary information. Hence learners do not see the printed information of their partners so that they must communicate in ways that talk-in-interaction occurs in the world beyond the classroom. Implicit in listening to one another is the negotiation of meaning that occurs to interpret meaning and arrive at understanding of the message or information being shared (Shrum & Glisan, 2016, pp. 239–240).

(2) *How does oral interpersonal communication differ from presentational communication?* While interpersonal communication is two-way communication that is negotiated between and among speakers, **presentational communication** is one-way communication to an audience of listeners (or readers/viewers) in which the message usually cannot be clarified or negotiated. Many classroom tasks that teachers label "interpersonal" are in reality "presentational." The following are examples of activities that are frequently and mistakenly thought to be interpersonal forms of communication.

- Scripted dialogs/conversations or skits performed in front of the class

- One student "reporting" to another student (e.g., "Tell your partner about how you spend your weekend."). Often these reports amount to little more than students reading prepared written texts to each other.

- Role play activities in textbooks in which Student A knows what Student B will say and vice versa—i.e., there is *no* information gap.

It is important to note that presentational tasks have a place in the classroom, but they should be used within a meaningful context and with the audience in mind, and they should not be confused with interpersonal communication.

(3) *What types of tasks prompt oral interpersonal communication?* Tasks must be meaningful and interesting and feature a larger topical goal. For example, learners might interview one another to find out about preferences for leisure-time activities; they might use this information to report on most popular and least popular preferences of the class. The larger purpose of this type of task might be to prepare learners to interview a native speaker of the target language in order to learn about cultural differences and similarities as well as to provide a context for authentic interpersonal communication beyond the classroom. It is important to note that the task of learners working in pairs to complete mechanical exercises or talking about form in English does *not* constitute interpersonal communication in which learners express their thoughts, opinions, feelings and share information in the target language.

Learners must listen to one another to complete the task and cannot know in advance how other learners will respond. Therefore, it is important that Student A does not know how Student B will respond and vice versa. Also, any printed information that learners have, such as cards that describe a role that the learner needs to assume or a particular situation or communicative goal, should be kept private and not shared with the conversational partner.

Learners should do something with the information they obtain from the task. In other words, a motivation is needed for engaging in the interpersonal task in the first place beyond a participation grade. If learners are interviewing one another, what will they do with the information they acquire? Learners could share it with the class for further whole-class discussion regarding trends among the student groups or they could use the information in a follow-up task that involves creation of a presentational product such as an advertisement, a PowerPoint presentation, a report using data from the class, or a brochure that takes a position based on the information they gathered.

(4) *What tools do learners need to engage in an interpersonal task?* Learners need specific language and strategies to negotiate meaning during the task. Prior to beginning the interpersonal task, learners benefit from recalling the type of language (e.g., grammar and vocabulary) that they might use, such as a particular verb tense, ways to ask questions, and specific expressions that might be used in the context. Recalling language needed for an upcoming task also should reflect the context of the task and should not be artificially separated from the topic or theme. Additionally, learners need explicit instruction and practice in using target language expressions for asking for clarification and checking comprehension such as "Did you mean that..." or "I don't understand what you are saying." Similarly, in assisting students in maintaining their conversations, the teacher can give them ***conversational gambits***, i.e., "devices that help the speaker maintain the smooth flow of the conversation" (Taylor, 2002, p. 172). Examples of gambits are: *Wait a minute; As I was saying; By the way; Let me think; Excuse me. I was going to say that....*

Some language teachers post a set of conversational gambits around the classroom for their learners to access during interpersonal tasks. After a month or so, they take them down once they realize that learners have acquired the expressions, no longer need the tool as a reference, and use the expressions actively. At this point, teachers may post a new set of expressions. Learners should review gambits with the teachers and learn what functions they serve, e.g., to make a point, interrupt, ask for repetition or clarification, restate a point, go back to a former idea.

(5) *What if learners speak in English during interpersonal tasks?* The research is clear about how learners mediate, or make sense of, their own learning during interpersonal tasks. According to Brooks, Donato, and McGlone (1997), learners mediate their learning in four ways:

- They talk about talk (engage in *metatalk*): Learners figure out what they need to say in the target language by interacting with their conversational partner(s), usually in the L1. They might say: "How do you say...?" or "That's a good word for that!"

- They talk about the task: Learners try to make sense of the task and confirm what is expected of them. Here is an example from the Brooks et al. research study in which the student is trying to establish the roles for both students in the task:

  "¿Tú quieres mi hablar mi hablo en español y tú oye oír?" ("You want me to speak and you listen?") (1997, p. 529). [Note: What the student said would literally be translated as, "You want my to speak my I speak in Spanish and you listen to listen?"]

- They speak in English: As learners think through a task, they mediate their work with the language that is immediately available to them, most likely the native language. However, as learners work through similar tasks, the use of English decreases substantially and in many cases disappears entirely.

- They whisper to themselves: Learners whisper to themselves to "rehearse" or engage in language play where they put stretches of speech together in new ways or try out new vocabulary and expressions. Whispering is done both in L1 and L2 but diminishes when tasks become more familiar.

In sum, it is helpful to remember that learners will naturally engage in these four types of verbal mediation as they become engaged in oral interpersonal tasks and that a developmental perspective is needed when assessing learners' growth in interpersonal communication, that is performance needs to be assessed across tasks and not on one isolated task.

(6) *What types of teacher behavior promote a classroom discourse community?* At the heart of developing a discourse community is the role that the teacher assumes. It is challenging to promote a community if the teacher is always on center stage, imparting knowledge in a one-directional manner, and preoccupied with "covering" textbook material. In this regard, learners are relegated to the role of audience, note takers, and rote imitators of what the teacher tells them to say. On the contrary, the contemporary role of the teacher is to wear a variety of hats depending on lesson goals and classroom circumstances, including that of facilitator who is on the side at times while learners assume a greater central role. In this regard, perhaps one of the most important teacher behaviors that builds a discourse community is to provide what Walsh calls **interactional space** by increasing wait time, resisting the urge to "fill the silence," and by promoting extended learner turns that allow time to think and plan utterances (2011, p. 168). Offering learners more interactional space enables them to co-construct meaning more effectively as a result of the additional thinking or rehearsal

time and turns-at-talk they are afforded. With turn-taking slowed down and wait time increased, learners often feel less anxiety and provide more elaborate responses.

Consequently, with increased space, the teacher can assume a bigger role in *shaping* learner contributions (i.e., providing **scaffolding**) by assisting them in what they want to say, asking for more details, and responding in meaningful ways to the message learners communicate. Sometimes shaping entails providing modeling, help with vocabulary, and requesting clarification to help move the topic forward. In this regard, overt error correction is not given a central focus in everyday classroom discourse; instead errors that cause misunderstandings are addressed within the context of requesting clarification and negotiating meaning. (See HLTP #4, Chapter 4, for a discussion of the role of focus on grammatical form.) Of course, as discussed earlier, the IRF pattern is key to promoting a classroom discourse community. It should also be noted that these types of teacher behaviors provide models to learners that they indeed imitate as they interact with their peers in pairs and groups. Simply observing the talk of learners during pair and group work will reveal that learners imitate the discourse patterns of the teacher. In classes with heavy doses of IRE, it is found that rather than engaging in information exchange, asking follow up questions, or requesting clarification, learners will often simply evaluate each other's utterances and terminate the exchange.

(7) *How can oral interpersonal communication be assessed?* While not every task needs to be formally assessed, teachers constantly track learners' progress through informal means of assessment such as through checklists, observation, and interaction with individual students. A tool that many teachers have found useful for assessing student-to-student interactions is TALK Scores, developed by Donato (Shrum & Glisan, 2016). The acronym TALK stands for:

- T = Is the student TALKING in the target language?
- A = Is the student performing at an acceptable level of ACCURACY?
- L = Is the student ON TASK and LISTENING to partner?
- K = Is the student KIND and COOPERATIVE?

Each letter of the word TALK represents one performance objective to be observed during a pair or small-group activity. During the activity, the teacher generally selects only one objective to observe. The goal could be that, at the end of one or two weeks, for example, students have been observed on all four performance objectives ("a round"). See Shrum and Glisan (2016) for the complete TALK Scores Template and ideas for assigning points.

PART 1: Engaging Learners in Oral Classroom Communication (Between Teacher-Student)

Deconstructing the Practice

What sets this HLTP apart from the others addressed in this text is that it permeates everything that teachers do in their classrooms. To this extent, it can be viewed as a "way of doing business" that is based upon beliefs concerning the role of the teacher in a more contemporary paradigm in which he or she is not always the imparter of knowledge on center stage.

It is critical to understand that this particular HLTP develops *over time* as the teacher and learners get to know one another, as their bank of shared understandings and experiences grows, and as learners' language abilities develop. The enacting of this practice consists of 5 inter-related steps:

1. **Familiarity With and Among Students**: Essential for growth of any type of community is that the members know one another well. Teachers must get to know their learners as quickly as possible and provide opportunities for learners to get to know them and their peers. This familiarity results in the teacher and learners understanding the worlds of others in the classroom, including not only their routines, habits, and interests, but perhaps more importantly, what matters to them in life, their opinions, joys, fears, disappointments. The relationships that can develop over time in a language classroom can also lead to respect, tolerance, and civility for others—which are building blocks for meaningful interaction and sharing of ideas and opinions. Classroom members can get to know one another through interactive tasks in the TL such as surveys, polls, and interviews; sharing of photos and experiences; and out-of-class experiences such as field trips, interaction with target language communities, and community service projects. It should be noted that these examples involve open-ended and creative responses—it is difficult to become familiar with one's classmates if the usual practice is to complete grammatical exercises in the textbook.

2. **Contexts for Interaction:** Fostering interactions that will connect members of the classroom community necessitates finding contexts and topics that will motivate the learners to talk and exchange ideas. The teacher and learners share a common context—the school and community—which can serve as an endless source of relevant and important topics to prompt sharing. Do students play on sports teams? participate in other extra-curricular activities? have part time jobs? Is there an important event coming up in the near future such as a championship game, homecoming, a dance, a study abroad trip? What events are happening in the community outside of the school, or what topics are being discussed in the community (e.g., an upcoming election year, a report of school violence, a change to a school policy)? Beyond the local community, what are the hot topics or news events that could be brought into the classroom community for exploration and discussion? While some may think that these types of topics are only pertinent to learners at high levels of linguistic ability, these topics can be explored even with novice learners. For example, the class could explore the topic of the Academy Awards by simply talking about the attire of the actors on the red carpet, rank-ordering their movie preferences, or surveying the films that the class has or has not seen (for novice learners) to a critically important topic such as recent concerns about diversity within the Academy Awards (for intermediate and advanced learners). Another avenue for ensuring an equal role for all members of the discourse community is to have learners suggest topics that would motivate them and their peers to discuss.

3. **Spontaneous Interaction/Chit-Chat:** Building a discourse community entails finding every opportunity possible for engaging in spontaneous interaction and even in chit-chat with learners. This informal dialogue goes a long way toward building a discourse community between the teacher and learners and among learners. The teacher could be available to chat as learners enter the class within contexts of interest, as discussed above (often this is down time), between activities,

to begin the class before the actual lesson begins, or at the end of class. All of this time can be put to productive, yet enjoyable, use and strengthen the connection among members of the class. Another possibility is to use meaningful chit-chat to replace what has become known as the traditional warm-up when the teacher typically asks known-answer questions such as "What's the weather like?" or "What's the date today?" Research in conversational analysis has found that interpersonal communication that occurs at these non-instructional moments, such as when handing out papers, reflect discourse that invites participation and is informative, engaging, and spontaneous. Additionally, a study by Hall and Smotrova (2013) revealed that teacher sidebar comments (e.g., *Hmm...where did I put those papers?*) results in learners expressing a positive disposition toward the teacher and builds a classroom community.

4. **Humor**: Humor is not only effective for language learning since it lessens anxiety about using the language, but it also contributes to a positive environment that bonds community members (Pomerantz & Bell, 2011). Over time, as familiarity among learners increases, humor can be used to refer to common understandings and shared experiences that have come to occur gradually as time has progressed.

5. **IRF and Interactional Space**: Earlier in this chapter two strategies were explored as being key to facilitating oral interpersonal communication and nurturing a discourse community. It is virtually impossible to develop a discourse community in a classroom that features pervasive use of the IRE interaction pattern given that the focus is exclusively on form rather than on the meanings that forms construct. Therefore an important step in enacting this HLTP is to integrate as much IRF as possible to validate learners' contributions by engaging them in multiple turns-at-talk and by moving conversations forward (see earlier discussion). Similarly, providing learners with sufficient interactional space by increasing wait-time and offering scaffolding assistance can motivate students to participate and reduce anxiety.

Rehearsing the Practice

The following tasks are provided to practice ways to engage learners in spontaneous TL use in the classroom as a way to develop a discourse community over time.

1. Script out what you as the teacher might say in exchanges with learners at the following times in your classroom. It should be noted that, with natural discourse, you cannot anticipate how it will unfold or how students will respond when you enact the practice with real learners. However, you can think about and plan how you might initiate the exchange and what the content of such an interaction might be.

   a. an exchange between the teacher and a student who is entering the classroom prior to the start of class
   b. an exchange between the teacher and the class that might occur in place of the usual warm-up to start the class
   c. an exchange between the teacher and a student that might occur near the end of an activity while other students are still working
   d. an exchange between the teacher and the class during the last 2 minutes of the class period as students are preparing to leave the room

2. If you are currently teaching or participating in a field experience in a K-12 classroom, try out your ideas from #1 above by initiating these exchanges with your learners. You might find it helpful to refer to External Mediational Tool #2A in this chapter's Appendix A to mediate your work. As indicated above, given that the exchanges will occur in natural discourse, you cannot predict in advance how learners will respond or how exchanges will unfold. Write a brief observation report on how learners responded during the exchanges. State whether you think learner responses were predictable or unpredictable and why. Then think about how your analysis of these exchanges might influence future exchanges with learners in the context that you selected.

Assessing the Practice

Use Rubric #2A in this chapter's Appendix B to self-assess your interactions above. As an alternative, you could ask a colleague to observe the interactions and provide feedback using the rubric.

Note: Rubric #2A would most effectively be used by an observer (i.e., teacher educator, mentor teacher, colleague, peer) after observing several days of class interactions so that evidence of a discourse community could be more readily apparent. Observing only a few interactions within one class session is likely to be insufficient in judging the quality of the classroom discourse community.

PART 2: Designing and Conducting Oral Interpersonal Pair and Group Tasks (Between Student-Student)

Deconstructing the Practice

The HLTP of designing and conducting oral interpersonal pair and group tasks will be deconstructed by first carrying out a model interpersonal task designed for pairs of students. Imagine that you are a student learning the target language that you teach. If possible, work with a colleague in the language you teach (or, in the case of pre-service teachers, with a peer in the language you are preparing to teach) to engage in this pair activity together. This task involves talking to a friend on the phone and making plans. In preparation for completing this task, answer the following questions with your partner:

1. In your target language, what do you say when you call a friend on your cell phone? How do you answer the phone when receiving a call?

2. How do you invite a friend to do something? What are some things you could invite a friend to do?

3. How do you accept the invitation?

4. What will the two of you have to decide?

Now each of you should take a role (Student A and Student B). See Figure 2.1 for the role play situations. Look only at your own role play card and not at your colleague's/ peer's card! To make this activity real, you could enact it over the phone. If this is not possible, you should sit back to back to simulate a phone call. Carry out the task in your target language.

THE INVITATION BY PHONE: STUDENT A	THE PHONE CALL: STUDENT B
You call a good friend and invite him/her to go out to do something with you (e.g., see a movie, have dinner, go to the gym, or something else). Make the call and make small talk first. Then make the invitation. You will have to figure out together the details (such as the day, time, where you meet, etc.). Ask questions so that you are clear on the plans. After you end the call, be prepared to tell your roommate what the plan is.	You receive a call from a good friend inviting you to do something. Answer the phone and listen carefully to what he or she says. You will need to ask questions to decide how to respond. Also you will need to keep in mind what's currently on your calendar as you discuss the invitation. After you end the call, be prepared to tell your roommate about it.

Figure 2.1. **Oral Interpersonal Task: The Phone Call**

[These situations appear on separate cards or pieces of paper so that each student sees only his/her role.]

Deconstructing this interpersonal task involves examining it from two perspectives: (1) planning the task, and (2) conducting the task with learners. In fact, "planning for instruction" is a large grain-size HLTP of its own. See the Oral Interpersonal Task Planning Template in Figure 2.2.

Planning for the task is accomplished through the following steps:

1. The overarching theme, topic, or big idea is the springboard for the task and provides the context within which interpersonal communication will take place. This information comes from the unit or lesson that has been planned using a backward-design approach, through which the objectives or end results are identified first and are used to chart the path for the types of assessments and experiences that should occur in class for learners to achieve these results. For our model interpersonal task, the theme is "social plans."

2. The unit objective addressed is "Learners will be able to make social plans with others." This objective is addressed in a lesson plan and consequently the teacher decides to create an interpersonal task that could address this objective.

3. The next step is to design a task that fits the context and that would be engaging for learners. It should be noted that this task could be slightly altered to incorporate cultural information by telling learners that they are to imagine conducting the activity during a study abroad trip in a country where the language is spoken. In this way, cultural norms would need to be taken into account, such as what types of activities people might do in their leisure time and at what time of the day, among other considerations.

ORAL INTERPERSONAL TASK PLANNING TEMPLATE

Language & Level of Class:

Overarching Theme/Topic:

Objectives of Task: Learners will be able to...

Interpersonal Task:

      Student A

      Student B

Language function(s) needed to carry out the task:

Key vocabulary for the task:

Key grammatical structures for functions:

Communication strategies:

Cultural knowledge needed (if applicable):

Follow-up: What do students do with the information they shared?

***Figure 2.2.* Oral Interpersonal Task Planning Template.**

Source: Adapted from Glisan & Adair-Hauck, 2015.

4. In designing the task, the teacher considers the specific language and cultural knowledge that learners will need to complete the task, specifically

   a. Language functions such as asking for information, stating an opinion, ordering a meal

   b. Vocabulary related to the functions

   c. Grammatical structures needed to carry out the functions

   d. Communication strategies such as asking for clarification or assistance in saying something, circumlocuting in the absence of a word (see Chapter 1)

   e. Cultural knowledge— i.e., cultural products, practices, perspectives.

Sometimes the language needed is that which students are still in the process of learning and practicing within the unit/lesson, while at other times the activity may be an end-of-unit/lesson task that involves the synthesis of language and vocabulary already learned.

5. In terms of pair activities that are role plays and/or involve a Student A and Student B role, as part of the planning, the teacher creates a card or paper that can be given to each student and that depicts the instructions to the student. It is critical that each student keep this information to himself/herself (it's a secret!) so that each student does not know in advance what the other will say.

Conducting the task involves the following steps:

1. Group students into pairs and seat them facing one another. In the case of a "phone call" scenario, seat them back-to-back to simulate the authentic context of not having visual support during a phone conversation. Another option is to actually have students use their cell phones and call each other; again, they should not see each other's face to simulate talking by cell phone. How teachers seat students is important. For interpersonal communication, it works best to have students face one another to prompt interaction and back-and-forth exchanges. Additionally, it helps to prevent students from looking at one another's card/paper. In this regard, students could also be asked to use their cell phones to do face time, in which case they would see one another on their cell phone screens.

2. Preview the activity orally with learners and conduct the preparation phase (refer back to the questions in the model activity) to activate background knowledge and target language.

3. Tell learners how much time they have to complete the task (set a timer on the computer or use a simple kitchen timer with loud buzzer) and what they should do if they have questions or need vocabulary. Indicate that you are circulating around the class to monitor progress and provide assistance.

4. Teachers often play music softly in the background, which can simulate more of an authentic environment for interpersonal communication.

5. Tell learners what they will be expected to do after the activity is over. The following are some examples of follow-up activities for the model interpersonal task that could be done depending on the linguistic level of learners:

    •   Follow-up at the Novice level: Tell your roommate about your plans with your other friend so that he or she knows you will be gone. What are you going to do and when?

    •   Follow-up at the Intermediate level: Describe the plan to your roommate with vivid details about the activity, place where you will go, why you are interested in that activity.

    •   Follow-up at the Advanced level: Report to your roommate how your phone call unfolded. What was the invitation? What did you say? What did your friend say? What are you going to do together and when? How do you feel about the plans?

6. Develop a way to signal to learners when to begin and end the activity. For example, in the case of the model activity, which is a phone call, the teacher might make the sound of a phone ringing orally or by playing a sound setting on a cell phone, and to indicate that students should stop talking, the clock timer could sound or the lights could be dimmed.

Rehearsing the Practice

The following tasks are provided to practice ways to engage learners in oral interpersonal communication in the TL. You might find it helpful to review the features of interpersonal communication presented earlier in this chapter before you begin.

1. In this task, you will use the interpersonal task that you enacted in the previous section above. Using the template shown in Figure 2.2, complete the planning for the interpersonal task that you enacted above for the target language that you teach. You might complete this task with a colleague or classmate so that you have an opportunity to reflect together and discuss your concerns and thoughts.

2. Now use the template to design your own interpersonal task for the target language you teach. You might find it helpful to refer to External Mediational Tool #2B.1 in this chapter's Appendix A to recall the steps you might take as you plan this task.

3. a. If you are a pre-service teacher enrolled in classes, ask two peers to (1) enact the task and (2) evaluate it using the reflective questions in Figure 2.3. Have a discussion with your peers to obtain their feedback. Are there changes you need to make to the task as a result of this feedback? If so, describe them.

   b. If you are an in-service teacher, conduct your activity with a class of your learners. You might find it helpful to refer to External Mediational Tool #2B.2 in this chapter's Appendix A to recall possible steps in conducting this task with real learners. If possible, either record the activity or ask a colleague to observe it. Later, use the questions in Figure 2.3 to self-assess the effectiveness of the task (along with your colleague if you were observed). If you could conduct this activity again, what changes would you make to it and why?

Assessing the Practice

Use Rubric #2B in this chapter's Appendix B to self-assess your interpersonal activity. As an alternative or in addition, you could ask a colleague to observe the interaction and provide feedback using the rubric.

Putting the Practice into a Larger Context: Instructional Goals and Challenges

In this chapter, the larger HLTP of building a discourse community has been deconstructed in terms of two smaller grain-size practices: engaging learners in oral classroom communication and designing and conducting oral interpersonal pair and group tasks. Because high-leverage teaching practices are never enacted in a vacuum, it is important to view them within the larger context of language teaching and learning. The building of a discourse community is critically important in a language program considering that

- the national *World Readiness Standards for Learning Languages* cite the ability to "communicate with other people..." as a basic assumption about the need for study of language and culture (National Standards in Foreign Language Education Project, 2015, p. 7);

- students themselves most often state the ability to communicate with others as the main reason they choose to study language;

- within the sociocultural framework (see discussion in Chapter 1 and earlier discussion in this chapter), our linguistic, cognitive, and social development is constructed through interaction with tools and others (Lantolf, 1994; Vygotsky, 1978; Wertsch, 1994); and

- the oral interaction addressed in this chapter through the theme of building a discourse community will mediate the learning of other aspects of language including its linguistic features, cultures, connections to other disciplines, and interaction within target-language communities.

Beyond the larger purposes of building a discourse community, this HLTP also addresses larger teaching challenges (Kennedy, 2016). One of these challenges for all teachers regardless of their content areas is enlisting student participation. According to Cohen (2011), teachers are members of the "human improvement" professions, such as fitness training and psychotherapy, in which a key measure of one's success lies in the clients' willingness to improve themselves (cf. Kennedy, 2016, p. 11). In the case of teachers, they cannot succeed unless their students choose to learn. Plenty of anecdotal evidence abounds

---

Reflective Questions for Evaluating Oral Interpersonal Tasks

1. Did you need to listen to your partner in order to complete the task?

2. Was the task engaging; that is, were you motivated to listen to your partner to complete the task?

3. Did the task promote the negotiation of meaning or conversational adjustments? If so, when? Please explain.

4. Did the task require the use of vocabulary and grammatical structures indicated on the planning template? Any comments?

5. Did the task require cultural knowledge?

6. Do you have any suggestions that might increase the interactivity of the task?

Figure 2.3. **Reflective Questions for Evaluating Oral Interpersonal Tasks.**

Source: Adapted from Glisan & Adair-Hauck, 2015.

regarding learners in language classes who are reticent to speak, or who are labeled as being too timid, too anxious, too worried about not speaking accurately, or simply too unmotivated. Eliciting student participation in a language class is key to discovering how they are making sense of the language to which they are exposed, how they are progressing, and how motivated they are to communicate with the language.

Another larger challenge that this HLTP helps teachers face is classroom management. Encouraging learners to share their worlds and thoughts with the teacher and peers often motivates them to become involved in the class and to be socially invested in the growing discourse community that they are helping to shape. In this regard, learners should not feel threatened or afraid to express their feelings, reactions, or thoughts for fear of reprisal from the teacher and/or peers. That is, there should be an air of "comfort" to speak. Finally, teaching is particularly personal and interpersonal work on the part of teachers, who do what they do at least in part because of their own personalities and needs (Kennedy, 2016). Thus this HLTP prompts teachers to engage in self-reflection regarding how they can draw upon their own personalities and belief system to nurture the discourse community that is so pivotal in today's language classrooms.

For Further Reading

Brooks, F. B., Donato, R., & McGlone, J. (1997). When are they going to say "it" right? Understanding learner talk during pair-work activity. *Foreign Language Annals, 30,* 524–541.

Celce-Murcia, M. (2007). Rethinking the role of communicative competence in language teaching. In E. A. Soler & M. P. Safont Jordà (Eds.), *Intercultural language use and language learning.* Netherlands: Springer.

Cohen, D. K. (2011). *Teaching and its predicaments.* Cambridge, MA: Harvard University Press.

Glisan, E. W., & Adair-Hauck, B. (2015). *Keeping it interpersonal in the L2 classroom.* Presentation for the Pittsburgh Public Schools World Language Faculty. February 21, 2015, Pittsburgh, PA.

Hall, J. K. (1995). "Aw, man, where we goin'?" Classroom interaction and the development of L2 interactional competence. *Issues in Applied Linguistics, 6,* 37–62.

Hall, J. K. (1999). The communication standards. In J. K. Phillips & R. M. Terry (Eds.), *Foreign language standards: Linking research, theories, and practices* (pp. 15–56). Lincolnwood, IL: National Textbook Company.

Hall, J. K. (2004). Language learning as an interactional achievement. *The Modern Language Journal, 88,* 607–612.

Hall, J. K. (2010). Interaction as method and result of language learning. *Language Teaching, 43,* 202–215. doi:10.1017/S0261444809005722

Hall, J. K. (2012). *Teaching and researching language and culture (2nd ed.).* Harlow, UK: Pearson.

Hall, J. K., & Smotrova, T. (2013). Teacher self-talk: Interactional resource for managing instruction and eliciting empathy. *Journal of Pragmatics, 47:*75–92.

Johnson, K. (1995). *Understanding Communication in Second Language Classrooms.* Cambridge: Cambridge University Press.

Kennedy, M. (2016). Parsing the practice of teaching. *Journal of Teacher Education, 67*(1), 6–17.

Lantolf, J. P. (1994). Sociocultural theory and second language learning. *The Modern Language Journal, 78,* 418–420.

Mehan, H. (1979). What time is it, Denise?: Asking known information questions in classroom discourse. *Theory Into Practice, 28*(4), 285–294.

National Standards in Foreign Language Education Project (NSFLEP). (2015). *World-Readiness standards for learning languages.* Alexandria, VA: Author.

Pica, T., Holliday, L., Lewis, N., & Morgenthaler, L. (1989). Comprehensible output as an outcome of linguistic demands on the learner. *Studies in Second Language Acquisition, 11,* 63–90.

Pomerantz, A., & Bell, N. D. (2011). Humor as safe house in the foreign language classroom. *The Modern Language Journal, 95,* Supplementary Issue, 148–161.

Shrum, J. L., & Glisan, E. W. (2016). *Teacher's handbook: Contextualized language instruction.* 5th ed. Cengage Learning: Boston, MA.

Taylor, G. (2002). Teaching gambits: The effect of instruction and task variation on the use of conversation strategies by intermediate Spanish students. *Foreign Language Annals, 35,* 171–189.

Tharp, R. G., & Gallimore, R. (1991). *The instructional conversation: Teaching and learning in social activity.* Santa Cruz, CA: The National Center for Research on Cultural Diversity and Second Language Learning.

Toth, P. (1997). The pragmatics of foreign language communities. Paper presented at the 1997 meeting of the American Association of Applied Linguistics, Orlando, FL.

Toth, P. (2004). When grammar instruction undermines cohesion in L2 Spanish classroom discourse. *The Modern Language Journal, 88,* 14–30.

Toth, P. (2011). Social and cognitive factors in making teacher-led classroom discourse relevant for second language development. *The Modern Language Journal, 95,* 1–25.

Vygotsky, L. S. (1978). *Mind in society: The development of higher psychological processes.* Cambridge, MA: Harvard University Press.

Walsh, S. (2011). *Exploring classroom discourse: Language in action.* London: Routledge.

Wells, G. (1993). Re-evaluating the IRF sequence. *Linguistics and Education, 5,* 1–38.

Wells, G. (1999). *Dialogic inquiry: Toward a sociocultural practice and theory of education.* New York: Cambridge University Press.

Wertsch, J. V. (1994). The primacy of mediated action in sociocultural studies. *Mind, Culture, and Activity, 1,* 202–208.

Appendix A

External Mediational Tool #2A:
Engaging Learners in Oral Classroom Communication
(Between Teacher-Student)

1. Get to know your learners and help them to become familiar with one another.

2. Find contexts and topics that will motivate learners to talk and exchange ideas.

3. Find every opportunity possible for engaging in spontaneous interaction and in chit-chat with your learners.

4. Use humor to refer to common understandings and shared experiences that have come to occur in your classroom gradually as time has progressed.

5. Integrate as much IRF as possible, engage learners in multiple turns-at-talk, and move conversations forward; provide learners with sufficient interactional space by increasing wait-time and offering scaffolding assistance to motivate learners to participate and reduce anxiety.

External Mediational Tool #2B.1:
Designing and Conducting Oral Interpersonal Pair and Group Tasks
(Between Student-Student)

PLANNING FOR THE TASK

1. Use the overarching theme, topic, or big idea as the springboard/context for the task.

2. Address the unit/lesson objective.

3. Design a task that fits the context and would be engaging for learners.

4. Consider the specific language and cultural knowledge that learners will need: language functions, vocabulary, grammatical structures, communication strategies, cultural knowledge.

5. Create a card or paper for each learner with instructions to that learner (this card/paper is a secret!).

External Mediational Tool #2B.2:
Designing and Conducting Oral Interpersonal Pair and Group Tasks
(Between Student-Student)

CONDUCTING THE TASK

1. Group students into pairs and seat them facing one another.

2. Preview the activity orally with students and conduct the preparation phase.

3. Tell students how much time they have to complete the task.

4. Play music softly in the background (optional).

5. Tell students what they will be expected to do after the activity is over (follow-up).

6. Develop a way to signal to students when to begin and end the activity.

Appendix B

RUBRIC: HLTP #2A: Engaging Learners in Oral Classroom Communication (Between Teacher-Student)*

	EXCEEDS EXPECTATIONS	MEETS EXPECTATIONS	DEVELOPING	UNACCEPTABLE
Shared Experiences and Knowledge of Members of Discourse Community	The experiences and knowledge that the teacher and students share about one another are the foundation of the discourse community.	Evidence that teacher and students share some experiences and/or some knowledge about one another.	Teacher makes some attempt to connect to students' worlds and/or to connect them to one another.	Little evidence that teacher knows students and their worlds or makes an effort to connect to them or connect them to one another.
Meaningful Contexts for Interaction	Meaningful contexts that engage students are the basis for all class activities.	Contexts for interaction are meaningful and most are engaging.	At least half of the contexts for interaction are meaningful, but may not engage students fully.	Contexts are determined largely by textbook content and are usually devoid of meaning.
Spontaneous Interaction/ Chit-Chat	Entire class features back-and-forth spontaneous interaction with teacher.	Evidence of spontaneous interaction and chit-chat at times throughout class.	Sporadic evidence of spontaneous interaction.	Virtually all interactions are scripted or conducted in a planned manner.
Integration of Humor	Humor is an integral part of the class.	Humor is used throughout much of the class by teacher and students.	Periodic insertion of humor by teacher.	Little evidence of humor in class. When it exists, it is inserted by students on their own.
Use of IRF	The IRF discourse pattern is central to the functioning of the classroom.	Evidence of primarily IRF discourse pattern.	Combination of IRF and IRE discourse patterns.	Class is dominated by the IRE discourse pattern.

*All communication referred to in rubric is carried out in the target language.

RUBRIC: HLTP #2B: Designing and Conducting Oral Interpersonal Pair/Group Tasks (Between Student-Student)*

	EXCEEDS EXPECTATIONS	MEETS EXPECTATIONS	DEVELOPING	UNACCEPTABLE
Context/Theme of Activity & Objective	Task occurs within a meaningful and engaging context. It addresses the objective in a creative way and includes appropriate linguistic and cultural knowledge and communication strategies to be used.	Task occurs within a meaningful context. It addresses the objective and includes appropriate linguistic and cultural knowledge and communication strategies to be used.	Task occurs within a meaningful context but does not fully address the objective. Appropriate linguistic and cultural knowledge are addressed but communication strategies to be used may be lacking.	Task does not occur within a context and/or does not address the objective. Appropriate linguistic and cultural knowledge as well as communication strategies to be used are lacking.
Nature of Task & Linguistic Level	Real-world task motivates learners to communicate at an appropriate level. Learners must listen to one another and negotiate meaning to complete task.	Real-world task prompts learners to communicate at an appropriate level. Learners must listen to one another and negotiate meaning to complete task.	Task prompts learners to communicate. However, learners may not have to listen to one another and/or negotiate meaning to complete task. Level of task may not be appropriate.	Task does not prompt much communication or is inappropriate for the linguistic level. And/or learners may not have to listen to one another or negotiate meaning to complete task.
Preparation for Task	Activates background knowledge and language needed for task in a learner-centered and interesting way.	Activates background knowledge and language needed for task.	Activates either background knowledge or language needed for task, but rarely both.	No preparation for task or preparation is inadequate.

	EXCEEDS EXPECTATIONS	MEETS EXPECTATIONS	DEVELOPING	UNACCEPTABLE
Conducting/ Management of Task	Authentic environment for 2-way communication is simulated (e.g., music is playing in background). Students are seated in a way that facilitates 2-way communication. Start and finish times are signaled. Teacher monitors task and provides assistance as needed.	Students are seated in a way that facilitates 2-way communication. Start and finish times are signaled. Teacher monitors task and provides assistance as needed.	Seating of students does not facilitate 2-way communication. Start and finish times may not be signaled. Teacher may not monitor task and/or provide assistance as needed.	Management of task is lacking inasmuch as seating does not facilitate 2-way communication and teacher does not monitor task or provide assistance as needed.
Follow-up Activity	Real-world follow-up activity is engaging. Learners share information from interpersonal task in a creative way.	Real-world follow-up activity prompts learners to share information from interpersonal task in a meaningful way.	Follow-up task prompts learners to share information from interpersonal task.	Follow-up task is absent or ineffective in prompting learners to share information from interpersonal task.

*All communication referred to in rubric is carried out in the target language.

CHAPTER 3

HLTP #3: Guiding Learners to Interpret and Discuss Authentic Texts

PART 1: Guiding Learners to Interpret Authentic Texts

PART 2: Leading a Text-Based Discussion

Acquiring new perspectives and insights through text-based discussions is a skill that goes beyond the foreign language classroom and situates language learning within a broader educational mission.

The discussion of the HLTP dealing with the use of the target language (TL) (see Chapter 1) revealed that interesting talk and text in the target language are necessary for learners to develop language and cultural proficiency. In this regard, not only do learners need to attend to the teacher's spoken language in the TL but also to the language that occurs in the form of **authentic texts**—i.e., texts, be they printed, audio, or video, that are created for various social and cultural purposes *by* and *for* monolingual, bilingual, or multilingual users of the TL and various other cultural groups. The term *authentic*, when referring to foreign language classrooms, also implies that the text has not been simplified or edited for the purpose of foreign language instruction. Additionally, authentic texts, in the way the term is used in this chapter, have a sociocultural purpose (e.g., to inform, entertain, argue, teach a life lesson) that goes beyond simply providing contrived, artificial, and unmotivated examples of the target language to learners, as is the case in most textbook material. Further, meaningful TL use and IRF patterns of discourse (see Chapter 2) can only exist within interesting contexts and engaging topics, which culturally relevant authentic texts provide. A body of research in language pedagogy has confirmed the essential role of authentic texts in the learning of language and culture (Galloway, 1998; Villegas Rogers & Medley, 1988). In this regard, authentic texts prompt goal-oriented communication in cultural contexts as opposed to providing only opportunities to "practice" the language (Tomlinson, 2012). Thus, it is essential that novice teachers be able to integrate authentic texts into their classroom practice as a vehicle for introducing engaging content, topics, and culture. Further, in the larger educational context, the ability to interpret texts and engage in text-based discussions has been given critical importance in the *P-21 Framework for 21st Century Skills Learning* to enable learners to succeed in today's information age (Partnership for 21st Century Skills, 2011). Thus, this practice is justified as being high-leverage not only for foreign language instruction but also for meeting broader educational goals.

In practice, interpretation and discussion go hand-in-hand; that is, we discuss to develop interpretations and we share interpretations of texts in conversations about them. This larger grain-size HLTP of guiding learners to interpret and discuss authentic texts consists of two smaller grain-size practices that support each other but that can be deconstructed independently:

1. guiding learners to interpret authentic texts, and
2. leading a text-based discussion.

The deconstruction and practice of each smaller grain-size practice will illustrate how interpretation can be supported by discussion and how discussion about interpretations should be carried out.

ACTFL/CAEP Standards addressed: #1a, 1b; #2a, 2c; #3a, 3b; #4a, 4b, 4c; #5a, 5b

Research and Theory Supporting the Practice

The overarching HLTP of guiding learners through texts so that they have meaningful content to explore and discuss is supported by research in (1) interpreting authentic texts, and (2) the role of social interaction in meaning-making, acquiring new knowledge, and exchanging ideas and opinions based on the content of authentic texts.

The national *World-Readiness Standards for Learning Languages* document has identified the following standard regarding interpretive communication: "Learners understand, interpret, and analyze what is heard, read, or viewed on a variety of topics" (National Standards in Foreign Language Education Project, 2015, p. 55). This communicative mode involves listening, reading, and viewing as they pertain to tasks such as listening to a news broadcast, reading a novel, or viewing a film. In the twenty-first century, this mode has been expanded to include information literacy and media literacy that learners develop as they engage with a wide variety of print and non-print materials including multimedia (Partnership for 21st Century Skills, 2011). Clarification of the message is typically not possible in the interpretive mode because the creator of the message is absent, i.e., the reader of a newspaper or online article is not able to ask the author for clarification of the article's content.

Research in language education continues to confirm the benefits of exposing learners to culturally authentic texts to support overall language learning and the development of interpretive skills (Bacon, 1992; Herron & Seay, 1991; Maxim, 2002). Studies have shown that even beginning learners experience success in interpreting authentic texts if they receive assistance and scaffolding from the teacher and learn to use strategies for making meaning of texts (Maxim, 2002). In fact, research has revealed that learners demonstrate a higher level of comprehension of texts read in their unedited, authentic forms as opposed to more simplified versions created by the teacher to ostensibly simplify the task (Vigil, 1987; Young, 1993, 1999). This is undoubtedly due to the fact that authentic texts contain redundancy (i.e., natural repetition of language) and contextual richness that support meaning in pivotal ways. Unfortunately, some language textbooks still include unauthentic texts that feature unnatural use of vocabulary and grammar, which pose greater difficulty for learners than do texts in their authentic form. Teachers can enable students to experience success with an authentic text by *editing the task, not the text*—i.e., designing tasks appropriate for learners' linguistic levels without having complete comprehension and interpretation of the text as the goal (Shrum & Glisan, 2016). Additionally, maintaining task complexity while limiting learner involvement in the task is one of the major features of scaffolded instruction (Stone, 1993; Reiser & Tabak 2014).

It is important to note that the interpretive process involves not only *literal comprehension* of words and sentences, but also *interpretation* of the message, including cultural perspectives, opinions, and points of view about the text. Accordingly, "the interpretation of cultural meanings is a critical component" of the interpretive mode (National Standards in Foreign Language Education Project, 2015, p. 55). Interpretation involves the process of **inferencing**, defined by Hammadou as "a thinking process that involves reasoning a step beyond the text using generalization, synthesis, and/or explanation" (2002, p. 219). In more colloquial terms, this is often called "reading or listening between the lines." Individuals engage in making inferences when they can draw conclusions or make predictions about the text when those ideas are not explicitly stated in the text.

According to current research, the interpretive process is constructivist in nature. That is, listeners and readers derive meaning from a text by interacting with the text together with their knowledge of the target language, their background knowledge and world experiences, their knowledge of how discourse is organized in texts, their pragmatic knowledge that accounts for the author's communicative intent beyond literal meaning, their short-term memory, their use of interpretive strategies, and their degree of motivation and anxiety about interpreting authentic texts (Nassaji, 2007; Tafaghodtari & Vandergrift, 2008). Meaning-making is *not* achieved by means of translation from the target language to English! Bernhardt (2005) has described the reading process (and, by extension, listening and viewing) as a "juggling or switching process" in which certain "knowledge sources assist or take over for other knowledge sources that are inadequate or nonexistent" (p. 140; c.f. Shrum & Glisan, 2016, p. 177). For example, learners might begin to interpret a text in a **top-down manner** initially by processing meaning in chunks as a result of applying background knowledge and using contextual clues. This often occurs with texts that have a familiar context and those that are explored for enjoyment such as novels. In the face of misunderstanding, the reader may switch to **bottom-up processing** by resorting to more sequential processing and analysis of language parts; for instance, the reader may stop to ponder the meaning of a word or re-examine the previous sentences for clues to meaning. The current view of the interpretation process is that learners use both top-down and bottom-up processing in concert. More specifically, according to Bernhardt, learners may compensate for the absence of knowledge in one area by drawing on knowledge from another; for example, in the absence of L2 vocabulary, learners use the context to make guesses about possible meaning. Further, interpretation does not develop in a linear manner as do speaking and writing, i.e., one does not learn to comprehend first words, then phrases, then sentences, and then paragraphs, as is the case in learning to speak and write in the target language. Instead, depending on the familiarity of a text, learners glean meaning from the entire text, piecing together stretches of language within the context.

The meaning-making process described above is also a social phenomenon. More specifically, learners interact with a text as they select the characteristics that they think are most important for deriving the meaning of the text. Further, learners acquire additional ideas and points of view about a text's meaning through interactions with others—i.e., text-based discussions. This pivotal notion of social interaction reflects the sociocultural view of language learning that has been discussed in the previous two chapters as being key to other high-leverage teaching practices.

The literature in foreign language pedagogy proposes the implementation of **instructional conversations (ICs)** as a vehicle for facilitating discussions with students on topics of interest and intellectual challenge, such as those based on an authentic text (Goldenberg, 1991; Hall, 1999; Todhunter, 2007). ICs, while focusing on a text or engaging topic, provide opportunities for learners to develop language and conceptual knowledge about a meaningful topic. In these conversations, the teacher takes on the role of discussion facilitator, asking assisting questions (see Chapter 2) to help learners elaborate on their contributions, and connecting learners' background knowledge and experiences to the conversation (Hall, 1999). In this regard, the teacher may model how learners might approach the discussion, focus briefly on form when faced with difficulty using a particular grammatical structure, link a learner comment to what was said previously, provide direct teaching when additional information about the text or topic is necessary, and offer expressive reactions to learner contributions (e.g., "I didn't know that!") (Shrum & Glisan, 2016, p. 243). ICs based on an authentic text unfold in an unpredictable manner and serve to develop interpersonal communication by incorporating the IRF pattern of classroom interaction (see Chapter 2).

Considerations about Guiding Learners to Interpret and Discuss Authentic Texts[3]

(1) *How do I select an authentic text?* One myth in selecting an authentic text is that texts represent different levels of interpretive proficiency, i.e., specific text types can be associated with novice, intermediate, and advanced levels of proficiency. According to Adair-Hauck, Glisan, and Troyan, "any text can be interpreted at a variety of linguistic levels" (2013, p. 34). However, there are several important factors to keep in mind when selecting authentic texts. First, texts should be *context-appropriate* by reflecting contexts and topics that learners are exploring and/or in which they are interested. Secondly, they should be *age-appropriate*—texts that capture the interest of elementary school learners might not intrigue high school learners. Finally, texts should be *appropriate for the linguistic level of learners*, meaning that they "should have enough language that students can recognize so that they can use these recognizable portions on which to scaffold meaning" (p. 33). It should be noted that this does not mean that teachers should attempt to locate texts that have only the vocabulary and grammar that learners have studied, which would be fairly impossible to undertake anyway. As an alternative, teachers should consider carefully the degree of contextual support that a text offers in terms of factors such as length (longer texts may be easier to comprehend because there is more context), organization (texts with a story format facilitate comprehension), and linguistic and non-linguistic signaling clues such as connector words (e.g., "on the other hand") and charts, subtitles, pictures (Adair-Hauck, Glisan, & Troyan, 2013). Of course, as mentioned earlier, the key in supporting learners in interpreting any text is to design tasks appropriate to their linguistic level while challenging them to enhance their interpretive abilities.

(2) *Should the focus be on literal or interpretive comprehension?* Both literal and interpretive comprehension skills should be developed. Language textbooks often do an ineffective job in this regard inasmuch as they typically present a series of questions that learners can answer simply by matching the language of each question with what appears in the text in a retrieval sort of fashion. Lee and VanPatten (1995) call this the **"look-back-and-lift-off"approach** since one only has to do a matching game. In fact, learners can find the answers to these types of questions without even knowing what either the questions or answers mean. In sum, learners' ability to lift off answers directly from the text does not ensure that they have comprehended the main ideas and supporting

---

[3] For other guidelines and more detailed explanations of those provided in this list, see Chapter 6 of Shrum and Glisan (2016).

details of the text or are able to interpret the text's social or cultural purpose, authorial point of view, tone, and intended readership.

(3) *Is making inferences appropriate for more advanced learners?* Even novice learners can engage in interpretive or inferencing tasks. Some may think that inferencing can only be done by more advanced learners, but even children are able to draw inferences. Think about how children read a story and we ask them questions such as "What do you think will happen next?" "What kind of person do you think X character is?" "What was your favorite part of the story?" Teachers can guide learners to draw inferences from the time they begin to listen, read, and view texts in the target language.

(4) *What type of preparation do learners need prior to interpreting a text?* Learners benefit from activities that prepare them for the interpretive tasks by activating their background knowledge, target language vocabulary/expressions, world experiences, and cultural insights. This preparation can be used as a tool to mediate their interpretive process when reading the text.

(5) *Should interpretive tasks always be done in the target language?* Research shows that students tend to perform higher on interpretive tasks if they are assessed in their native language due to the possibility that they will not understand questions and tasks posed in the TL and may be limited in their ability to demonstrate in the TL what they have comprehended (Godev, Martínez-Gibson, & Toris, 2002; Lee, 1986). Additionally, textual misinterpretations are easier to identify when students make their comprehension visible in their dominant language. However, there is a caution here. This is not to say that English should be used exclusively for checking comprehension, but rather that some comprehension tasks could be done in English so that what is assessed is learners' interpretive skill and not their ability to understand complicated questions in the target language. Another way to think about the use of English (the students' L1) in assessing text comprehension and interpretation is from the perspective of what constitutes a valid assessment. The goal of comprehension tasks is not to assess students' ability in the presentational mode of communication, i.e., in how well they can express text comprehension in the target language. For example, sometimes learners report that they often understand the text but do not understand the comprehension questions or how to express their comprehension in the target language. Also, presenting some comprehension questions in English, or even just asking students to give the main idea in English, keeps students from resorting to the "look-back-and-lift-off" strategy. It should be noted that the role of the TL is to serve as the language of communication when interpreting and discussing the text with others once overall comprehension has been achieved.

(6) *Does reading aloud a printed text in class promote comprehension?* When learners are asked to read parts of a printed text aloud in class, they typically do not attend to meaning but instead are preoccupied with the pronunciation of individual words. In fact, it is unlikely that the other learners are paying much attention to meaning either while their peers read aloud. If teachers choose to use reading aloud as a classroom management strategy (i.e., to focus students' attention on the text), they should provide time for learners to read the text silently to process meaning before beginning the interpretation and discussion cycle (Shrum & Glisan, 2016).

(7) *How can learners be motivated to read/listen/view authentic texts?* Teachers should consider providing frequent opportunities for learners to select their own authentic texts of interest and interpret them. Learners will be motivated to explore texts if they are given some opportunities to select those in which they have an interest.

(8) *What role does collaboration with peers play in the interpretation of a text?* Learners should be given opportunities to collaborate to make meaning with a text. Within a sociocultural view of language development, learners can progress in their understanding and language use if they work with others.

(9) *What strategies can I use to encourage learner participation in text-based discussions?* First, teachers should ensure that learners have multiple turns in a conversational exchange, sufficient time to offer their ideas, and opportunities to take the floor. Secondly, teachers should accept a variety of responses from learners, including short answers where they would naturally be appropriate, as in responses to yes-no questions. Thirdly, teachers can assist in fostering discussions that are coherent by expecting learners to respond to ideas offered by their classmates and connect those ideas to their own. Finally, teachers should assume the role of facilitator as they offer scaffolding and assistance to move the discussion forward when necessary (adapted from Shrum & Glisan, 2016, p. 244).

PART 1: Guiding Learners to Interpret Authentic Texts

Deconstructing the Practice

A necessary practice leading to a text-based discussion is to assist learners in comprehending and interpreting authentic target language material of various kinds. To this end, guiding learners to interpret authentic texts will be deconstructed by exploring a model of interpretive tasks designed around an authentic text in Spanish. The reading and tasks presented here are adapted from the 2013 *Implementing Integrated Performance* text by Adair-Hauck, Glisan, and Troyan.[4] Deconstruction of this practice involves examining it from three perspectives: (1) selecting an authentic text, (2) planning the sequence of interpretive tasks, and (3) conducting the interpretive tasks with learners. It should be noted that the interpretive work should not occur in isolation but should be viewed as part of a larger instructional practice, that is, participation in a text-based discussion. Text-based discussions, which will be deconstructed later in the chapter, complement interpretive work by students and teachers. Because the practice of guiding learners to interpret authentic texts is discussed by means of the model, you might work with a colleague in the language you teach (or, in the case of pre-service teachers, with a peer in the language you are preparing to teach) to complete the tasks as if you were students learning Spanish.

Selecting the authentic text: The text presented here, a website about using the metro in Madrid, Spain, was selected by the teacher because it fit well into the novice-level unit on vacations, in which the culminating activity is planning a virtual vacation to Madrid. Students learn about the metro prior to interpreting this text. Factors that were considered in selecting this text included:

---

[4] Many thanks to José Pan, Spanish teacher in the Edison (NJ) School District, for designing this IPA, which is adapted for use here.

- topic familiarity, context-appropriateness, level of interest: These criteria go a long way to motivate students to make an effort to interpret the text.

- age-appropriateness for a beginning-level high school Spanish class: High school students would be apt to use the metro both at home and abroad.

- linguistic level: The text has organizational features that facilitate comprehension such as subtitles, visuals, a chart; enough familiar language to mediate understanding; contextual clues to unknown language (e.g., cognates, paraphrased words and expressions, visuals to represent meaning); topic divisions by paragraphs.

- strategy use: Learners could use strategies in interpreting this text such as guessing meaning in context, using visual support as clues to meaning, and bringing their background knowledge and world experiences to the meaning-making task.

In addition, this text addresses unit and lesson objectives that were identified through backward-design planning (see Chapter 2). In this vein, it could be used not only to facilitate the development of interpretive abilities but also as the basis for text-based discussion.

Planning the sequence of interpretive tasks: There are several popular models suggested in language pedagogy research for guiding students through texts. The model presented here draws on characteristics of two approaches: The Interactive Model for Developing Interpretive Communication by Shrum and Glisan (2016) and the Integrated Performance Assessment (IPA) by Adair-Hauck, Glisan, and Troyan (2013). Both of these approaches guide learners through the text through the following sequence of tasks:

(1) *Pre-reading/Pre-listening/Pre-viewing:* Learners are prepared for the text and their interest is piqued by previewing the text, activating their background knowledge and world experiences, and anticipating pertinent vocabulary and text language. Although this section could be done in either the target language or English, it may be more effective to use English for beginning language learners who may not have the target language necessary to respond to the questions.

"You are on vacation with your family in Madrid. You all decide to head out and go sightseeing but no one is sure what would be the best way to travel throughout the city. You head downstairs to the hotel lobby and sign on to the Internet to see what would be the best means of transportation. Your web search leads you to the following web page [see figure on the next page]."[5]

1. Look at the title and visuals in the text. What mode of transportation is being discussed?

2. What experiences do you have using this mode of transportation?

3. Why might you want to read this article?

4. What vocabulary and expressions in Spanish do you expect to read?

(2) *Skimming for Main Idea(s):* Once background information is activated, to begin the Comprehension Phase, learners skim the text for a few minutes to identify the overall main idea. In the case of an audio or video text, learners would listen to/watch the text for the first time.

---

[5] This web article highlights the advantages of using the Madrid metro system to get around the city and provides practical information regarding how to navigate the metro. It describes how to buy a subway ticket and how to travel from station to station. Ticket prices are listed and the reader can click on several words that are links to the full metro map, stops where certain businesses are located, among other types of information.

- Now skim the article for a minute or two. Using information from the article, describe in English the main purpose of the webpage. The most expeditious way to find out whether learners understood the gist of the text is to elicit the main idea in their own words in English. Nonetheless, more advanced language learners might do this in the target language.

WEB MADRID
Guía de Madrid

Transportes
- Introducción
- Metro
- En coche
- Aparcamientos
- Trenes
- Aeropuerto
- Taxis
- Autobuses

Guía de Madrid
- Historia
- Alojamiento
- La ciudad
- Transporte
- Aprende a...
- Información útil
- De compras
- Madrid gratis (o casi)

◄ **Metro** ►

Sin duda, viajar en el Metro de Madrid es la forma más rápida de desplazarse. La continuidad del paso de sus trenes junto con la inexistencia de atascos hacen de este medio de transporte el ideal cuando llevas prisa.

Las líneas del Metro de Madrid crecen casi cada año, y disponemos ya de una de las mejores redes de toda europa.

¿Quieres ver el plano? Pincha aquí.

Cuando entres en el metro, puedes pagar en la taquilla o directamente (si ya dispones de billete) dirigirte a los tornos de entrada que te permiten el paso. Te advertimos de que en muchas estaciones disponen de varias entradas/salidas, pero sólo hay una taquilla, con lo cual puede que no veas a nadie en la entrada. Para ello encontrarás unas máquinas expendedoras que funcionan bastante bien, incluso admiten billetes de mil y dos mil pesetas para que puedas comprar tu billete.

Moverte en metro, aunque al principio parezca complicado, es bastante sencillo. Puedes moverte libremente dentro de la red siempre que no estés más de tres horas dentro. Frente al plano busca las paradas de origen y destino. Imagina el recorrido más corto, algunas veces merece la pena hacer más estaciones y menos trasbordos (cambios de líneas). Ahora consiste en dirigirte a la línea que has elegido (marcadas por colores y por números) y ver la dirección en la que quieres ir. La dirección esta marcada por la estación final (por ejemplo: "linea nueve, Herrera Oria", irás hacia arriba según ves el plano). No te preocupes por los trasbordos. Siempre que quieras cambiar de línea tendrás señalada en cada estación todo lo que precises para moverte. Encontrarás además flechas indicativas en cada pasillo. Es casi imposible perderse en el Metro de Madrid.

El metro además, cuenta con algunas estaciones con comercios así como de una exposición en distintas estaciónes, especialmente la de Retiro (línea 2, roja). En la estación de sol tienes una comisaría para denuncias de delitos cometidos en su interior.

En los vestíbulos de las estaciones de Atocha-Renfe, Chamartin y avda. de América, existen cabinas e información atendidas por agentes de Metro de Madrid. En el resto de las estaciones puedes dirigirte a cualquier agente de la empresa para solicitar la información que precises. Además, todas las estaciones disponen de megafonía que informa de las posibles incidencias sobre el servicio. También puedes solicitar información puntual a través de los interfonos amarillos dIspuestos en todas las estaciones.

Las tarifas actualmente son la siguientes:

Horario	6:00 a 1:30
Precio*	Billete sencillo: 145 pts Metro bus (10 viajes)**: 760 pts

* Los niños deberán pagar billete a partir de los 4 años.
**Válido para ambos transportes

- Students could also identify 8 words in the text that relate to the metro system. Identifying key content words such as nouns, verbs, and adjectives, helps learners to make meaning of the text.

(3) *Scanning for Important Details:* After learners identify the overall main idea of the text, they scan for important details. In this text, they could find

(a) The place where one can purchase a metro ticket.
(b) How the metro lines are marked to help you find your way.
(c) The price of tickets for children.
(d) The hours the subway is open.

As an alternative, learners could also match main ideas to key details. This section might be done in English to avoid the likelihood of learners resorting to the "look-back-and-lift-off" strategy, which will not confirm that they understood these details. It should be noted that, during the planning process, teachers will need to decide when the use of L1 might occur in any of the interpretation phases.

(4) *Interpretive Phase: Guessing Meaning in Context:* In this phase learners work with vocabulary to help them begin to interpret meaning.

In the text we are interpreting, use the context to guess the meaning of the following in English:

1. ***desplazarse*** (paragraph 1)
2. *¿Quieres ver el **plano**?* (paragraph 2)
3. *"**es bastante sencillo**"* (paragraph 5)

Depending on the type of text that learners are interpreting, they could also be asked to identify words or expressions that deal with specific themes or content areas in the text.

(5) *Interpretation/Discussion Phase:* In this part of the Interpretation Phase, learners use the text to discuss and make inferences in the target language. From this point forward, all interactions regarding the text should be carried out only in the target language. Learners could discuss the interpretation questions in pairs or small groups to maximize participation and then share opinions with the whole class. This phase will be explored in further detail in the second small grain-sized practice of this HLTP, leading a text-based discussion, later in this chapter.

It should be noted that learners can also engage in interpretive communication by

- analyzing the organizational features of the text (e.g., compare/contrast, story format, cause/effect, problem/solution);

- identifying the author's perspective (e.g., factual, historical, comic, moral/religious);

- identifying cultural perspectives (e.g., products, practices, perspectives; comparisons between target and native cultures).

See Adair-Hauck, Glisan, and Troyan (2013) for further details on these three types of interpretive tasks.

(6) *Creativity Phase:* Learners continue to use the information from the text to create their own meaning in the interpersonal and then presentational modes.

For the Interpersonal Phase, one option is for learners to discuss the information they read in this article with others (such as friends or family) so that they can plan to travel around Madrid using the subway. A second option would be a role play in which learners engage in an interaction with someone in the metro to find out additional information.

For the Presentational Phase, learners create a presentational product based on the text they interpreted. A possible task might be

> Create a brochure about how to navigate the Madrid metro, using information from the text. Find additional information from other Internet sources. Include visuals to support your message. You will share this brochure with your classmates to help them prepare for their trip to Madrid. Use five new words/expressions that you learned in the text. You might have a classmate read your first draft and react to it in terms of both content and accuracy.

As an alternative, learners could present a short talk that is illustrated with multimedia (e.g., PowerPoint) about the use of the metro in Madrid. Teachers should strive to create a real audience for learners' presentational products (other than just the teacher!) and to help learners have the audience in mind as they create oral or written presentational products.[6]

This approach to guiding learners through an authentic text also reflects how the three modes of communication are intertwined in the world beyond the classroom. That is, we often read/listen to/view a text, then talk about it with a friend or co-worker, and may incorporate it into a presentational product such as writing a letter to the editor of a local newspaper.

<u>Conducting the series of tasks</u> described above involves the following steps:

1. Introduce the text in a way that piques learners' interest. Visuals, maps, and realia can be used to motivate learners to want to interpret the text. Provide a purpose for learners to interpret this particular text or ask them to think about what purpose the text might serve them, who the intended audience might be, and why a person might read or view this text. For example, a simple recipe can become an occasion for deep and thoughtful interpretation. Scanning the recipe for specific information can suggest additional purposes beyond the superficial conclusion that the purpose of the text is to learn how to prepare a dish. For example, the number of servings can suggest if the person is planning a large party or a dinner for two, the nature of the recipe (a dessert, a main course, a healthy option) can indicate the dietary preferences of the reader, and cultural information accompanying the recipe can contribute to identifying the overall purposes, readers, and reasons for the text. Even an innocent recipe can be used to help students "read between the lines" or to assess if they are reading at all! Finally, state explicitly how interpreting this particular text addresses your long-term unit goals and/or big idea for the unit.

    Additionally, connect what you have already done in the unit with the text.

2. Implement the main idea and important details phases in class so that you can see immediately whether or not learners have comprehended the key elements of the text.

---

[6] See Shrum and Glisan (2016) for an extension task called *Intertextuality*, in which learners compare the text with a second text that they interpret. For this particular metro reading, learners might listen to a public service announcement about using the metro in Madrid and compare this information to what they read in the first text.

3. Following the scanning for important details activity, provide time for learners to read/listen to/view the entire text so that they can process meaning. This activity could also be done outside of class for homework once the main idea and details have been discussed in class. It is critical to stress to students the ineffectiveness of translating from the target language to the native language, since this is a laborious activity that does not typically result in an interpretation of the text, particularly in drawing inferences, i.e., one could translate an entire text and still not arrive at an understanding of it.

4. For the various types of interpretation activities, including discussion of inferences and cultural perspectives, learners could collaborate in pairs or groups and share opinions afterwards with the entire class by means of a discussion. Students benefit from working with one another, which also provides an avenue for developing interpersonal communication in the target language.

Rehearsing the Practice

The following tasks are provided to practice ways to guide learners through an authentic text. Before you begin, you might find it helpful to (a) review the features of interpretive communication presented earlier in this chapter, and (b) access External Mediational Tool #3A in this chapter's Appendix A to assist you in guiding students through the text.

1. Select an authentic text in the target language that you teach or are preparing to teach for a specific level of instruction. The text may be a printed text, audio segment, or video text. Justify your choice of text according to

   - context appropriateness

   - age appropriateness

   - appropriateness for linguistic level of learners (including organizational features as described in earlier section of chapter).

2. Develop a series of interpretive tasks for this text according to the model presented earlier. For now, skip the Interpretive/Discussion Phase, which you will return to complete in the next section of this chapter. Justify your use of either the target language or English in the tasks that check comprehension of the text. State explicitly the amount of English that would be used in the interpretive tasks in terms of an approximate percentage or number of utterances.

3. a. If you are a pre-service teacher enrolled in a teaching or practicum class, ask one or two peers to (1) read/listen to/watch the text and (2) complete the tasks you designed. Have a discussion with your peers to obtain their feedback. Are there changes you need to make to your interpretive tasks as a result of this feedback? If so, describe them.

   b. If you are an in-service teacher, conduct your interpretive activity with a class of your learners. If possible, either record the activity or ask a colleague to observe it. Later, self-assess the effectiveness of the task (along with your colleague if you were observed). If you could conduct this activity again, what changes would you make to it and why?

Assessing the Practice

Use Rubric #3A in this chapter's Appendix B to self-assess your interpretive series of tasks. As an alternative or in addition, you could ask a colleague to observe the interpretive lesson that you taught and provide feedback using the rubric.

PART 2: Leading a Text-Based Discussion

Deconstructing the Practice

Leading a discussion on the authentic text provides an avenue for learners to interpret the text by making inferences and exchanging ideas and opinions with others. Further, it offers opportunities for developing oral interpersonal communication while fostering the larger classroom discourse community (see Chapter 2). It should be noted that, while learners should have the text being discussed in front of them during the conversation, discussions are designed to be *spontaneous* in nature—that is, learners should not *read* scripted answers to questions posed by the teacher. This part of the HLTP is enacted by means of the following steps:

1. Prior to beginning a class discussion, be sure that learners have demonstrated comprehension of the main idea(s) and important details of the text (see first two phases presented earlier) so that they feel confident in stating their opinions and interpretations about the text and further meaning-making with one another.

2. The first time that you engage your class in this type of discussion, give learners a few rules to follow. You can print and distribute the rules for discussion and/or have them posted in the classroom for everyone to see. Notice that you will need to teach your learners some key expressions for participating in a conversation and/or make these resources available to them during the discussion. The following are some discussion rules that can be taught to students to create a coherent discussion rather than a series of teacher questions and student answers.

    (a) Instead of raising your hands to be called upon, take the floor to speak using the appropriate expressions in the target language (e.g., "Excuse me, but I'd like to say that....") (if the teacher approves of this process).
    (b) Comment on what someone else has said before you add something so that a connected, coherent discussion occurs. Accordingly, look at your classmates as you speak rather than stare at the teacher.
    (c) Do not monopolize the conversation, but you are expected to contribute something to the discussion.
    (d) Ask questions about parts of the text that you do not understand or are confused about—this is also considered a form of participation.
    (e) Ask your classmates for clarification and/or further details if you do not fully understand their points. This is a natural feature of participating in a discussion.
    (f) Use information from the text to support your opinions, given that the discussion is based on the text itself. Share your interpretations and opinions, but support what you say with textual evidence, e.g., quotes from the text, uses of specific kinds of words.

(g) Be respectful of the contributions of your peers to the discussion, as all opinions are welcome and make the discussion engaging.

(h) Make every attempt to use language that you have learned to communicate what you what to say. Ask your teacher for vocabulary only when you cannot think of any other way to express an idea without using a particular word or expression. Communicative success in a discussion is not based on the use of correct grammar but on your ability to get your meaning across in the target language in any way you can (This is to prevent the entire discussion from turning into "How do you say...?").

(i) Offer as much detail as possible, challenging yourselves to speak in longer, more detailed sentences.

3. Arrange the desks in a circle or semicircle to facilitate face-to-face conversation.

4. Sit in the circle, at least for the first few times that you facilitate the discussion. Once learners become comfortable with the discussion format, you may want to sit outside of the circle to give learners more control over managing the discussion; this would be particularly effective to do in the case of more advanced classes. The decision that you make regarding where to sit will also depend on how large your classes are and on the role you need to play in managing learner behavior (i.e., to keep students on task and engaged).

5. Ask questions one at a time for discussion. You could project them onto a screen for learners to see as well as hear. Avoid giving the class the entire list of questions to prevent students from planning their responses to other questions in advance. Questions should elicit inferences by students as opposed to having one "correct" answer in the text. The following are two examples of discussion questions for the authentic text presented here on the metro in Madrid:

- *¿Por qué dice el autor: "Las lineas del Metro de Madrid crecen casi cada año y disponemos ya de una de las mejores redes de toda Europa"?* [Why do you think that the author states: "The Madrid metro lines grow almost every year and we have at our disposal one of the best metro systems in all of Europe."?]

- *¿Por qué piensan que sea importante que los estudiantes estadounidenses sepan algo sobre el metro de Madrid antes de viajar a esta famosa ciudad? Usen información del texto para apoyar sus ideas.* [Why do you think that it is important for American students to have an understanding of Madrid's metro before traveling to this famous city? Use information from the text to support your ideas.]

Note that one of these questions was designed to engage learners in drawing inferences from the text and one was an opinion type of question. In both cases, learners are asked to use information from the text to respond. This is important to remember because otherwise students could offer opinions on questions without using the text at all.

While enacting this practice, it is critical that the teacher demonstrate specific *types of teacher behaviors* that will facilitate the text-based discussion in a *challenging*, yet *non-threatening* manner:

- Tolerate silences during the discussion and avoid filling the pauses with your own talk. In this way, learners will feel pressure to initiate their own talk. Give learners sufficient time to think of what they want to say.

- Avoid the temptation to respond to the contribution made by each learner by adding your own thoughts and information, as this will disrupt the natural flow of the conversation. In this regard, avoid the IRE pattern of interaction (see Chapter 2).

- Do not call learners' attention to language errors during the discussion unless they impede understanding (e.g., "Did you mean to say that...?") (see Chapter 6). Instead, keep a list of common errors that you can bring to their attention at another time when it is more appropriate to focus on grammatical form.

- Direct your gaze to any learner, not just the one who has the floor.

- Choose to participate when you need to ask for clarification (i.e., ask assisting questions), encourage the learner to say more about a particular point, or react in some way (e.g., "How surprising!") (see Chapter 6). Do not cut off an exchange with one learner prematurely to ask another learner to participate.

- Since this is a text-based discussion, be vigilant that students are referring back to the text during the discussion. If they stray from the text, bring them back to it. Keep everyone on course and know when to interrupt and how.

- Teach learners **gambits** for taking the floor (e.g., "Wait a minute, as I was saying....")— don't just let them begin to talk; see Chapter 2 (Taylor, 2002).

- Permit short responses where they naturally would occur, as in yes/no questions, but elicit more detailed responses when additional information is needed using prompts such as: "Can you say more about this point?" "Tell us more about why you said this." "Is there something in the text that made you think this way?"

- Provide direct teaching when necessary (i.e., a teachable moment) to provide information on a topic or review a structure that is needed in the discussion; these moments will occur spontaneously in the conversation (suggestions adapted from Kramsch, 1987).

- Conclude the discussion by eliciting some statements that would provide a summary of the ideas that had been shared. At the conclusion of a discussion, it is always a good idea to provide a few summary comments so students feel the discussion was productive and information generated in the discussion was worthwhile and important. Many learners complain that discussions often seem to go nowhere and have no point. As you listen to the discussion take a few notes on three to four main points that you want to highlight at the conclusion of the discussion. These points can also be posted on a discussion board, reviewed at the beginning of the next class, or used as a launching point for a follow-up discussion (list adapted from Kramsch, 1987).

In addition, as learners engage in text-based discussions over the course of time, you might want to gradually remove yourself from the discussion so that learners take more ownership of it. Further, students could take turns leading the discussion.

Rehearsing the Practice

The following tasks are provided to practice ways to engage learners in text-based discussions.

1. Create a list of gambits in the target language you teach or are preparing to teach that would be useful for your learners to use during task-based discussions. More

specifically, create a list of 5 gambits for novice-level learners, 5 for intermediate-level learners, and 5 for advanced-level learners.

2. Using the authentic text that you selected for your rehearsal of the first practice presented in this chapter, create a list of 5 possible questions in the target language that you could use to elicit inferences and discussion (see #5 above).

3. Using the questions that you prepared in task #2, anticipate 3 different types of student responses to each question. Explain the nature of each student response, e.g., misunderstanding, appropriate response, incomplete response. Then based on these student responses, provide a teacher response in terms of IRF (see Chapter 2).

4. Before beginning Task a or b below, you might find it helpful to access External Mediational Tool #3B in this chapter's Appendix A for a review of the guidelines for conducting a text-based discussion.

    a. If you are a pre-service teacher enrolled in teaching or practicum classes, conduct this text-based discussion with some of your peers and practice the teacher behaviors presented earlier. Ask a few of your peers to be observers. Afterwards, elicit observer and participant feedback on the effectiveness of the discussion. What changes do you need to make for future discussions?

    b. If you are an in-service teacher, conduct this text-based discussion with a class of your learners. If possible, either record the activity or ask a colleague to observe it. Later, self-assess its effectiveness (along with your colleague if you were observed). If you could conduct this discussion again, what changes would you make to it and why?

Assessing the Practice

Use Rubric #3B in this chapter's Appendix B to self-assess your text-based discussion. As an alternative or in addition, you could ask a colleague to observe the discussion that you facilitate and provide feedback using the rubric.

Putting the Practice into a Larger Context: Instructional Goals and Challenges

In this chapter, the larger HLTP of guiding learners to interpret and discuss authentic texts has been deconstructed in terms of two small grain-size practices: guiding learners to interpret authentic texts and leading a text-based discussion. In educational settings at all levels, including language classes, acquiring information from texts and exploring that information through discussion and exchange with others are critical abilities for becoming educated individuals. Acquiring new perspectives and insights through text-based discussions is a skill that goes beyond the foreign language classroom and situates language learning within a broader educational mission. The ability to interpret and discuss texts fosters many of the twenty-first century skills, which, in addition to communication, include information, media, and technology literacy. Further, through this HLTP, learners acquire skill in collaborating with others, engaging in critical thinking and problem solving, as well as demonstrating creativity and innovation. Finally, learners practice social and cross-cultural skills as they interact and problem solve with their peers, which also supports flexibility and adaptability (Partnership for 21st Century Skills, 2011).

These HLTPs also address a larger teaching challenge that confronts all educators. In light of the fact that teachers need to be certain of what their learners have understood, teachers must be on a continual search for ways to expose their learners' thinking (Kennedy,

2016). This is essential so that the teacher can make instructional decisions in terms of whether to remediate, elaborate, or continue on to new topics and skills. The need to make student thinking visible becomes more daunting as the social distance between the teacher and students widen (Jackson, 1986). As Kennedy explains, "social distance grows as students become younger, come from different social classes or cultural groups, speak different languages, live in different family structures, or have learning disabilities that the teacher has not yet experienced" (2016, p. 12). In these instances, teachers must work more deliberately to confirm the degree to which their learners understand. The two-part HLTP presented in this chapter is a mediational tool for exposing learner understanding. First, the approach to guiding students through authentic texts serves to reveal what students have comprehended and interpreted and to facilitate the development of interpretive communication. Secondly, text-based discussion provides a venue for learners to illustrate (1) how they comprehend and understand texts, and (2) how these understandings are informing and shaping their own knowledge, ideas, and opinions. It should be noted that the role of the teacher as guide and facilitator in these practices is key to narrowing the social distance gap that is a challenging variable in typical classroom settings.

A final thought to conclude this chapter is that the practice of guiding learners through interpreting and discussing authentic texts is linked closely to the two HLTPs presented in earlier chapters—facilitating target language comprehensibility and building a classroom discourse community. In all of these practices, comprehensibility of the target language—be it oral or printed— and social interaction in the TL are pivotal to making meaning and bringing about understanding.

For Further Reading

Adair-Hauck, B., Glisan, E. W., & Troyan, F. J. (2013). *Implementing Integrated Performance Assessment.* Alexandria, VA: ACTFL.

Bacon, S. M. (1992). The relationship between gender, comprehension, processing strategies, and cognitive and affective response in foreign language listening. *The Modern Language Journal, 76,* 160–178.

Bernhardt, E. B. (2005). Progress and procrastination in second language reading. *Annual Review of Applied Linguistics, 25,* 133–150.

Galloway, V. (1998). Constructing cultural realities: "Facts" and frameworks of association. In J. Harper, M. Lively, & M. Williams (Eds.), *The coming of age of the profession* (pp. 129–140). Boston: Heinle & Heinle.

Godev, C. B., Martínez-Gibson, E. A., & Toris, C. C. M. (2002). Foreign language reading comprehension test: L1 versus L2 in open-ended questions. *Foreign Language Annals, 35,* 202–221.

Goldenberg, C. (1991). *Instructional conversations and their classroom implication.* Washington, DC: The National Center for Research on Cultural Diversity and Second Language Learning. (ERIC Document Reproduction Service No. 341–353).

Hall, J. K. (1999). The communication standards. In J. K. Phillips & R. M. Terry (Eds.), *Foreign language standards: Linking research, theories, and practices* (pp. 15–56). Lincolnwood, IL: National Textbook Company.

Hammadou, J. A. (2002). Advanced foreign language readers' inferencing. In J. A. Hammadou Sullivan (Ed.), *Literacy and the second language learner* (pp. 217–238). Greenwich, CT: Information Age Publishing.

Herron, C. A., & Seay, I. (1991). The effect of authentic oral texts on student listening comprehension in the foreign language classroom. *Foreign Language Annals, 24,* 487–495.

Jackson, P. W. (1986). *The practice of teaching.* New York, NY: Teachers College Press.

Kennedy, M. (2016). Parsing the practice of teaching. *Journal of Teacher Education, 67*(1), 6–17.

Kramsch, C. (1987). Interactive discourse in small and large groups. In W. Rivers (Ed.), *Interactive language teaching* (pp. 17–30). Cambridge, UK: Cambridge University Press.

Lee, J. F. (1986). Background knowledge and L2 reading. *The Modern Language Journal, 70,* 350–354.

Lee, J. F., & VanPatten, B. (1995). *Making communicative language teaching happen* (2nd ed.). New York: McGraw-Hill.

Maxim, H. H., II. (2002). A study into the feasibility and effects of reading extended authentic discourse in the beginning German language classroom. *The Modern Language Journal, 86,* 20–35.

Nassaji, H. (2007). Schema theory and knowledge-based processes in second language reading comprehension: A need for alternative perspectives. *Language Learning, 57,* 79–113.

National Standards in Foreign Language Education Project. (2015). *World-Readiness standards for learning languages.* Alexandria, VA: Author.

Partnership for 21st Century Skills. (2011). *21st century skills map for world languages.* Washington, DC: Author. Retrieved from http://www.actfl.org/sites/default/files/pdfs/21stCenturySkillsMap/p21_worldlanguagesmap.pdf

Reiser, B. J., & Tabak, I. (2014). Scaffolding. In R. K. Sawyer (Ed.), *Cambridge handbook of the learning sciences,* 2nd ed. (pp. 44–61). New York, NY: Cambridge University Press.

Shrum, J. L., & Glisan, E. W. (2016). *Teacher's handbook: Contextualized language instruction.* 5th edition. Boston, MA: Cengage Learning.

Stone, A. C. (1993). What is missing in the metaphor of scaffolding? In E. A. Forman, N. Minnick, C. Addison Stone (Eds.), *Contexts for learning, sociocultural dynamics in children's development* (pp. 169–183). New York: Oxford University Press.

Tafaghodtari, M. H., & Vandergrift, L. (2008). Second/foreign language listening: Unraveling the construct. *Perceptual and Motor Skills, 107,* 99–113.

Taylor, G. (2002). Teaching gambits: The effect of instruction and task variation on the use of conversation strategies by intermediate Spanish students. *Foreign Language Annals, 35,* 171–189.

Todhunter, S. (2007). Instructional conversations in a high school Spanish class. *Foreign Language Annals, 40,* 604–621.

Tomlinson, B. (2012). Materials development for language learning and teaching. *Language Teaching, 45,* 143–179. doi: 10.1017/S0261444811000528

Vigil, V. D. (1987). Authentic text in the college-level Spanish I class as the primary vehicle of instruction. Unpublished doctoral dissertation. University of Texas, Austin.

Villegas Rogers, C., & Medley, F. W., Jr. (1988). Language with a purpose: Using authentic materials in the foreign language classroom. *Foreign Language Annals, 21*, 467–478.

Young, D. J. (1993). Processing strategies of foreign language readers: Authentic and edited input. *Foreign Language Annals, 26,* 451–468.

Young, D. J. (1999). Linguistic simplification of SL reading material: Effective instructional practice? *The Modern Language Journal, 83,* 350–366.

Appendix A

External Mediational Tool #3A:
Guiding Learners to Interpret Authentic Texts

1. Select an authentic text in terms of topic familiarity, context-appropriateness, level of interest; age-appropriateness; linguistic level; strategy use by students.

2. Guide students through sequence of interpretive tasks:

    a. Pre-reading/Pre-listening/Pre-viewing: Introduce text in a way that piques interest.

    b. Skimming for main ideas and Scanning for important details: Conduct these in class.

    c. Provide time for students to read/listen/view entire text.

    d. Interpretive phase: Guessing meaning in context

    e. Interpretation/Discussion phase (see Tool #3B)

    f. Creativity phase

    Remember: Stress to students the ineffectiveness of translating from TL to English. Conduct interpretation tasks in pairs/groups.

External Mediational Tool #3B:
Leading a Text-Based Discussion

1. Prior to beginning the discussion, be sure that learners have demonstrated comprehension of the main idea(s) and important details of the text.

2. The first time that you engage your class in this type of discussion, give learners a few "rules" to follow regarding expectations for how they contribute to the conversation.

3. Arrange the desks in a circle or semi-circle to facilitate face-to-face conversation.

4. Sit in the circle, at least for the first few times that you facilitate the discussion.

5. Ask questions one at a time for discussion. Key teacher behaviors:

   a. Tolerate silences during the discussion and avoid filling the pauses with your own talk.

   b. Avoid responding to each student utterance by adding your own thoughts and avoid IRE.

   c. Ignore language errors unless they impede understanding.

   d. Direct your gaze to any learner, not just the one who has the floor.

   e. Participate when you need to ask for clarification, encourage the learner to say more about a particular point, or react in some way.

   f. Be vigilant that students are referring back to the text during the discussion.

   g. Teach learners gambits for taking the floor.

   h. Permit short responses where they would naturally occur, but elicit more detail when additional information is needed.

   i. Provide direct teaching when necessary.

   j. Conclude the discussion by eliciting some statements that would provide a summary of the ideas that had been shared.

Appendix B

RUBRIC: HLTP #3A:
Guiding Learners to Interpret Authentic Texts

	EXCEEDS EXPECTATIONS	MEETS EXPECTATIONS	DEVELOPING	UNACCEPTABLE
Nature of Text	Authentic text. Content and topic of text make a perfect fit with unit theme and are appropriate for age and linguistic level of learners. Text is engaging for learners. Text has multiple types of organizational support (e.g., visuals, subtitles) to facilitate comprehension.	Authentic text. Content and topic of text are pertinent to the unit theme and are appropriate for age and linguistic level of learners. Text is of interest to learners. Text has organizational support to facilitate comprehension.	Authentic text. Connection between content/ topic of text and unit theme are not obvious, but text is appropriate for age and linguistic level of learners. At least some element of text is of interest to learners. Some organizational support.	Unauthentic text, which may be from a textbook program. And/ or content and topic of text may not be pertinent to unit theme and/or not appropriate for age or linguistic level of learners. Text may not be of interest to learners. Lack of organizational support.
Preparation for Interpreting Text	Teacher activates background knowledge and language needed for interpreting text in a learner-centered and interesting way.	Teacher activates background knowledge and language needed for interpreting text.	Teacher activates either background knowledge or language needed for interpreting text, but not both.	No preparation for interpreting text or preparation is inadequate.
Approach to Guiding Learners Through Text	Teacher guides learners through both literal and interpretive comprehension tasks in an engaging manner. Teacher focuses on global meaning initially, then on important details, and finally on interpretation (i.e., inferencing).	Teacher guides learners through both literal and interpretive comprehension tasks. Teacher focuses on literal comprehension first and then on interpretive comprehension (i.e., inferencing).	Teacher guides learners through mainly literal tasks with a lesser focus on interpretive tasks. Teacher may focus on details at the expense of global meaning.	Teacher uses a traditional approach to exploring texts (e.g., translation, focus on literal meaning). And/ or teacher may edit the text instead of the task in order to bring the text to the level of learners.

(continued on next page)

RUBRIC: HLTP #3A (*continued*)

	EXCEEDS EXPECTATIONS	MEETS EXPECTATIONS	DEVELOPING	UNACCEPTABLE
Use of TL and English	Teacher uses the TL to the maximum extent and elicits maximum TL use from learners. Teacher may use English for appropriate reasons and provides justification for it.	Teacher uses the TL and elicits TL use from learners. Teacher may use English for appropriate reasons and provides justification for it.	Teacher uses a combination of TL and English but use of English may not be justified. Teacher elicits some TL use by learners but misses some opportunities to do so.	Overuse of English and/ or use of English with no justification or inadequate justification. And/or little TL use by learners.
Integration of 3 Modes of Communication	Teacher uses text as the basis for both interpersonal and presentational communication in creative and engaging real-world tasks.	Teacher integrates interpersonal and presentational communication within work on text.	Teacher integrates either interpersonal or presentational communication but not both. And/or interpersonal tasks may consist of answering questions about the text. Tasks may not reflect natural communication occurring in world beyond classroom.	Integration of interpersonal and presentational communication with text is lacking or absent.

RUBRIC: HLTP #3B: Leading a Text-Based Discussion*

	EXCEEDS EXPECTATIONS	MEETS EXPECTATIONS	DEVELOPING	UNACCEPTABLE
Seating Arrangement & Classroom Atmosphere	Learners are seated so that they see all of their classmates' faces. Climate of lesson is challenging, engaging, and non-threatening.	Learners are seated in a way so that they see the majority of their classmates' faces. Climate of lesson is engaging and non-threatening.	Learners are seated so that they see some of their classmates' faces. Climate of lesson is non-threatening but not totally engaging.	Learners are seated in traditional row format and/or do not see their classmates' faces. And/or climate of lesson is boring and/or threatening.
Questions Asked during Discussion	Questions require learners to engage in inferencing from the text, critical thinking, and sharing of opinions.	Questions require learners to engage in inferencing from the text and some critical thinking and sharing of opinions.	Questions are a combination of retrieval-type questions from text and inferencing-type. Little evidence of critical thinking and/or sharing of opinions.	Questions are largely retrieval-type questions or are opinion-type questions that do not require learners to refer to information in the text.
Role of Teacher in Discussion	Teacher is facilitator and offers assistance and guided as necessary to move discussion forward.[1] Teacher is an equal partner in discussion, responding to learners' contributions by giving expressive reactions or prompting for further details (IRF). Teacher gazes around the room, not just at the learner who has the floor.	Teacher is facilitator and offers assistance and guided as necessary to move discussion forward. Teacher responds to learners' contributions by giving expressive reactions or prompting for further details (IRF). Teacher tends to look at each student who has the floor.	Teacher is mostly facilitator and offers assistance as necessary but engages in periodic teacher talk that may not be relevant. Teacher tends to look at each student who has the floor.	Teacher directs discussion and learners respond to the teacher. Teacher takes the floor and engages in teacher talk often. Teacher looks at each student who has the floor. Pervasive use of IRE.

(continued on next page)

RUBRIC: HLTP #3B (*continued*)

	EXCEEDS EXPECTATIONS	MEETS EXPECTATIONS	DEVELOPING	UNACCEPTABLE
Scaffolding/ Assistance by Teacher	Teacher activates background knowledge and TL and gives learners gambits prior to discussion. Teacher offers assistance, including models for more complex language learners might use. Teacher provides some direct teaching within the context of the discussion, only when asked by learners.	Teacher activates background knowledge and TL and gives learners gambits prior to discussion. Teacher offers assistance, mostly through vocabulary. Teacher provides direct teaching within the context of the discussion, when s/he deems it necessary to guide and move discussion forward.	Teacher activates background knowledge and TL prior to discussion. Teacher offers assistance often, mostly through vocabulary. Direct teaching may be excessive.	Teacher offers little assistance other than to correct language errors. Direct teaching is pervasive and provided out of context.
Interaction of Learners in TL	Learners engage in a lively discussion in the TL in which they look at one another, respond to what their classmates said, and offer opinions and expressive reactions.	Learners engage in discussion in the TL in which they look at one another, respond to what their classmates said, and offer opinions.	Learners engage in some discussion and look at one another periodically. They offer opinions but seldom respond to what their classmates said. There may be some use of English.	Little to no interaction among learners. Learners gaze at and respond directly to teacher. There may be excessive use of English by learners.

[1] For more advanced classes or when learners gain more experience with text-based discussions, the teacher may be mostly a spectator to the discussion other than when asked by learners to offer assistance.

*All communication referred to in rubric is carried out in the target language.

Chapter 4

HLTP #4: Focusing on Form in a Dialogic Context Through PACE

To know grammar means, therefore, the ability to use language forms for real communicative purposes and not just to display knowledge of rules for sentence formation, verb paradigms, and exceptions to linguistic rules....

This chapter deals with one widely researched, theorized, and debated aspects of language teaching and learning—teaching grammatical structures, or what will be referred to in this chapter as, **focus on form**. By using the term *focus on form*, we distinguish lessons designed around teaching the grammar point of the day from lessons that draw attention to form in meaningful cultural texts and contexts, for larger communicative purposes, and for expressing and interpreting social and cultural meaning in various modes of communication.

The *World-Readiness Standards for Learning Languages* states that communication is at the core of foreign language learning (National Standards in Foreign Language Education Project, 2015), and, in this regard, previous chapters have explored communicating comprehensibly in the target language, creating a classroom discourse community, and interpreting and discussing authentic texts. If human communication is at the core of foreign language learning, learning how to assist students to investigate, explain, and reflect on forms of language that constitute this communication is essential. From this communicative perspective, teaching language forms requires understanding that grammatical forms offer language users a variety of abilities for accomplishing activities in the everyday world, for example, to interpret meaning, to express ideas and opinions clearly, to act in socially and culturally appropriate ways, and to use language strategically when words may fail us. As Hall (2001/2003) states, we learn to take action with our words.

The overarching HLTP in this chapter is focus on form through dialogic inquiry in a meaningful context as it is carried out in the PACE approach (Adair-Hauck & Donato, 2016). PACE, an acronym for Presentation, Attention, Co-Construction, and Extension, will be deconstructed and detailed within each of the four phases of the model. We have selected the PACE approach because it (a) maximizes the teacher's and students' use of comprehensible target language (see Chapter 1), (b) fosters a discourse community in which students and teachers investigate cultural texts and the role of form in making meaning in these texts (see Chapter 2), and (c) promotes interaction, interpretation, and text-based discussion (see Chapter 3). Through the interactive presentation of cultural texts (e.g., stories, folktales, legends), a rich context is created for dialoguing with learners about the relationship of forms to their meanings and uses.

ACTFL/CAEP Standards addressed: #1a, 1b; #2a, 2c; #3a, 3b; #4a, 4b, 4c

Research and Theory Supporting the Practice

In their book, *How Languages are Learned* (2013), Lightbown and Spada present no fewer than eight theoretical and research-based approaches that attempt to explain the complexities of focusing learner attention on the formal aspects of the language and the processes involved in how learners internalize and use language structures for communicative purposes. Given the diversity of approaches, types of research studies, and theoretical opinions, it is no wonder that a recurring question raised by new and experienced teachers alike is "How can I best teach grammar to my students?"

Based on numerous studies of the various approaches and theories associated with learning the formal aspects of a language, one conclusion is clear. Focusing attention on form is clearly beneficial and allows learners to make progress as language users (e.g., Donato, 1994; Gass & Selinker, 2001; Lantolf & Poehner, 2014; Paradis, 2009; Swain, 1995). Focus on form can emerge spontaneously when learners experience gaps in knowledge, when they try to express themselves, or when they discuss their comprehension and interpretations of texts (Davin & Donato, 2013; Poehner, 2008). This spontaneous approach is referred to as **noticing the gap** (Swain, 1995) indicating that when learners encounter aspects of the language that they do not know in speech or writing (the gap), their attention shifts to the formal aspects of language to help them convey their ideas.

Teachers can also deliberately plan for focus on form in the context of listening to, reading, and interpreting texts. Teachers can direct attention to a particular useful form for making meaning, an approach that will be presented in this chapter as one part of the PACE model. Pre-selecting a form on which to direct learners' attention is not to be confused with the **'grammar point of the day' approach to lesson planning**. That is, the goal is not just to teach the form but to explore how the form serves a larger communicative purpose.

Two Research Perspectives on Focus on Form

A majority of the research on the acquisition of the formal properties of language can be summarized in studies of two opposite and distinct approaches, deductive and inductive presentations of language forms. Induction and deduction represent ways that an individual reasons and processes information. When individuals begin with a high-level generalization (e.g., a rule of some kind) and then apply this generalization to a specific problem they need to solve (e.g., expressing meaning in language), they are said to be using *deductive* forms of reasoning, logic, and thinking. Conversely, when individuals arrive at a generalization (e.g., a rule) by observing specific forms of evidence (e.g., example sentences and utterances), they are said to be reasoning *inductively*. When applied to the classroom, **deductive instruction** involves teacher-fronted explanations of language rules followed by student application of these rules in mechanical and eventually communicative activities, often only if time allows. Deductive presentations of grammar rules is what occurs in most foreign language classrooms and the approach with which most beginning teachers are familiar because of their own language learning experiences. Further this approach is characteristic of the vast majority of language textbooks, which present a series of grammar rules, followed by practice that proceeds on a continuum from mechanical to communicative.

An **inductive presentation**, on the other hand, involves the teacher providing multiple examples of the use of a form, or what is called in the literature 'input flooding' (Trahey & White, 1993), from which learners are expected to arrive at some generalization or rule. A well known inductive approach is Processing Instruction (VanPatten, 2004).

There are several important points that need to be acknowledged when reviewing studies of approaches to teaching grammar. First, in real classrooms with real learners, it is highly unlikely that either of these two approaches could be implemented in their pure and unadulterated forms. Second, the studies of these approaches are often carried out in laboratory conditions, for example, one-on-one with a researcher or in classes in which procedures for instructions are strictly specified and constrained to ensure fidelity and validity of the research study. Third, the goal of many studies on focus on form is not exclusively to arrive at a pedagogical recommendation per se or to situate the teaching of form in the many contextual factors that make up a class (e.g., student motivation, age of the learners, classroom resources, teacher proficiency and preparation). Rather, these studies have the goal of understanding the psychology of language learning and how learners process language when they encounter it in the world both in and out of the classroom. This is not to dismiss the good work of focus on form researchers but only to point out that a large gap needs to be bridged when trying to connect findings of highly controlled studies to practice and the laboratory setting to what actually happens in classrooms.

The Shortcomings of Deductive and Inductive Approaches

In teacher-fronted deductive presentations, grammatical rules are presented stripped of a meaningful context with little or no attention to how particular language rules apply to communicative situations beyond the classroom. Because emphasis is on learning the rule of the day's lesson and applying the rule to isolated sentences, learners often have little personal investment in the lesson, are not engaged in analyzing the language, lack motivation, and do not develop the ability to use language forms to convey meaning when interacting in the target language (Wong & VanPatten, 2003). In essence, language learning is reduced to a course in linguistics and decontextualized language analysis most often at the sentence level.

On the other side of the instructional dichotomy is the inductive approach, which is based on the notion that providing target language input to learners, which is comprehensible and structured in ways that makes a form obvious, enables learners to induce, or figure out on their own, how language forms and structures operate. The responsibility for learning is placed on the learners; the teacher's role is one of providing comprehensible sentences illustrating the target language form that learners are expected to reflect upon and analyze. One limitation of this approach is that a purely inductive approach does not guarantee that learners develop accurate understandings about language forms, meaning, and, use (Adair-Hauck, 1993; Donato, 1994; Lantolf & Poehner, 2011, 2014) because their thinking is never made visible and is only indirectly available through the utterances they produce.

Focus on Form as a Social Process

The approach to teaching the formal properties of language (e.g., sound systems, morphology, syntax, discourse coherence) that is presented in this chapter considers the essence of language to be social action, something that exists in use and in communication (Hall, 2001, 2003). In this view, language is not comprised of internal structures located exclusively in the heads of individuals. Rather, language is considered to be fundamentally social, comprised of linguistic resources whose meanings are located in our everyday communicative activities and practices. From this perspective, language learning is not simply the acquisition of grammatical structures for their own sake. Rather, language learning is fundamentally a social process. That is, learning the forms and functions of language occurs in social actions and interactions, such as expressing personal feeling and opinions, requesting goods and services, sharing information, directing one's own actions through self-talk, interpreting what others say, communicating to reach mutual understandings, and expressing personal identities, to name a few (Young, 2008, 2009).

To know grammar means, therefore, the ability to use language forms for real communicative purposes and not just to display knowledge of rules for sentence formation, verb paradigms, and exceptions to linguistic rules, or what Larsen Freeman (2003) refers to as **inert knowledge**. In other words, the goal of language instruction is not the mere mastery of a list of grammatical rules with the hope that at some point learners will be able to apply these rules quickly and efficiently in some feat of mental gymnastics. On the contrary, focus on form must always occur in a meaningful context and must make visible to the learner how a particular language form is used for the various modes of communication, how forms construct social and cultural meanings, and how they address larger communicative goals and purposes (Adair-Hauck & Donato, 2016). Moreover, whenever teachers turn students' attention to form, it must always be at the service of constructing and facilitating meaning making.

Considerations about Focus on Form

(1) *Why can't I just explain the rule and let students do the exercises in the book?* Knowledge of form is conceptual. Knowledge about the language system goes far beyond simply reciting textbook **rules of thumb** (Lantolf & Poehner, 2014), e.g., "add an –e to make the adjective feminine, delete the subject pronoun to form a command, or place direct and indirect objects before the verb." Textbook rules are often incomplete and inadequate for understanding how forms function as meaning-making resources in social and cultural contexts.

   Conceptual knowledge of language deals with the types of language choices one makes to express intended meaning and the reasons why one form rather than another has been selected in acts of communication for one's intended meaning. Lantolf and Poehner (2014) state that conceptual language knowledge is systematic and generalizable and not linked to any one specific situation of use, such as only knowing how to use a grammatical form in a textbook exercise but unable to use the form in other circumstances or even to recognize how a form can apply across contexts. For example, a conceptual understanding of past tense narration in Romance languages requires understanding the speaker's perspectives on past actions (verbal aspect) as initiating, habitual, completed, or sequential in order to tell or comprehend a narrative. The concept of verbal aspect contrasts sharply with the rules of thumb for the uses of past tenses that are presented at sentence-level rather than in a narrative and as predictable forms cued by certain time expressions in sentences such as "every day" or "at 10:00." These rules of thumb, as appealing as they may seem to students for arriving at the correct verb form, actually complicate the use of the structure when learners eventually discover that their handy rules do not apply to all situations.[7]

(2) *Why do students still make errors after I explain the rule?* Learning how to use forms to make meaning is developmental. It is very common to observe that even after

---

[7] For an in-depth discussion of the role of explicit declarative (metalinguistic) knowledge in language learning and acquisition, see Paradis (2009).

the most skilled and engaging deductive presentation of a grammatical structure, students continue to make errors, struggle to express themselves, or appear not to make progress and rely only on previously learned material. Language learning is developmental in the sense that changes over time can be observed. These changes in language knowledge take place through a process called ***restructuring***. When learners restructure their knowledge of language based on the interaction of new information with what they already know, it may be observed that a burst of progress appears where students seem "to get it;" at other times learners seem to backslide and begin to make errors that they had not previously made. These errors are proof that language learning is developmental and often result from the learners' **overgeneralizing** how a form works and using it in contexts to which it does not apply (e.g., after learning about the typical pattern of English past tense formation, the learner may produce the form *I eated). The important point to remember is that not all errors are created equal and in some cases what appears to be a mistake is actually evidence of the learner's progress toward restructuring and an emerging conceptual understanding of the formal properties of language (see #1).

The process described above can be described by the concept of **U-shaped Learning**, as depicted in Figure 4.1.

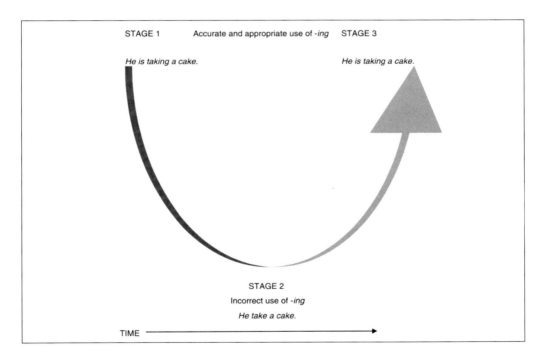

Figure 4.1. **U-Shaped Learning** (Gass, 2013, p. 263)

In Stage 1, the learner produces a correct form, perhaps as a result of attention on the form in classroom practice. In Stage 2, the learner begins to produce the form with errors, due to a number of factors, e.g., a demanding communicative situation or the introduction of a new new grammatical information, such as the use of the simple present tense verb forms in Stage 2. Finally, in Stage 3, the learner again uses the correct form, after having restructured his or her understanding of the new form and incorporating what was known into new information. U-shaped behavior is often the reason why learners may appear to "go backwards" in their use of a particular grammatical structure after they have learned and practiced it in our classroom. Parents often worry that their children are having developmental language problems when they observe that one day the child is saying "I fell down" and weeks later the child is heard to say "I falled down." Teachers are also sometimes frustrated and bewildered when learners appear to regress in this same way. U-shaped learning can help us understand the process of acquiring grammatical knowledge and how errors may not always be a result of forgetfulness or carelessness. Rather, it is a natural process of analyzing the language system based on the everyday communicative activities and practices in which they encounter new ways of expression and meaning making.

(3) *How do I address the issue of my students just wanting me to explain grammatical rules to them?* Teachers need to re-orient their learners' traditional ways of thinking about grammar instruction so that they understand why they are being asked to dialogue about language form, meaning, and use. Students need to understand how languages are acquired and that mastery of a long list of language rules is limited in its usefulness for meaning making. Students (and teachers) also need to understand why grammatical structures are concepts rather than simple rules to follow for word formation and that concepts develop out of a process of observation, dialogue, hypothesis testing, and language use. Unlike deductive and inductive approaches to reasoning about form where the responsibility for learning is placed entirely on the teacher or on the learner, students need to understand that focus on form requires collaborative dialogue between teachers and learners. In this dialogue, the teacher guides students in interpreting cultural texts (see Chapter 3) in which particular forms of the language are represented and modeled and later explored in reference to the relationship between the form (past tense verb forms), its meaning (the action and how and when it occurred), and function (narrating, recounting, or reporting) in the text. The importance of guiding students to observe forms in action, to hypothesize about their relationship to textual functions and social actions, and to develop the ability to arrive at language conceptualizations is more important than the memorization of language rules. Learners also need to be made aware that language classes are places where they *learn how to learn* languages so that they can reflect on and analyze language that they encounter when the teacher is not present. By mediating learners' relationship with form through dialogue, the teacher does more than simply teach a rule that may or may not be usable for acts of communication. By guiding students to observe and analyze form, the teacher equips students with the important ability to continue learning and expanding their language knowledge beyond the formal instruction of the classroom and without reliance on the teacher for explanations.

Deconstructing the Practice

The high-leverage teaching practice that has been chosen for focus on form is a Dialogic Story-Based Approach called PACE (Adair-Hauck & Donato, 2016). This approach reconciles the polarized views of deductive and inductive approaches. It allows teachers and students to work together to build understandings of form as they are encountered in meaningful texts. The approach invites the learner to experience meaning through an engaging, coherently organized text and then construct *concepts* about target language structures through discussion and dialogue with the teacher. PACE is based on research in second-language acquisition examined in earlier chapters. Further, the research conducted on PACE has illustrated its effectiveness in promoting learners' interpretive comprehension and grammatical understanding when compared to either deductive or inductive approaches (Adair-Hauck & Donato, 2016).

The PACE model makes use of a core text in the form of an interesting story from the target language culture(s). Stories are excellent ways to present language forms to learners because stories naturally create a context, are meaningful, and can be made relevant to the learners' lives. Additionally, because stories are organized in ways that we use to make sense of the world (e.g., characters, sequential actions, emotional reactions, settings, conflicts, resolutions), they support understanding, retention, and recall (Oller, 1983; Kennedy, 2006; Sousa, 2011). Think about a time that you heard a familiar story in the foreign language that you speak and how your comprehension increased because of your familiarity with the topic, genre, or plot. Stories can also contain dialogue, explanations, academic information, and cultural products, practices, and perspectives, and, therefore, within the body of a single story, examples of various text types and sources of information can often be found (Tannen, 2007).

PACE will be deconstructed into four parts, each part associated with one letter of the acronym (for additional information about the PACE model, see Adair-Hauck and Donato, 2016 and Toth & Davin, 2016):

(1) **PRESENTING** orally a short text in the form of a story from the target language culture or an authentic text in print for more advanced classes (see Chapter 3 for the definition of authentic texts).

(2) Calling learners' **ATTENTION** to a particular form in the text that is important to the text's meaning and so that the teacher and learners establish a joint focus of attention.

(3) **CO-CONSTRUCTING** an explanation of the form with the teacher through class discussion and dialogue.

(4) **EXTENDING** and using the form in a new context related to the theme and/or cultural content of the story.

These four steps of the model work in harmony and support each other as will be shown in the following explanation of the practice.

Step 1: PRESENTATION PHASE

<u>Select the story for</u> **PRESENTATION**: Selecting a culturally authentic story is one of the most important steps in developing a PACE lesson. Without an appropriate story that (a) is relevant and age-appropriate to the learners, (b) contains an engaging plot and characters, (c) reflects some aspect of the culture(s) of target language communities, and (d) contains an interesting theme that can be expanded upon, the steps of the PACE lesson will lack a meaningful context that is the foundation upon which focus on form occurs. The teacher should consider how the target culture is represented in terms of cultural products, practices, and perspectives (National Standards in Foreign Language Education Project, 2015). Further, the story must be linguistically appropriate for the learners. Not all texts are created equal and some texts may be better suited for learners at different levels of language development (see Chapter 3). The story needs to contain natural occurrences in sufficient quantity of the particular form on which learners will focus attention and discuss at a later time with the teacher and each other. Further, it should lend itself to

actions that are stageable, that is, actions that can be made visible and can be demonstrated with the use of props, visuals, and/or dramatization.

One of the questions that teachers often ask is whether they can create their own stories for a PACE lesson. Inventing a story is not advisable. The danger is that teachers will often create a story that is made up of a series of sentences that feature a grammatical point in an unnatural manner and with little redeeming cultural value. Additionally, creating a story requires writing talent and knowledge of the elements of a good story, skills that many teachers do not possess simply because they are not authors. For these reasons, creating one's own text should be avoided.

<u>Plan and Prepare the Story for Presentation</u>. After having selected the appropriate story for presentation, plan on how the story will be told to the class, how interactions will be carried out during story telling, and how long the story presentation will last. The Presentation Phase of the PACE model is not reading a story aloud to a class. It is based on telling the story and this requires practice. Rehearse the story before telling it to the class. A good idea is to observe professional storytellers on YouTube or at local children's museums for the techniques and strategies they use to engage an audience in a story. If forgetting parts of the story is a concern, create a story skeleton. A story skeleton is a tool that summarizes the story in sequence by using a few key words and phrases. Having a small index card on which the story skeleton is printed can be used as a reference when telling the story. In an upper-level class in which the focus might be on literature and literacy, the teacher may opt to present a printed text to the class rather than use oral storytelling. In this case, the Presentation Phase should follow guidelines for the use of authentic texts (see Chapter 3).

When planning the story, also include when in the story the teacher will interact with the class. For example, students might have images that they hold up and show at certain parts of the story, be cued to supply key words that reoccur in the story, or are asked questions that anticipate what happens next.

<u>Tell the Story.</u> The teacher must be familiar with the story before telling it to the class. While the teacher does not need to have the story completely memorized, reading it directly from the script will result in a dull presentation that will quickly lose students' interest. The story should be made accessible through storytelling simplifications. Because this story is told orally and not read as a printed text, the teacher can make language modifications to make meaning more understandable for learners such as using vocabulary that the students have learned, using shorter, less complex sentences, and making use of paraphrases (see Chapter 1 for ways to modify language for increased comprehensibility). However, care should be taken to be certain that these simplifications do not result in a sanitized, unnatural text that may result from trying to provide multiple illustrations of the form in question rather than establishing the story's meaning. Clearly the form that has been selected for focus needs to be present in sufficient quantity but the form also needs to be illustrated with sufficient quality. In addition, the teacher should use props, visuals, and dramatization to support meaning and heighten interest. While some teachers may prefer to use PowerPoint slides, it should be noted that the lesson will be more animated if props and visuals are used since learners can use them to dramatize the story or demonstrate comprehension.

During storytelling, opportunities for interaction with the storyteller need to be provided. Telling the story should not become time for students to listen passively to the teacher. Professional storytellers use many strategies to involve the audience while the story is being told. For example, students can signal their comprehension of certain parts of the story by holding up visuals, completing teacher utterances with key words from the story, answering questions that ask students to anticipate what will happen next, or dramatizing the story as it is being told (see "Planning the story" above). The story needs to be considered a text from which students can learn language in the context of what they already know. In this way, learners can learn *through* language and not only learn *about* language in the form of grammar rules and demotivating and uninspiring exercises.

Time the Story. Depending on the level of the class and the story selected, the storytelling event can last a few minutes or can be distributed in logical sections across several days. What is important in deciding how much of the story to tell and how long to spend on the storytelling event is the level of the class and the amount of content and language that learners can handle without overwhelming them or frustrating their meaning making abilities.

Checking Comprehension. It is essential that learners demonstrate comprehension of the story before proceeding to focusing on grammatical form. In addition to checking comprehension as the story is told (see previous discussion), the teacher might also engage learners in discussion of the story and/or ask some comprehension questions after the story presentation and before proceeding to the next phase.

Step 2: ATTENTION PHASE

Calling learners' ATTENTION to a meaningful form is the second phase of PACE. It is fairly well known that joint focus of attention of particular forms is necessary for language learning to occur and that often, in the absence of explicit direction from the teacher, learners may not focus attention on relevant parts of the text if left on their own. The purpose of the Attention Phase is to direct learners to *notice* some aspect of language relevant to the story and represented in sufficient quantity. According to the Noticing Hypothesis (Schmidt, 1990, 2001), the learner must first *notice* or become aware of a language feature before it can be learned or acquired (see also Gass, 1988, and Lightbown and Spada, 2013). The Attention Phase lasts *only a few minutes* and is carried out by highlighting a recurrent form on a written text. Highlighting a repeated form can be done in many ways—by underlining, by using a different font, a different color, or italics. Once attention has been established, the teacher may ask students to make observations about structural and functional similarities across highlighted forms. For example, the teacher may ask students to look at the highlighted forms and write down three similarities that they see or ask students if they recall hearing the forms in the story. The point is that calling attention to a particular form is a precursor to the next phase of the model. Without this joint focus of attention, exploring the uses of the form with students will not be possible.

Step 3: CO-CONSTRUCTION PHASE

During the Co-Construction Phase, the teacher assists learners in developing the concept of the target structure highlighted in the Attention phase. Learners and teacher may co-construct the structure, meaning, and function of a grammatical form through, for example, a series of well-chosen questions asked by teacher. These questions may ask students to find patterns, to compare the use of one form with another, or to state what role the particular form plays in the text. For example, learners can determine if a form functions to describe a character or setting, establish the circumstances of actions, indicate the narrator's perspective on a past event as habitual or completed, or appraise the situation as positive or negative.

A key element in this phase is that the teacher and learners engage in a dialogic interaction to arrive at a description and explanation of the grammatical concept. That is, **dialogic grammar instruction** is not a one-way inquisition by the teacher but rather an instructional conversation between the teacher and learners. Sometimes learners may not be able to understand the grammatical aspects through teacher questioning alone but may require direct instruction on part on the part of the teacher. Dialoguing and constructing educated guesses about form, meaning, and use may also be first conducted in student pairs or small groups. After the initial small group discussion, the learners may share their hypotheses with the class for further discussion and refinement.

Another reason to envision and approach grammar instruction as dialogic interaction rather than a teacher lecture about grammatical rules relates to Vygotsky's concept of the **Zone of Proximal Development (ZPD)** (Vygotsky, 1978, 1986). One of Vygotsky's most significant contributions to understanding how individuals learn and develop is his reconceptualization of the child (in our case language learners) as having two levels of development—(1) what they can currently do alone and without support, and (2) what they can potentially do with assistance of others, such as peers or adults. Our traditional way of thinking about learners' development of grammar concepts is based on assessments of their abilities when working alone, for example, based on how they answer a teacher's direct question, complete a textbook exercise, or perform on a summative paper-and-pencil test. Although this type of assessment may indicate something about the learners' actual (in the sense of current) level of development of a grammatical concept and their ability to use it, it fails entirely to consider the learners' potential for improvement if provided help, for example with dialogic assistance by the teacher or by some other material tool, such as a textbook, charts and graphs, checklists, or models. Moreover, the concept of learning potential and the ZPD requires teachers to diagnose the ZPD in each learner so that the assistance given can realistically be used by learners to mediate concept development about grammar, that is, so that the assistance is neither too easy and therefore unnecessary or incomprehensible to the learners and therefore ineffective and unusable. The Co-Construction phase of the PACE lesson is the time when teachers actively seek to discover students' respective ZPDs. Through conversations about grammar rather than teacher-fronted lectures about rules, the learners' ZPDs can be made visible. Through dialogic interaction about what learners observed in action in the Presentation Phase and focused on in the Attention Phase, the teacher can identify the ZPD of the learners and work to mediate their conceptual knowledge about grammar and influence their future performance with these new grammatical understandings.

Figure 4.2 illustrates an example of a dialogic interaction that might take place in the Co-Construction Phase. Notice that, in addition to its structural properties, the discussion focuses on the *functions* of the grammatical form, in this case, the imperative form of the verb. As students explore the various uses of this form in the context of the story that they heard, they begin to develop a conceptual understanding of the imperative, the meaning of these verb forms, and its communicative purposes. As discussed earlier, this conceptual understanding stands in stark contrast to the grammatical rules of thumb featured in most textbooks in which rules for imperative formation are given with little attention to the multiple uses that the imperative can play beyond giving an order, as the transcript below illustrates. The dialogic interaction below is based on the African tale in French, *Le bras, la jambe, et le ventre*; for the entire story, see Adair-Hauck & Donato, 2002). The form being co-constructed is the imperative or command form that has been noticed in the Attention Phase.

SAMPLE DIALOGIC INTERACTION IN CO-CONSTRUCTION PHASE

T: What similarities do you see among these forms [points to the boxed forms]? What letters do you see repeated and how are these letters pronounced? Let's see if we can come up with THREE similarities. Tell me THREE things that are the same about all these verbs. They are verbs, right?

S: Yeah, verbs and they all end in *-ez*.

T: They all end in *-ez* (circles the *-ez* on each verb). Is there something else that's similar about these forms?

S: The subject pronoun... well, it's not there.

T: Very good point. Look, there's no subject pronoun before these verbs (points to each box). Look, it's missing. Why isn't there a subject pronoun?

S: You don't need it? (rising intonation)

S: I think it's implied.

T: Yes, it's implied. This means there is no need to indicate the person we are talking to. The sons know that the father is talking to them and no one else. There's something else that's similar about these sentences without a subject pronoun. Look closely at the text.

S: Well, they all end with an exclamation point.

T: Sure, they all end in an exclamation point.

T: Can any of you guess how these words in the boxes are used and for what purpose? Can you guess when we would use these kinds of utterances?

S: Is it to tell someone they should do something or not do something? (rising intonation)

T: Yes, that's it! They are command forms. Some of these verbs are telling someone to do something, like *Quittez mon village* to tell someone to get out my village. So tell me again why the subject does not have to be said?

S: There's no need to say the subject, or, well, it's just 'you' but you don't need to say it. You are talking to the person directly so you don't need to say 'you.'

T: So go back to the text and tell me who is saying these commands. What is the relationship between the two people?

S: The father is giving his sons commands, giving them orders.

T: So what might this mean about the kind of person who can use these commands? Can we use them with your parents, your younger brother or sister, your pet, your teacher?

(*continued on next page*)

***Figure 4.2.* Sample Dialogic Interaction in Co-construction Phase**

(Donato, original material, 2016, based on Adair-Hauck & Donato, 2002)

S: I think you can't use them with someone older than you or someone you should respect. If you use them with people who are older they might think you disrespect them. Like you are bossing them around.

T: Good thinking. Commands can't be used with just anyone. People can think you're being rude. Well how about these commands *Ne soyez pas ingrats*, *N'oubliez pas tous les services que votre mère et moi avons faits pour vous!*, and *Ne soyez pas égoïstes*. Are these really orders? Commands? Like "Stand up" and "Sit down" and "Close the door"? Think about it. What do these mean when the father says these things to his sons? Discuss this with your partner for a few minutes.

[after a few minutes pairs of students report their thinking]

Ss: Well we think it's more like advice, like telling the sons to never forget all the good things their mother and father did for them. He also gives them advice before they leave home not to be selfish and ungrateful.

T: I agree with you. Not all commands are orders to do things. Sometimes a command gives us a warning like when someone is going to touch something hot we might say *Fais attention, c'est chaud!* Sometimes a command just gives good advice, like "Take good care" or "Forgive and forget," or "Never give up," or "Take your vitamins." Where in the text does the father give advice to his sons?

S: When he says *Ne soyez pas ingrats* and *Ne soyez pas égoïstes*. It's like advice for when they go on their trip and how they should behave with other people.

T: I also think we know it's advice because it is not something they have to do right now but all the time. It's something they need to remember all the time. So we see different uses of this form of the verb with no subject pronoun—sometimes it's *a command* and tells someone to do something immediately like a teacher tells the class to "Open your books now to page 30," sometimes it's *a warning* like at the zoo "Don't feed the animals; they may bite," and sometimes it's *advice* for life like "Get plenty of exercise,' "Be kind to others,' or "Brush your time at least two times a day."

Figure 4.2. **(continued)**

The Co-Construction phase may be done in English depending on the level of learners and the complexity of the grammatical form. However, depending on the complexity of the topic of discussion, it may be possible to simplify the discussion so that the target language can be used. In this case, the teacher could ask questions and give options to students, for example, "Is this a statement or a question?" It is also important to note that teachers who use PACE for the first time may resort to constructing the grammatical structure *for* students rather than *with* students. Students may not be used to making observations about language and may be reluctant to participate in dialoguing about language. Over time and with experience, students will begin to learn to dialogue about form and internalize the assistance of the teacher for making their own observations about the language of texts. Students learn and retain information about grammatical form more effectively if they can be supported in exploring the language of a text and constructing form, meaning, and use with the teacher and each other. The challenge for the teacher is to use various strategies for helping students to notice the form and develop hypotheses concerning how to construct it.

One important strategy that a teacher may use comes from the work in **Dynamic Assessment** (Lantolf & Poehner, 2007, 2011; Poehner, 2007; Davin & Donato, 2013). This approach to assistance maintains that feedback to learners should move from **implicit help** (e.g., What is similar about these words?) to more **explicit help** (e.g., What part of each word is the same?), if students are not able to make use of the more implicit forms of help that the teacher provided (see further discussion of implicit and explicit feedback in Chapter 6). Dialoguing with students about form is not simply telling the students an answer, but supporting their thinking about the form by providing graduated assistance that helps them focus attention, make hypotheses, draw conclusions, and resolve problems. In the co-constructed example of the forms and functions of imperatives, this type of **graduated assistance** is clear.

Another challenge for the teacher is the need to re-conceptualize grammar as a concept rather than just as a rule. For this reason, before beginning to discuss a form with students, teachers should have a clear idea of how the language form works beyond a simplistic rule for word formation or word order. As stated in the introduction to this chapter, we learn how to take action with our words (Hall, 2001, 2003). All discussions of form should show students how certain language choices that they make allow them to perform certain communicative actions with different kinds of people, in various settings, and for different reasons; see how this is accomplished in the co-construction script above. Several studies of concept-based grammar teaching have been conducted and resources are available to inform teachers about new ways to describe language that go beyond what the form is to how it is used in texts of various kinds (see for example, Derewianka and Jones, 2010; Troyan, 2016).

Step 4: EXTENSION PHASE

The final phase of PACE is the Extension Phase in which learners use the new grammatical concept in creative and interesting ways. This phase may take multiple class lessons to complete and can include a variety of engaging tasks in the interpersonal and presentational modes of communication such as information-gap activities, role plays, games, paired interviews, or writing projects. Not all extension activities need to focus on the theme of the story. They may be personalized to a unit theme or students' interests and extend the story in new directions. What is important to note is that extension activities are not worksheets in which students fill in blanks with grammatical structures. Rather, extension activities need to provide opportunities to create personal meaning with others based on the phases of the PACE model which have come before. The extension phase allows the learners to use use the form (and possible other story elements) in an interpersonal exchange or in the creation of a product that incorporates and extends the target structure in a new and meaningful context. This final phase enables us to close the structure of the lesson. The lesson starts with a whole text, moves to noticing a particular structure, dialoguing about the form and use of the structure with the teacher and others in class, then ends with the students' self-selected use of the structure in oral interactions with others as well as in creative projects, documents, or presentations. For example, if a poem was used for the Presentation Phase, students may write their own poems based on the theme, add an extra stanza to the poem, convert the poem into dramatic script and perform it, or illustrate the poem. They could also reflect together on ways in which they might interpret the poem and how the poem relates to them personally. The importance of the Extension Phase is to provide evidence that the students can use the form in their own way and for their own purposes and that they can generalize the use of the form across different contexts of use. This phase also allows the teacher to assess how well the students have grasped the form and function and decide whether additional dialoguing about the form is needed.

Rehearsing the Practice (See this chapter's Appendix A, External Mediational Tool #4a: PACE Model at-a-glance)

1. Selecting and Analyzing Your Story (Appendix A, External Mediational Tool #4b)

Find a story that you will use for the presentation phase of a PACE lesson. The story you select will be used for various parts of the rehearsal. Review the section of the chapter on selecting a story for presentation. After selecting your story, summarize briefly the story for the class, indicate cultural products, practices, or perspectives in the story, and identify the grammatical form that is illustrated in sufficient quantity in the story. State how the form is used in the story in terms of its meaning and use. For example, present perfect verb forms (1) mean that specific actions indicated by the meaning of the verb have taken place in the past, are completed, and do not occur cyclically, repeatedly or habitually in the past, and (2) these forms function to move the narrative forward by presenting a series of sequential actions in the past. Use the chart shown in Figure 4.3 below to organize your thinking.

TITLE OF STORY	BRIEF SUMMARY & CULTURAL CONTENT	FORM	MEANING	FUNCTION

Figure 4.3. **Selecting and Analyzing PACE Story**

(Original material developed by Heather Hendry)

2.   Planning Storytelling (Appendix A, External Mediational Tool #4c)

Based on a story you have selected, (a) decide on how long it will take you to tell the story, (b) what materials (e.g., visuals, props, PowerPoint slides) you will use during story telling to make meanings clear, and (c) at least two kinds of interactions you will have with the students to involve them during storytelling. That is, what will you ask students to do so that they are actively involved in the storytelling and not passively listening to you? Next, (d) select a few vocabulary words that you anticipate that students will not know or will find hard to understand from context, list these words, and decide how you will establish the meaning of these words in the context of the story. Finally, (e) decide on what types of language modifications you will make to increase comprehensibility, to enter and re-enter the target form, and to meet the language level of the learners.

3.   Practicing Storytelling

Based on what you prepared in number 2, present your story (or part of your story if you plan on telling your story across several days) to your methods or field experience class (or to a class in the school where you teach). After your presentation, discuss with your peers or a colleague (a) your students' level of comprehension, (b) your students' level of interest in the story, and (c) the effectiveness of your interactive involvement activities during storytelling. Allow your peers/colleague to make additional observations, if necessary. You may also have specific questions about your story presentation and should feel free to ask these questions.

4.   Planning for Attention and Co-Construction (Appendix A, External Mediational Tool #4d)

Using the story you presented and the analysis of the form you have selected, complete the chart that appears in Figure 4.4.

5.   Preparing for Dialogic Interaction

Return to the chart above and review the scripted questions you have prepared. Organize the questions from implicit assisting questions (e.g., What do you notice here?) to explicit assisting questions (Listen to how I pronounce X and compare it to Y. What differences do you hear in the pronunciation?). Show examples of the highlighted form from the story to the class and try out questions to see if your classmates make the kinds of observations you have in mind. Also note how your questioning may need to move from implicit prompts to more explicit prompts depending on the contributions of the class.

6.   Developing Extension Activities

Based on your story and the form that has been selected for teacher-student exploration, prepare at least two Extension activities (one in the Interpersonal mode and one in the Presentational mode) that allow students to make use of the form in a meaningful and purposeful way. Justify why you have selected these extension activities based on the theme of the story, its cultural content, and/or student interest. State how long it will take to carry out the extension activities and what interactions or product(s) the students will prepare and present.

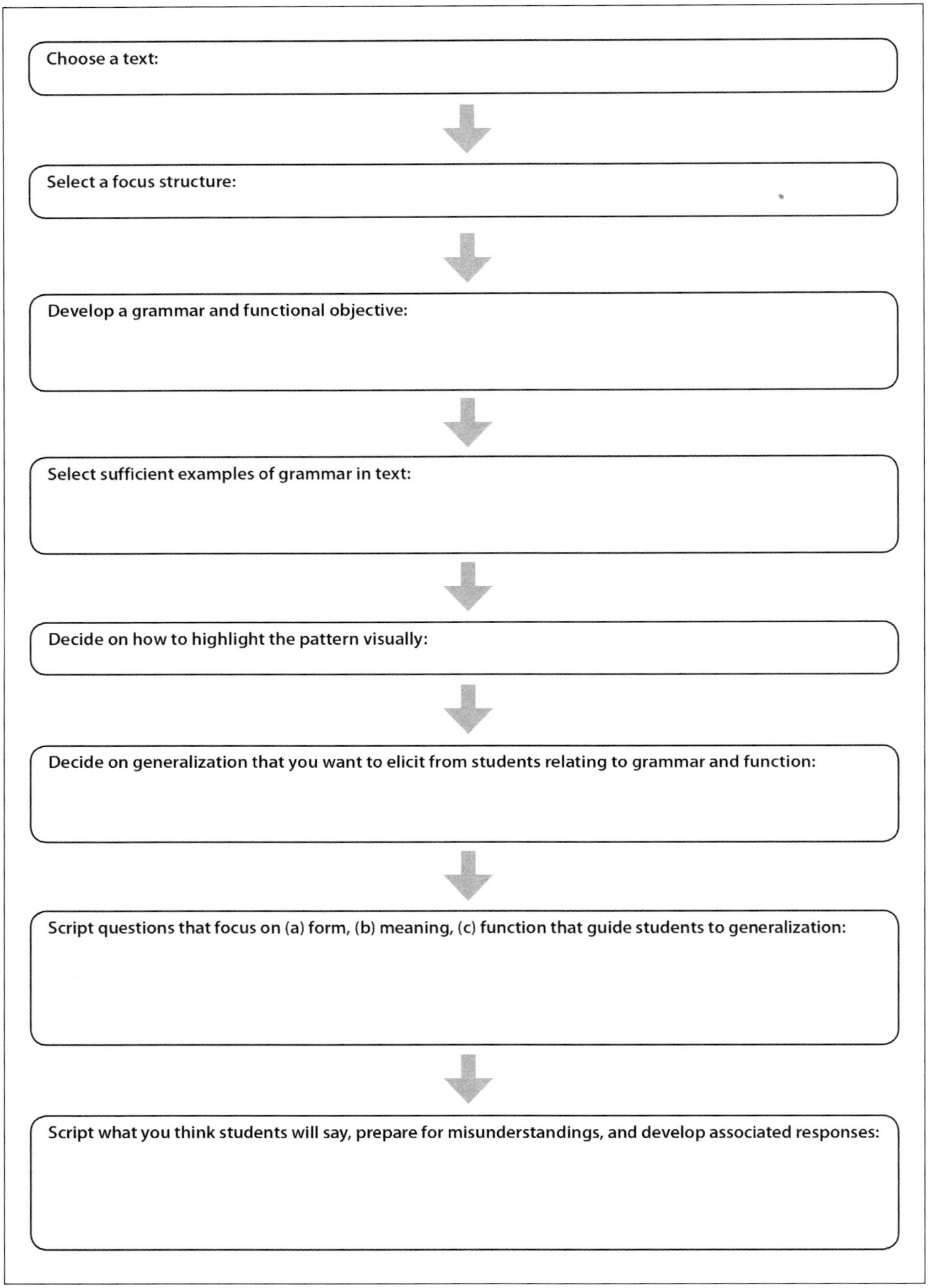

Choose a text:

Select a focus structure:

Develop a grammar and functional objective:

Select sufficient examples of grammar in text:

Decide on how to highlight the pattern visually:

Decide on generalization that you want to elicit from students relating to grammar and function:

Script questions that focus on (a) form, (b) meaning, (c) function that guide students to generalization:

Script what you think students will say, prepare for misunderstandings, and develop associated responses:

Figure 4.4. **Planning for Attention and Co-Construction**

Assessing the Practice

Use Rubric #4 in this chapter's Appendix B to self-assess your PACE lesson. As an alternative or in addition, you could ask a colleague to observe the discussion that you facilitate and provide feedback using the rubric.

Putting the Practice into a Larger Context: Instructional Goals and Challenges

In this chapter, focus on form has been presented and deconstructed through an approach that emphasizes whole texts, collaborative investigation of form and function, and students' independent use of language forms for meaning making. In addition to trying to solve the intractable problem of making grammar instruction meaningful and memorable, the PACE approach addresses several larger educational concerns. It is commonplace to hear that schooling needs to develop students' critical thinking skills and that foreign language instruction is one way to meet this instructional goal. However, simply memorizing rules for language formation without investigating and reflecting on how language forms serve communicative purposes and how changes in forms signal changes in meaning is far from what it means to engage in critical thinking. By allowing students to observe language in action, hypothesize about the form and function of words and expressions, dialog with the teacher and each other, and come to conclusions about how language choices effect meaning, students develop analytical abilities about language that go far beyond text-based language rules and formulaic expressions.

Additionally, this approach is not a return to discovery learning in which learners are expected to figure out for themselves what has taken linguists years to understand. Through the assistance of the teacher during rich conversations about form, text, and context, students investigate language by thinking critically and analytically about form-function connections. They learn to talk about language in a new way and begin to understand that the forms of language are *choices* that a speaker or writer makes to express particular meanings and not just *rules* for generating grammatically correct sentences. In this way, foreign language learning supports students' metalinguistic awareness that can be applied to their first language and to the use of language in their lives.

By using authentic cultural texts, language learners develop global perspectives and explore ways of believing and valuing that are different from their own. Stories provide a cultural context for exploring the products, practices, and related perspectives that can support students' work in other subject areas, such as social studies, art, music, and world literature classes. The texts of stories are often hybrid forms that incorporate elements of narrative and expository text and thus can present academic information that may connect to other academic disciplines and contributes to students' overall academic development.

Finally, the PACE approach directly address the goal areas of the *World-Readiness Standards for Learning Languages* (National Standards in Foreign Language Education Project, 2015). Through stories and analysis of the language of texts, students develop all modes of communication, encounter cultures and communities in a globalized world, and can investigate, explain, and reflect on the different ways that meanings can be expressed across different languages and communities. In this way, the goals of the standards are integrated and are not isolated and artificially separated.

For Further Reading

Adair-Hauck, B. (1993). *A descriptive analysis of whole language/guided participatory versus explicit teaching strategies in foreign language instruction* (Doctoral dissertation). University of Pittsburgh, Pittsburgh, PA.

Adair-Hauck, B., & Donato, R. (2002). The PACE Model: A story-based approach to meaning and form for standards-based language learning. *The French Review, 76,* 265–296.

Adair-Hauck, B., & Donato, R. (2016). PACE: A story-based approach for dialogic inquiry about form and meaning. In Shrum, J. L., and Glisan, E. W., *Teacher's handbook: Contextualized language instruction,* 5th edition. Boston, MA: Cengage Learning.

Davin, K., & Donato, R. (2013). Student collaboration and teacher-directed classroom dynamic assessment: A complementary pairing. *Foreign Language Annals, 46,* 5–22.

Derewianka, B. & Jones, P. (2010). From traditional grammar to functional grammar: Bridging the divide. *NALDIC Quarterly, 8*(1), 6–17.

Donato, R. (1994). Collective scaffolding. In J. P. Lantolf & G. Appel (Eds.), *Vygotskyan approaches to second language acquisition research* (pp. 33–56). Norwood, NJ: Ablex.

Gass, S. M. (1988). Integrating research areas: A framework for second language studies. *Applied Linguistics 9*(2), 198–217.

Gass, S. M. (2013). *Second language acquisition: An introductory course* (4th ed.). New York: Routledge.

Gass, S. M., & Selinker, L. (2001). *Second language acquisition: An introductory course.* London: Lawrence Erlbaum Associates.

Hall, J.K. (2001/2003) Classroom interaction and language learning, *Ilha do Desterro, 41,* 17–39.

Kennedy, T. J. (2006). Language learning and its impact on the brain: Connecting language learning through the mind through content-based instruction. *Foreign Language Annals, 39,* 471–486.

Lantolf, J. P., & Poehner, M. E. (2007). *Dynamic assessment in the foreign language classroom: A teacher's guide.* University Park, PA: CALPER Publications.

Lantolf, J. P., & Poehner, M. E. (2011). Dynamic assessment in the classroom: Vygotskian praxis for second language development: Bringing the past into the future. *Language Teaching Research, 15,* 323–340. doi: 10.1177/1362168810383328

Lantolf, J. P., & Poehner, M. E. (2014). *Sociocultural theory and the pedagogical imperative in L2 education.* New York: Routledge.

Larsen-Freeman, D. (2003). *Teaching language: From grammar to grammaring.* Boston: Thomson Heinle.

Lightbown, P., & Spada, N. (2013). *How languages are learned* (4th ed.). New York: Oxford University Press.

National Standards in Foreign Language Education Project (NSFLEP). (2015). *World-Readiness standards for learning languages.* Alexandria, VA: Author.

Oller, J. W. (1983). Some working ideas for language teaching. In J. W. Oller & P. A. Richard-Amato (Eds.), *Methods that work* (pp. 3–19). Rowley, MA: Newbury House.

Paradis, M. (2009). *Declarative and procedural determinants of second languages.* Amsterdam: John Benjamins Publishing Company.

Poehner, M. E. (2007). Beyond the test: L2 dynamic assessment and the transcendence of mediated learning. *Modern Language Journal, 91,* 323–340.

Poehner, M. E. (2008). *Dynamic assessment: A Vygotskian approach to understanding and promoting second language development.* Berlin: Springer Publishing.

Schmidt, R. W. (1990). The role of consciousness in second language learning. *Applied Linguistics 11*(1), 17–46.

Schmidt, R. W. (2001). Attention. In P. Robinson (Ed.), *Cognition and second language instruction* (pp. 3–32). Cambridge: Cambridge University Press.

Sousa, D. A. (2011). *How the brain learns (4th ed.).* Thousand Oaks, CA: Corwin Press.

Swain, M. (1995). Three functions of output in second language learning. In G. Cook & B. Seidlhofer (Eds.), *Principle and practice in applied linguistics: Studies in honour of H. G. Widdowson* (pp. 125–144). Oxford, UK: Oxford University Press.

Tannen, D. (2007). *Talking voices: Repetition, dialogue and imagery in conversational discourse.* New York: Cambridge University Press.

Toth, P. D. & Davin, K. J. (2016). The sociocognitive imperative in L2 pedagogy. *Modern Language Journal, 100*(Suppl. 2016), 148–168.

Trahey, M. & White, L. (1993). Positive evidence and preemption in the second language classroom. *Studies in Second Language Acquisition 15*(2), 181–204.

Troyan, F. J. (2016). Learning to mean in Spanish writing: A case study of a genre-based pedagogy for standards-based writing instruction. *Foreign Language Annals, 49,* 317–335. doi: 10.1111/flan.12192

VanPatten, B. (2004). *Processing instruction: Theory, research, and commentary.* Mahwah, New Jersey: Lawrence Erlbaum Associates

Vygotsky, L. S. (1978). *Mind in society: The development of higher psychological processes.* Cambridge, MA: Harvard University Press.

Vygotsky, L. S. (1986). *Thought and language.* Cambridge, MA: MIT Press.

Wong, W., & VanPatten, B. (2003). The evidence is IN: Drills are OUT. *Foreign Language Annals, 36,* 403–424.

Young, R. F. (2008). *Language and interaction: An advanced resource book.* New York: Routledge.

Young, R. F. (2009). *Discursive practice in language learning and teaching.* Malden, MA: Wiley-Blackwell.

Appendix A

External Mediational Tool #4a: PACE Model At-a-Glance

1. **Presentation:** Present orally an authentic story, folktale, or legend from the target language culture.

2. **Attention:** Call learners' attention to a particular form in the text that is important to text's meaning and so that the teacher and learners establish a joint focus of attention.

3. **Co-construction:** Teacher and learners co-construct an explanation of the form through class discussion and dialogue.

4. **Extension:** Extending and using the form in a new context related to the theme and/or cultural content of the story within the interpretive, interpersonal, and presentational modes of communication.

External Mediational Tool #4b: Selecting and Analyzing a PACE Story

TITLE OF STORY	BRIEF SUMMARY and CULTURAL CONTENT	FORM	MEANING	FUNCTION

External Mediational Tool #4c: Planning for Storytelling

DOES MY STORYTELLING FEATURE THE FOLLOWING CHARACTERISTICS?

❑　Does the story engage learners' interest?

❑　Does the teacher simplify the story as needed to support comprehension?

❑　Does the teacher use props, visuals, and dramatization to support meaning-making?

❑　Are students actively involved in the telling of the story?

❑.　Does the teacher check learners' comprehension of the story?

External Mediational Tool #4d: Planning for Attention and Co-Construction

Choose a text:

Select a focus structure:

Develop a grammar and functional objective:

Select sufficient examples of grammar in text:

Decide on how to highlight the pattern visually:

Decide on generalization that you want to elicit from students relating to grammar and function:

Script questions that focus on (a) form, (b) meaning, (c) function that guide students to generalization:

Script what you think students will say, prepare for misunderstandings, and develop associated responses:

External Mediational Tool #4e: Planning for Extension Activities

DO MY EXTENSION ACTIVITIES...?

❏   integrate the grammatical form naturally?

❏   reflect personalized use of language and students' interests?

❏   feature the grammatical form within the interpretive, interpersonal, and presentational modes of communication?

❏   provide opportunities to create personal meaning?

Appendix B

RUBRIC: HLTP #4: Focusing on Form in a Dialogic Context Through PACE

	EXCEEDS EXPECTATIONS	MEETS EXPECTATIONS	DEVELOPING	UNACCEPTABLE
Selection of Authentic Story	Story is relevant and age-appropriate, contains an engaging plot and characters as well as an interesting theme. Story contains natural occurrences of grammatical structure. Cultural products, practices, perspectives are reflected in story. Story lends itself to stageable actions.	Story is relevant and age-appropriate and contains an interesting theme. Story contains natural occurrences of grammatical structure. At least 2 aspects of the 3P culture paradigm are reflected in story. Story lends itself to stageable actions.	Story is relevant and age-appropriate but may not contain an interesting theme. Story is lacking in natural occurrences of grammatical structure. At least 2 aspects of the 3P culture paradigm are reflected in story. And/or only part of story lends itself to stageable actions.	Story is not relevant and/or age-appropriate. Plot and characters and/or theme are not engaging. And/or story either does not contain a sufficient number of occurrences of grammatical structure or contains a natural overabundance of grammatical structure. Cultural aspects are lacking. Story may be difficult to stage.
Presentation Phase	Teacher tells story in an engaging manner using props, visuals, and dramatizations, and simplifying language as necessary. Learners are actively involved throughout telling of story in a meaningful manner. Teacher integrates comprehension checking in a creative manner.	Teacher tells story using props, visuals, and some dramatization, and simplifying language as necessary. Learners are involved in the telling of story in a meaningful manner. Teacher checks comprehension either during or after storytelling.	Teacher tells story using some props and visuals but little dramatization. Learners are involved in the telling of story in some way, but attention to meaning may not be apparent in their participation. Limited checking of comprehension.	Teacher tells story without the use of props, visuals, or dramatizations. Little active involvement of learners in telling of story. And/or absence of comprehension checks.

	EXCEEDS EXPECTATIONS	MEETS EXPECTATIONS	DEVELOPING	UNACCEPTABLE
Attention Phase	Teacher calls learners' attention to form in an engaging/creative and dialogic manner.	Teacher calls learners' attention to form in a dialogic manner.	Teacher calls learners' attention to form in a partially dialogic manner.	Teacher either points out the form directly or may skip the Attention Phase.
Co-Construction Phase	Teacher engages learners in interaction in a creative manner to co-construct the form. Co-construction focuses on grammatical form, meaningful use, function that guides learners to conceptual understanding. Teacher provides graduated assistance that progresses from clear implicit to explicit questioning as needed.	Teacher engages learners in interaction to co-construct the form. Co-construction focuses mostly on grammatical form and secondarily on meaningful use and function. Teacher provides assistance that consists of clear and specific questions.	Teacher engages learners in interaction but may construct part of the form for learners. Co-construction focuses mostly on grammatical form. Teacher provides assistance in the form of questions, some of which may be too vague.	Teacher constructs the form for learners with the focus on grammatical form. Lack of questioning since information is given in a one-way manner from teacher to learners.
Extension Phase	Creative and engaging extension activities that integrate the grammatical structure naturally within interpretive, interpersonal, and presentational modes of communication. Focus of activities is on meaning making and personal expression.	Engaging extension activities that integrate the grammatical structure within interpersonal and presentational modes of communication. Focus of activities is on meaning making.	Engaging extension activities integrate the grammatical structure within either the interpersonal or the presentational mode of communication. Focus of activities is primarily on meaning making.	Extension activities integrate grammatical structure within the interpersonal and/or presentational mode of communication but not in an engaging or meaningful manner. Focus of activities is on manipulation of grammatical form.

CHAPTER 5

HLTP #5: Focusing on Cultural Products, Practices, and Perspectives in a Dialogic Context

Teachers and learners must be aware of how language instruction can be integrated with culture in ways that go beyond simply describing behaviors, learning about cultural customs, and memorizing historical facts.

Enabling learners to reflect on and analyze the cultures of target language communities is one of the primary goals of language instruction. To this end, teachers need to be able to engage learners in thoughtful conversations during which they are guided to make cultural observations, hypothesize about and interpret cultural meanings, and compare and contrast cultural perspectives that are unlike their own. As Cutshall (2012, p. 32) states, "in the best language education programs today, the study of another language is synonymous with the study of other cultures." From the perspective of the *World-Readiness Standards for Learning Languages* (National Standards in Foreign Language Education Project, 2015), to address the Cultures goal area, teachers must engage learners in target language-based investigations and explanations of cultural *products* and *practices* and their relationship to the cultural *perspectives* of the languages studied. The HLTP in this chapter is intended to provide a framework to support this goal.

The study of culture, as a topic in its own right, is often typically reserved for upper-level classes in which students are believed to have the level of language ability to handle critical cultural discussions. As a result, culture instruction for elementary-level learners is reduced to lessons that merely display **cultural *products*** (e.g., foods, monuments, currency, texts) or provide anecdotal information about **cultural *practices*** (e.g., greeting protocols, holiday celebrations, sporting events). This is not to dismiss the importance of introducing learners to various cultural products and practices that are different from their own. What this exclusive emphasis on the teaching of random cultural products and practices produces, however, is a view of culture as tourism or as behaviors that are strange, incomprehensible, or weird. An alternative to this limited approach to culture instruction is to view the study of cultural products and practices as the starting point for students to explore and interpret the deeper meanings of culture as a system of shared values and beliefs, i.e., **cultural *perspectives***. In this way, culture teaching is directly related to reflection on and analysis of the worldviews, ways of interacting and speaking, and the historical and local circumstances of speakers of other languages.

In this chapter, the HLTP that will be detailed and deconstructed will enable teachers to explore the relationship of cultural products and practices to cultural perspectives with their classes in comprehensible target-language interactions (see Chapter 1) in the discourse community that they have created (see Chapter 2). Using the *IMAGE Model for Exploring Cultural Perspectives*, teachers will be able to conduct dialogic interactions that scaffold (see Chapters 4 and 6) learners' cultural observations and lead them to well-reasoned conclusions about the deeper social and historical meanings of culture. This HLTP is applicable to all levels of instruction and is ultimately aimed at challenging stereotypical and negative views of culture that adolescent learners often bring to the task of learning new languages and cultures.

ACTFL/CAEP Standards addressed: #2a, 2b; 3a; 4a, 4b, 4c

Research and Theory Supporting the Practice

Conceptualizing Culture

The HLTP presented in this chapter is based on the concept of **culture as a system** of dispositions, values, actions, and assumptions that are located and reflected in various cultural products and practices—including communicative practices—of groups of people in sociocultural and historical contexts at particular moments in times and for specific social purposes (as discussed in Hall, 2012, and based on the work of Duranti, 1997, and Bhabba, 1994). This view contrasts sharply with the more traditional notion of culture as a fixed and stable body of knowledge shared by all members of groups living within the same geographical boundaries. As Hall points out, "culture is not located in an individual mind but in activity" (2012, p. 17). From this perspective, culture is not a universal property of nationalities but a dynamic system of beliefs, values, and worldviews that emerge in and are shaped by the shared social practices and products of a group or groups of individuals. To reflect on, analyze, and interpret culture requires uncovering, therefore, the *relationship* between the activities that people do, such as the products that they produce and use and the practices in which they engage, and the reasons for doing them. Examining this relationship leads to an understanding of cultural perspectives, that is, meanings, attitudes, values, beliefs, and concepts that underlie the cultural practices and products of a groups of individuals that are affiliated by a shared worldview.

Are Language and Culture Really Connected in Instruction?

It is often said that language and culture are intimately connected and one cannot be known without the other. However, as frequently as this claim is made, language and culture instruction is most often conducted as two separate instructional tasks with language reduced to the study of linguistic forms and functions, and culture reduced to factual knowledge about target language countries, periodic anecdotes from the teacher, or displays of cultural artifacts (Galloway, 1985). This separation of language and culture instruction is documented in a revealing study conducted by Kramsch (2012). In this study, Kramsch observed and interviewed an experienced German teacher and her students during and after a lesson based on a short authentic autobiographical account written for children on the bombing of Dresden. Prompts following the text asked teacher and students to engage in an interpretive discussion about the historical significance of the text, the symbolic value of the language used, and the author's cultural perspective reflected in his descriptions of the event.

Kramsch's analysis of the discussion and follow-up interviews with teacher and students revealed that, for this particular class, neither students nor teacher understood the language classroom to be a place where instruction engages the learners in the interpretive process of examining the values, symbols, and perspectives embodied in cultural products and practice, in this specific case the language and purpose of the authentic text, that is, the text as both product and practice. Rather, the teacher expressed the attitude that she had been trained to be only a facilitator of student talk and not as one who helps learners to understand the cultural values and authorial perspectives embodied in texts and other cultural products and practices. The students also seemed to believe that learning a language was totally distinct from learning about the culture of the speakers of that language. The students expressed the belief that the language instructor's role was to teach language forms and skills and their professors' role in other academic subject matter courses was to teach content. Although this is only one study, there is a great deal of anecdotal evidence that these beliefs about the learning of language and culture by both teachers and learners appear to be pervasive in language classrooms.

This traditional view underlying the relationship between language and culture underscores the fundamental importance of this HLTP to language instruction and the need to make teachers and learners aware of how language instruction can be integrated with culture in ways that go beyond simply describing behaviors, learning cultural customs, and memorizing historical facts (Kramsch, 2012).

Goals and Objectives for Integrating Language and Culture

Byram (1997, 2008) argues that an important goal of integrating culture instruction with language learning is to develop **cultural know-how** in learners, that is the ability to analyze, understand, and participate in cultures unlike their own. Among several features of know-how that he presents, three features are particularly relevant to the goals of this HLTP: (1) knowing *how to be and feel* when faced with cultures unlike one's own, (2) knowing *how to understand* cultural differences, and (3) knowing *how to engage* the self with cultures in contact. Knowing *how to be and feel* in cross-cultural situations involves a learner's disposition about cultural differences and includes curiosity, openness, and sensitivity to the perspective of others. Knowing *how to understand* cultures requires the knowledge and skill to observe, identify, interpret, and analyze cultural patterns, leading to an acceptance of difference where potential sources of misunderstanding, or even conflict, might occur. Finally, knowing *how to engage* the self with cultures requires learners to be committed to evaluating critically and rationally their own cultural perspectives compared to those of other sociocultural groups.

To achieve these goals, Schulz (2007) synthesizes various approaches to culture instruction, including Byram's know-how schema presented above. She identifies several fundamental objectives for culture learning that should guide instruction. These objectives include understanding the sociocultural, historical, and geographical conditions that influence cultures, dispelling cross-cultural stereotypes with information and evidence, and exploring culture-specific images and culture-specific uses of language. As will be shown, the approach to integrating cultural and language instruction through images, as presented in this chapter and enacted in this HLTP, is related closely to these goals and objectives outlined by Byram and Shultz.

Considerations about the Teaching of Culture

(1) *How do I approach culture so that my students don't dismiss the target culture as being "weird"?* Students may initially express negative attitudes and stereotypes when they learn about cultural differences. It has been shown that when learners experience a new culture, either during study abroad (Oberg, 1960) or during language instruction (West & Donato, 1995), they may pass through stages of resistance before understanding and accepting certain cultural ways of being and believing. Teachers need to realize that students' negative reactions are the first stage in developing cultural

understanding. Over time and with appropriate instruction, students can learn how to approach cultural differences with openness and understanding rather than resistance and negativity. For learners to develop this positive attitude, culture instruction must assist them to reflect on, hypothesize about, and analyze meanings and beliefs from the cultural insider's point of view. In this way, the learners' initial reactions to cultural differences as weird or unnatural will be gradually replaced with the ability to analyze and understand the complexity of cultural differences and, in so doing, to develop into true global citizens.

(2) *What if my students do not have enough target language to discuss cultural topics?* Teachers often think that addressing culture as a topic of discussion can only be achieved in advanced-level classes. Elementary-level classes are often restricted to discussions of cultural topics in English, displays of cultural artifacts, or anecdotes about the teacher's latest trip to a target language country. Chapters 1 and 2 emphasized the importance of comprehensible language use, target language interactions with students, and the need to develop a classroom discourse community from the start of instruction. The principles that were introduced and explained in these two chapters also apply to the teaching of culture lessons.

Teachers must ask themselves three important questions about the use of the target language during culture instruction. First, is the culture lesson appropriate for the level of the class or are the cultural concepts being introduced too complex for learners to talk about in the target language? Whenever instructional objectives are not appropriate to the level of the class, instruction will always degenerate into the learners' first language. When this occurs, it is a clear sign that the lesson objective was not well suited for the level of the student. Second, once an appropriate cultural investigation has been decided upon, how can the language be made comprehensible to promote talk-in-interaction about culture? Students can understand more than they can produce and seemingly complex cultural topics can be mediated in ways that are clear using the language that the students already know or that can be learned in the context of the culture lesson. Third, has the lesson been analyzed carefully for the language resources that learners need to allow for target language participation in the lesson? Related to planning for language is whether the teacher has identified discourse strategies to use for providing essential content language and grammatical structures as part of the culture lesson (see Chapter 1). The framework described below is intended to address the issue of language use during culture instruction through careful language planning and scaffolding of language production.

(3) *Is it sufficient to feature a cultural point in one lesson per week?* No. Culture permeates language teaching and cannot be reduced to isolated facts presented in a linear sequence one day a week during each week of a course. Culture is dynamic and the products and practices of a culture are interconnected in such a way that isolating one culture point prevents learners from understanding how various aspects of culture are the result of a rich network of historical, geographical, and social factors. Additionally, this approach may lead to learners' negative reactions to cultural differences since the culture is presented in a way that does not address the underlying reasons and insider perspectives on the culture fact being featured in the lesson. All language instruction must be embedded in cultural contexts. Even language itself is a reflection of cultural perspectives, which are made visible in the expressions, metaphors, and ways of describing the world that are unique across cultural contexts.

(4) *Is culture sufficiently addressed if the textbook has a cultural reading in each chapter?* In the traditional paradigm of language teaching, instruction was primarily about learning how to generate accurate language forms with the occasional note about culture as a diversion from the "real work" of the class. This approach manifests itself in the use of culture capsules, or short readings that are provided in textbooks about topics such as the history, customs, literary traditions, famous people, or geography of the target language being studied, to name a few. In much the same way as devoting one day a week to culture, relying only on these readings to address culture is not sufficient to develop the ability to interpret and understand deeply the sources and reasons for certain cultural practices and products. What is more, in the hands of teachers who do not understand how to address culture instruction, these texts are often used exclusively for reading instruction. The cultural content of the text is viewed only as a means for checking reading comprehension, not as core material for cultural exploration and discussion. Certainly the types of culture readings found in textbooks are useful as a starting point for learning about culture, but they are not sufficient for teaching culture in the ways described in the *World-Readiness Standards for Learning Languages* (National Standards in Foreign Language Education Project, 2015).

Deconstructing the Practice

The *IMAGE Model for Exploring Cultural Perspectives* in Figure 5.1, one approach to the teaching of culture, is based on (1) the work of Barnes-Karol and Broner (2010) on the use of images as a springboard to teach cultural perspectives, and (2) the work of Johnson and English (2003) on student analysis of images and texts about France to examine culture through a critical lens. The acronym *IMAGE* represent 4 steps of the model: **I**mages and **M**aking observations, **A**nalyzing additional information, **G**enerating hypotheses about cultural perspectives, and **E**xploring perspectives and reflecting further. The ***IMAGE* Model** guides the teacher through the planning stage, the enactment of the culture lesson itself, and follow-up tasks and assignments. The lesson is developed around a series of cultural images that will lead students to make cultural observations and draw conclusions. Dialogic interaction in the target language is promoted by a series of carefully scaffolded teacher questions in two categories: Fact Questions and Thought Questions. **Fact Questions** are those that ask students to make specific observations about what they see in the images, such as descriptions of settings, people, actions, and objects. **Thought questions** move the learners to a new level of analysis and require sharing opinions, hypotheses, and ideas. These two terms reflect clearly the function of these questions in the culture lesson and how the questions need to be designed based on the kind of information and ideas that learners are expected to provide at certain points in the lesson. The *IMAGE* culture lesson is structured around three major tasks that ask students to state what they *see*, what they *think*, and what they are still *wondering* about.

Deconstruction of this practice involves examining it from two perspectives: (1) planning the lesson and (2) enacting the lesson with learners in four steps, which will be explained in detail in the deconstruction section of the chapter. The deconstruction that follows will include concrete examples of ways in which novice teachers have enacted the instructional moves in the target languages they teach.[8]

---

[8] These novice teachers were graduate student teaching assistants in the Department of French and Italian Languages and Literatures and the Department of Hispanic Languages and Literatures at the University of Pittsburgh in Fall 2015.

The IMAGE Model for Exploring Cultural Perspectives

PLANNING STAGE: PREPARING FOR THE LESSON

A. <u>Who are the students?</u>

> For what course is your culture lesson designed? What year/semester of study is this course? What is the time frame for the lesson—A single class? Divided across several days? A week?
>
> _____

B. <u>What is the cultural content of lesson?</u>

> State the cultural product and/or practice you will show in the lesson and its/their relationship to a cultural perspective (that is, a value, belief, or meaning). What perspective(s) might your students explore? What images will you use?
>
> **Product/Practice** [Note: It is best to begin with a single product and/or practice; however, others may emanate in the lesson]:
>
> **Perspective(s):**
>
> **Images:**
>
> Set 1: _____
>
> Set 2: _____

Figure 5.1. **The IMAGE Model for Exploring Cultural Perspectives**

(Adapted from Donato, original material, 2015)

C. <u>What vocabulary do students need to participate in the lesson?</u>

List any **specific vocabulary** that students will need in this culture lesson. That is, what are the **essential vocabulary words** that are needed to understand your lesson? List this vocabulary. NOTE: Students will learn new vocabulary through your talk-in-interaction.

What **formulaic phrases** will you give to students to allow them to express opinions during a discussion? For example: "In my opinion," "I think that…," "I believe that…," "My opinion is…," "In general…" (for more examples, search on-line for *language for expressing opinions*).

D. <u>What grammar structures do students need to participate in the lesson?</u>

Are there any **specific grammatical structures** that will occur often in this lesson? **Be specific**, e.g., if students need *to describe*, what kind of **adjectives** or **adjectival phrases** will they use to achieve this function? If students need *to compare*, what **comparative forms** will be used in the lesson?

Figure 5.1. (**continued**)

ENACTING THE CULTURAL IMAGES LESSON

Step 1: <u>**I**mages and **M**aking Observations</u>

Begin the lesson by asking students to describe **the product** and/or **practice** that they see in the first set of images. Ask **FACT questions in the** TL (*What do you see?*). Write **THREE to FIVE FACT questions** here for each image. (*Space provided for three images but it is up to you to decide how many. Use as many or as few images as you like for this step*).

Image 1 is a picture of _____

Fact questions:

Image 2 is a picture of _____

Fact questions:

Image 3 is a picture of _____

Fact questions:

Step 2: <u>**A**nalyzing Additional Information about the Product and/or Practice:</u>

At this point in the lesson, what **additional information** will you provide in the form of **TEXT** or **DATA in the TL** on the cultural product or practice? What will you ask students to do with this information? This information should help students to **BEGIN TO THINK ABOUT PERSPECTIVES**. (*Space provided for two sources of information but it is up to you to decide how many*).

Informational source #1 is _____

With this information, I will ask students to _____

_____

_____

Informational source #2 is _____

With this information, I will ask students to _____

_____

_____

Figure 5.1. (**continued**)

Step 3: **G**enerating Hypotheses about Cultural Perspectives

Now show the second set of image(s) that prompt hypotheses about possible perspectives conveyed by the product and/or practice. Ask students to begin to **REFLECT** on perspectives. Ask **THREE to FIVE THOUGHT questions in the TL** (*What do you think?*). THOUGHT questions prompt students to think about possible **MEANINGS** of the product or practice. Since students are seeing the second set of images for the first time, you may begin this step with a few **FACT questions** to begin the interaction and encourage participation. (*Space provided for one image but it is up to you to decide how many. Use as many or as few images as you like for this step*).

Image #1 is a picture of _____

1. _____

2. _____

3. _____

4. _____

5. _____

Option 1 for Intermediate- or higher-level language classes:

Ask students to use the thought questions to hypothesize about and to state in their own words the *relationship of the product or practice to a cultural perspective*. This step should be carried out in pairs or small groups followed by a report back to class.

(a)   How you will carry out this part of the lesson?

(b)   What directions will you give to the students?

(c)   Can you anticipate any misinterpretations or cultural stereotyping that might occur? If yes, what might they be?

(d)   If misinterpretations occur or if students express cultural stereotypes, how will you respond?

Option 2 for Elementary-level language classes:

If you think your students will not be able to state a perspective in the target language on their own, provide a multiple-choice task. Write for the students *three possible perspectives* in the TL and ask students in pairs or small groups to (a) *select* one based on the images and information they have seen and analyzed and/or (b) *rank order* the three perspectives from the most to least important, obvious, comprehensive, interesting, etc. If possible, ask students to tell you WHY they selected or rank ordered the perspectives in this way.

Write the three perspectives for your images that you will give to students for their selection. Use comprehensible target language.

1. _____

2. _____

3. _____

***Figure 5.1.* (continued)**

Step 4: <u>**Exploring Perspectives and Reflecting Further**</u>

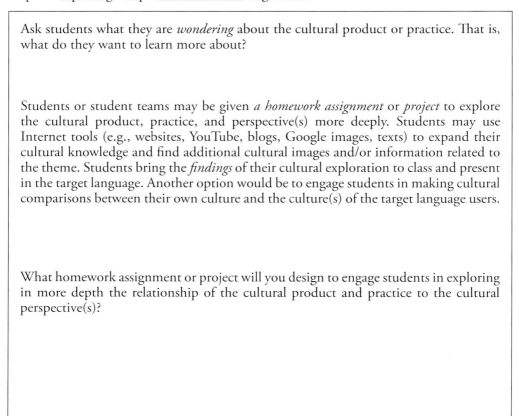

Ask students what they are *wondering* about the cultural product or practice. That is, what do they want to learn more about?

Students or student teams may be given *a homework assignment* or *project* to explore the cultural product, practice, and perspective(s) more deeply. Students may use Internet tools (e.g., websites, YouTube, blogs, Google images, texts) to expand their cultural knowledge and find additional cultural images and/or information related to the theme. Students bring the *findings* of their cultural exploration to class and present in the target language. Another option would be to engage students in making cultural comparisons between their own culture and the culture(s) of the target language users.

What homework assignment or project will you design to engage students in exploring in more depth the relationship of the cultural product and practice to the cultural perspective(s)?

Figure 5.1. (continued)

Planning the Lesson (In this chapter's Appendix A, External Mediational Tool #5a)

1. <u>Consider the level of the class and anticipate the time frame for the lesson</u>. This information will become important as you develop the plan for the specific tasks at each stage of the lesson. After planning the lesson, review the time frame to see if it is realistic.

2. <u>Decide on the cultural content of the lesson to be explored and the images you will use</u>. State the cultural product and/or practice that will be shown in images in the lesson and its/their relationship to a cultural perspective (or perspectives) that may emerge in the discussion. It is important that the teacher is clear on his or her views of the relationship of products and practices to cultural perspectives in order to support student thinking and interpretations later in the lesson. In other words, what specific cultural perspective(s) might students investigate, explore and reflect on in this lesson? How will your images (typically 4-5, but the number may depend on the scope of the lesson) lead students from observation to reflection and analysis.

Once the topic for cultural investigation has been identified, use the image function found in various Internet search engines to find appropriate images and information for each step of the lesson and/or use pictures that you or others have taken in places where the target language is spoken. It is important to note that we use the term *image* to mean all forms of visual representation, e.g., artifacts from target language countries, photos, and videos.

Two different sets of carefully sequenced images are necessary for the culture lesson. The first set of images used in Step 1 should clearly present the product and/or practice so that students can *identify* the focus of the cultural investigation and *describe* the product and/or practice. For example, in a lesson on the cultural meaning of the Chinese fan and its development over time (K. Y. Hua, personal communication, June 2016), several authentic Chinese fans (product) were shared with the class in addition to PowerPoint images of paintings from Ancient China in which fans were depicted and used (product and practice) as symbols of elegance and wisdom.

The second set of pictures to be used in Step 3 goes beyond static images of the product and/or practice and allows students to *explore* and *hypothesize* about possible cultural meanings and perspectives associate with the topic. In the Chinese lesson described above, a second set of images was used in this step showing images and artifacts of the uses of fans in contemporary Chinese society, for example, as household decorative art, as promotional material and advertisements, and as a tool for Tai Chi and Kung Fu.

3. <u>Anticipate the language that will be needed to participate in the culture discussion</u>. Keeping in mind what was learned in Chapter 1 about learning language through comprehensible talk-in-interaction and in Chapter 2 about how to promote oral interaction in a classroom discourse community, think about the kind of language that students will need to participate actively in the lesson. This language consists of vocabulary and formulaic phrases that learners may need to express opinions and ideas during the lesson—this language will need to be entered and re-entered in teacher presentations— and any specific grammatical structures that learners will use to explore the content of the culture lesson.

As an example, in a culture lesson that a teacher designed for an intermediate class on observing the differences between French comics and graphic novels and comic books in the US, she anticipated that students would need specific words to deal with the images she selected and the topic. For example, she selected words such as a "comic strip" (*une bande dessinée*) in anticipation of establishing the meaning of this word in the French context compared to her students' interpretive frame for this word. A few other words that she selected were "the readership" (*le lectorat*) to compare those who read comic books in each country, "a poster" (*une affiche*) for indicating the ways that comic books and comic conventions are advertised, and vocabulary pertaining to bookstores to describe the interiors of French bookstores that are devoted exclusively to comic book sales. This teacher also decided to provide students with more advanced ways of expressing opinions because, as she stated, "they have a tendency to always use the same ones when they speak so I will provide different expressions they may use on the board." She understood that expressing opinions would be very important in this lesson focused on exploring critically the perspective on French comics as commentary on serious social issues through the use of humor. In terms of grammatical structures, she did not anticipate many unfamiliar structures given the level of her class but realized that to describe what is observed in French and US comic books and then to compare them, students may need prepositions of location, ways of summarizing content, and comparative forms of adjectives and nouns.

Enacting the culture lesson in 4 steps

Step 1. <u>**I**mages and **M**aking Observations</u>. (Appendix A, External Mediational Tool #5b) In Step 1 of enacting the lesson, the teacher, using a PowerPoint presentation, shows the class the first image (or images) of a cultural product or practice to launch the interaction. Here the teacher should ask three to five Fact Questions in the target language to allow students to make detailed observations of the product or practice under investigation. Questions phrased with *what*, *where*, *when*, and *who* are useful ways to begin this interaction. The teacher could ask the questions to the whole class or provide a handout with questions for students to answer in small groups for later reporting back to class and for comparing responses.

For younger learners who may not find it engaging simply to sit, look, and describe, the teacher should plan activities that could be done in conjunction with image description. For example, middle school learners could dramatize the scene depicted in the image (see Chapter 4), point to various parts of the image in a TPR-type activity, display their comprehension using signaling activities (see Chapter 1), or be shown real objects that are found in the images to manipulate.

The goal of Step 1 is for students to have a clear understanding of the practice or product that they observe. For example, in a Spanish lesson beginning with an image of a 10 soles bill from Peru, students needed to identify the cultural product as currency, describe the symbols on the bill, and identify, with the help of the teacher or Internet resources, the portrait of the famous Peruvian air force hero, José Abelardo Quiñones Gónzales. Knowing this information was important before students could move to a discussion of how national identity and history are reinforced through the image of this aviator who sacrificed his life during the Ecuadorian-Peruvian war and who today is honored as a national hero symbolizing the strength and sacrifices of the Peruvian people.

Step 2. <u>**A**nalyzing Additional Information about the Product and/or Practice</u>. In Step 2 the teacher provides additional information in the target language about the cultural product or practice in the form of a *short text* or *data*. This additional information provides knowledge that students do not bring to the task and have probably not acquired elsewhere. Further, this information should help students begin to think about a cultural perspective embodied in the product or practice. Short texts, brief and carefully selected extracts from articles, or data in the form of graphs and charts are excellent ways to deepen cultural understanding and provide a new lens on the images that have been observed and described. There are many websites for finding short explanatory texts and accessible data charts about particular cultural practices and products. For example, in an ESL class on the cultural differences of coffee drinking in the US and in other parts of world, images of the interiors of coffee shops in the US and in Europe and Asia were complemented with a short text from the *Scientific American Blog Network* (D'Costa, 2011) on the culture of coffee drinkers. In a few well-chosen sentences cited from this article displayed on a PowerPoint slide, students' interpretations were confirmed, indicating that coffee drinking has become synonymous with work in the US compared to other countries where the perspective on coffee drinking is viewed as leisure-time activity for socializing with friends. In an Italian lesson on the culture of family mealtime in Italy, two pie charts comparing the frequency of meals at home vs. meals in restaurants in Italy and in the US showed graphically the importance of establishing family ties through meals in the home in Italy in contrast to a higher percentage of meals outside the home in the US. A final example from an ESL class, compared the types of side dishes that were ordered with McDonald's Happy Meals for children in 2011 and 2013. The bar graph used for Step 2 of the lesson indicated that in 2013 apples were ordered more frequently as a side dish for children compared to only french fries in 2011. What the data on these consumable products showed, therefore, was a changing perspective on what was considered healthy eating habits for children from 2011 to 2013. The important point is that clear and unambiguous **data visualization** and well-chosen texts that complement image analysis are powerful ways to engage learners in exploring cultural perspectives and the worldviews of other cultures and their own. Moreover, data are readily available on-line and can be found in a variety of comprehensible and accessible displays. Data displays are also excellent ways to promote observation and discussion in the target language. As illustrated in the *IMAGE* model, this new information is not provided in a unidirectional fashion (i.e., from teacher to students in the form of a lecture), but rather serves as an impetus for discussion and hypothesizing of cultural perspectives.

Step 3. <u>Generating Hypotheses about Cultural Perspectives</u>. Step 3 in the enactment of the culture lesson asks students to analyze, reflect, and hypothesize. After the first set of images and any text or data provided (Steps 1 and 2), the teacher shows a few new image(s) that will move the lesson forward, maintain student interest, and stimulate further reflection. Based on the scaffolding of the lesson up to this point and information provided, learners should be ready to begin to delve deeper into their cultural analysis. The teacher should prepare three to five target language Thought Questions for this step of the lesson. Thought Questions prompt students to think about possible meanings of the product or practice in their own terms and to elaborate on ideas and information that have been presented up to this point in pair or small group discussions using in the target language.

For example, in the French comic book lesson, the teacher addressed this stage of the lesson by asking students to discuss what message was represented by different cover illustrations on French and US comic books. In the Peruvian soles lesson, students were asked to compare symbolic images of heroes in the US with the depiction of the aviator on the 10 soles bill. In the ESL class, learners speculated on why eating habits of children changed between 2011 and 2013.

Two options are available for this part of the lesson. Option 1 is based on practices that were presented in Chapters 2 and 3—Building a discourse community and engaging students in interpreting and discussing authentic texts (here text can also be understood as images). For intermediate and advanced classes, teachers should design a prompt for discussion in pairs or small group. The discussion prompt should indicate that learners should share interpretations, support them with evidence from the lesson, and prepare a report of the contents of their discussion to the class for comparison, elaboration, and further discussion.

Option 2 can be used for elementary-level classes in which learners may not have all the language they need to state their hypotheses and interpretations adequately. To address the challenge of language use in elementary classes, it is suggested that teachers provide a list of three plausible perspectives in the target language. From this list, learners select one perspective that best reflects their thinking. When reporting back to the class on their choices, teachers can summarize the most popular interpretation, ask for justifications for choices, and elaborate upon them, if necessary. What is important if using this option is not to make the task into a multiple choice quiz with only one correct answer. As with all cultural interpretations, multiple readings of the data may be put forth, evaluated, and supported with observations and information. Learners should not be lead to believe that interpreting culture is simply a matter of stating the right answer. Rather, it is a process of arriving at an interpretation based on evidence allowing learners to explore the beliefs and values of various cultural communities and to move beyond their own cultural frames of reference, beliefs, and norms (see Brenner, 2010 on critical pedagogy and foreign language/culture education).

Step 3 brings closure to the lesson and provides learners with the opportunity to synthesize what they have seen and read, to state in their own words the relationship of the product and/or practice with a cultural perspective, and to compare observations. If the lesson has been carefully sequenced and scaffolded, learners should be able to make intelligent comments that go beyond stereotypical views of culture and superficial observations. What must be remembered during all phases of the culture lesson is that target language use is important and that the class should not devolve into an anthropology class taught in the learners' first language. The *World-Readiness Standards for Learning Languages* states clearly that to address the Cultures goal area, learners must use the *language* to investigate, explain, and reflect on the relationship of products and practices to cultural perspectives (National Standards in Foreign Language Education Project, 2015, p. 72).

Step 4. **E**xploring Perspectives and Reflecting Further. Step 4 extends the culture lesson beyond the classroom while providing additional opportunities for reflection and discussion about cultural perspectives. Learners should be given the opportunity to state what they may still wonder about, what questions remain, and what more they would like to learn about the topic. Observations of learner performance during the lesson and the lingering questions that the learners may have can lead the teacher to design out-of-class work for exploring the cultural product(s), practice(s), and perspective(s) more deeply. Individually or in teams, learners may be given an out-of-class assignment requiring the use of Internet tools (e.g., websites, YouTube, blogs, Google images, texts) to expand their cultural knowledge and find additional cultural images and information related to the lesson. Students then bring the findings of their independent cultural investigations to class and present their findings in the target language for class discussion. For example, in the Italian lesson on family, students were directed to a series of YouTube Italian commercials to explore the image of the Italian family further projected in the media. In a Spanish lesson on the symbolic value of the chili pepper in Mexican cuisine, students visited a Latino delicatessen and interviewed the owner on the uses of the chili pepper in his recipes, why he thought chili peppers were important to Mexican cooking, and why the use of the chili pepper was a characteristic of Mexican cooking. In the Spanish lesson on the Peruvian aviator represented on the country's 10 soles bill, learners researched other heroic figures in Latin American countries and compared the qualities of a hero in Latin America with their cultural concept of hero in the United States. These investigations have the potential to encourage critical thinking, motivate learners to reflect on cultural perspectives, and stimulate sharing of opinions and ideas in the target language.

Rehearsing the Practice

The following tasks reflect various steps of the planning tool and are intended to help you prepare a culture lesson with the assistance of instructor and peer feedback. Rehearsal Tasks 2-7 are based on a cultural product, practice, and possible perspectives that you want to explore with the class identified in Rehearsal Task 1. Therefore, selection of a series of images on a single cultural product or practice is required in order to complete all other tasks. Images should be put on PowerPoint for easy viewing and should be of high quality and clear. To prepare for the following tasks, first complete the two sections of the tool under planning—who are the learners and what is the cultural content of your lesson? The language of the lesson will be handled in a separate task below.

1. Identify a cultural product or practice that you want to explore with the class; then (a) select 3-5 images or other types of visual representations (e.g., manipulatives, artifacts, video) that you might use for your lesson and (b) describe how each image builds on the other and how the sequence of images leads students to making observations about cultural perspectives. Also, (c) state how the images help prevent cultural stereotyping that you anticipate that students may have. Share images with your peers and explain your rationale for image selection and sequencing. Listen to their reactions and suggestions and make refinements accordingly.

2. Practice writing *fact questions* and *thought questions* using the images you have selected in Rehearsal Task 1. Write 3-5 fact questions that you will ask for describing your images. Write 3-5 thought questions that move students beyond description to interpretation. Using your images, test your questions with the class to see if they elicit the kind of responses you expect.

3. Based on your cultural theme and your images, search on-line for data in the form of a chart or graph that can be used to add information to the lesson. Share the data with your peers to ensure that it is accessible and interpretable. If the data visualization is not easily understood, ask your peers why and, based on their feedback, find a replacement.

4. Realizing that you want the class to use the target language for the majority of the time in the lesson, complete the language section of the planning tool. Identify specific vocabulary related to your culture theme, any grammatical structures that reflect the functions of talk (e.g., compare and contrast, stating actions, providing descriptions) that will take place in the lesson, and a few well-chosen formulaic expressions that you will give to the students for expressing opinions and making observations. Explain how the language you have identified relates specifically to the lesson and provide an example in the context of the lesson of each language element you have listed.

5. Imagine your lesson is designed for beginners (first-year students or first-semester university students). You have decided that turning them loose on a group work discussion will result in a discussion in English. Write three plausible cultural interpretations about your images (and data) in language appropriate and comprehensible to the learners to be used for Option 2 in Step 3.

6. What types of interactive activities might be used during the culture lesson and where might these activities be located? In other words, in addition to class discussion and

pair and group work tasks, what other types of class involvement strategies beyond observation and discussion might be used in this lesson (e.g., role play, demonstrations, interpersonal communication tasks)?

7. Thinking beyond the classroom lesson, what assignment or project might you design to allow for further investigation and elaboration of the cultural content of the lesson? Design the assignment and decide how long it might take the learners to complete, what resources they might use to complete the assignment, and what form the assignment can take (e.g., report, presentation, visuals, additional data, selected texts). Finally describe how the project relates directly to the contents of the lesson and expands upon it.

8. If you are currently teaching, present your culture lesson to one of your classes. If videotaping is permitted in your school, record the lesson and show it to your colleagues for discussion of what worked well and where improvements are needed. If videotaping is not permitted, write a brief report and share your reaction to the lesson with your colleagues indicating where you thought the lesson went smoothly and as anticipated and where you noticed parts of the lesson that need to be re-worked. If you are not yet an in-service teacher but are enrolled in a practicum course, present your lesson to a class of your peers and elicit their reactions and suggestions.

Assessing the Practice

Use Rubric #5 in this chapter's Appendix B to self-assess your culture lesson. As an alternative or in addition, you could ask a colleague or peer to observe the lesson that you facilitated and provide feedback using the rubric.

Putting the Practice into a Larger Context: Instructional Goals and Challenges

We teach in an age in which global education and internationalizing the curriculum have become increasingly important and necessary. The world has become a smaller place due to social media, the Internet, and chat applications that connect people from all over the world with each other. To be prepared to live in today's world, students need to be global citizens and not just members of insular communities, unaware of a world beyond their own community boundaries. Foreign language education is well positioned to address the mandate of our schools and universities to internationalize curriculum and develop global understandings. But to achieve this goal, we must move beyond thinking about language instruction as only nouns, verb paradigms, and grammatical rules.

As the *Modern Language Association (MLA) Report* (Modern Language Association (MLA) Ad Hoc Committee on Foreign Languages, 2007) states that a major goal of language instruction is ***transcultural competence***, Kramsch (2012, p. 29) argues that transcultural competence does not mean the bland and meaningless co-existence of cultures under the happy banner of diversity. Rather, this concept means that learners are willing to engage in cultural explorations and are able to make informed and intelligent observations about patterns of cultural behavior unlike their own. To be transculturally competent, therefore, requires that our learners need to interact with others unlike themselves and work toward understanding difference rather than simply ignoring or tolerating it. As the *MLA Report* states emphatically, transcultural competence means that learners are taught to "comprehend speakers of the target language as member of foreign societies and to grasp themselves as Americans—that is, as members of a society that is [also] foreign to others" (Modern Language Association (MLA) Ad Hoc Committee on Foreign Languages, 2007,

p. 4). In this way, students can be emancipated from restrictive worldviews imposed on them by their own culture and can critically examine their place in the world and their relationship with others (Regan & Osborn, 2002).

A second educational concern related to the teaching of culture in foreign language classrooms is the importance of providing students with **culturally relevant pedagogy (CRP)** (Hall, 2008; Ladson-Billings, 1995, 2006) and **culturally responsive teaching**. Today's classrooms are linguistically, racially, and culturally diverse environments in which a teacher's understanding of the culture of his or her students and their frames of reference and students' understanding of each other are of paramount importance to build classroom community and to provide relevant instruction. Although CRP emphasizes that instruction must start where the students are and be grounded in their cultural realities, it cannot remain there, as Milner (2010) argues in his award-winning book *Start Where You Are, But Don't Stay There: Understanding Diversity, Opportunity Gaps, and Teaching in Today's Classrooms*. Enabling foreign language students to investigate, reflect on, and explain target language cultures (National Standards in Foreign Language Education Project, 2015) can be made relevant by designing instruction based on the cultural worlds that students bring to the classroom while simultaneously introducing and investigating cultural perspectives unlike their own. And this relationship moves in two directions. As students learn about their role as citizens in their own communities, the more they learn about being global citizens, and as they learn about the world, the more they understand their own local community.

Aronson and Laughter (2016) summarize the features of culturally relevant instruction gleaned from various approaches to CRP found in the literature. What is striking is that these features, described briefly below, parallel closely the goals of culture instruction in the foreign language classroom. For example, culturally relevant educators build on the knowledge and cultural assets that students bring with them into the classroom making the classroom inclusive of all students. The *MLA Report* (Modern Language Association [MLA] Ad Hoc Committee on Foreign Languages, 2007) also points out that teaching for transcultural competence involves enabling students to relate to fellow members of the students' own society (including the classroom community) who may speak languages other than English or who come from diverse familial heritages. In other words, culture instruction creates inclusive classrooms by its emphasis on critical reflection on the cultural diversity that exists in classrooms, schools, and in the world.

Culturally relevant educators are also said to have the ability to create instruction and classroom environments in which students learn both about their own and others' worldviews. Culture teaching, as an HLTP that all teachers must know and be able to carry out, supports this concept through critical reflections on cultures that are not always in the immediate classroom or community environments of the students. As described in the *World-Readiness Standards for Learning Languages* (National Standards in Foreign Language Education Project, 2015) and in the *MLA Report* (Modern Language Association [MLA] Ad Hoc Committee on Foreign Languages, 2007), classrooms need to be safe spaces where students reflect on the world and themselves in it from the perspective of other languages and cultures.

Finally, culturally relevant educators work in pursuit of social justice for all members of society and in the world. As described in the introduction to this chapter, language and culture are intimately connected and cultural values and worldviews can often be revealed in the metaphors and expressions that are commonplace in one's cultural world. Students can, therefore, explore culture through the lens of how language is used in a society's daily conversations, media, slogans, advertisements, and texts of various kinds, such as foreign language webpages, newspaper articles, and literature. Additionally, these discourses are often taken for granted but when analyzed closely can reveal deeply rooted ways of behaving and believing that include some social groups but marginalize others. Not all cultural practices and the perspectives that they engender are benign. For this reason, culture instruction is not just about knowledge of cultural facts. Culture lessons must also develop learners' ability to think critically about important equity and social justice issues in the world.

Developing students' critical thinking ability about culture is perhaps the most challenging to enact in the classroom (Brenner, 2010), but it is not any less important than other aspect of foreign language instruction. Reflecting on culture and conducting cultural investigations in the foreign language classroom, in the way described in this HLTP, contributes directly to this challenge and moves education closer to developing informed individuals who can operate with awareness and insight across languages and cultural boundaries.

For Further Reading

Aronson, B., & Laughter, J. (2016). The theory and practice of culturally relevant education: A synthesis of research across content areas. *Review of Educational Research, 86*(1), 163–206.

Barnes-Karol, G., & Broner, M. A. (2010). Using images as springboards to teach cultural perspectives in light of the ideals of the MLA Report. *Foreign Language Annals, 43*(3), 422–445.

Bhabba, H. (1994). *The location of culture.* London, Routledge.

Brenner, D. (2010). From core curriculum to core identities: On critical pedagogy and foreign language/culture education. In G. S. Levine & A. Phipps (Eds.), *Critical and intercultural theory and language pedagogy* (pp. 125–140). Boston, MA: Cengage Learning.

Byram, M. (1997). *Teaching and assessing intercultural communicative competence.* Clevedon, UK: Multilingual Matters, Ltd.

Byram, M. (2008). *From foreign language education to education for intercultural citizenship.* Clevedon, UK: Multilingual Matters, Ltd.

Cutshall, S. (2012). More than a decade of standards: Integrating "cultures" into your language instruction. *The Language Educator, 7*(1), 32–37.

D'Costa, K. (2011). *The culture of coffee drinkers.* Retrieved from http://blogs.scientificamerican.com/anthropology-in-practice/the-culture-of-coffee-drinkers/

Duranti, A. (1997). *Linguistic anthropology.* Cambridge: Cambridge University Press.

Galloway, V. B. (1985). *A design for the improvement of the teaching of culture in foreign language classrooms.* ACTFL project proposal. Yonkers, NY: American Council on the Teaching of Foreign Languages.

Johnson, S. P., & English, K. (2003). Images, Myths, and realities across cultures. *The French Review, 76*(3), 492–506.

Hall, J. K. (2012). *Teaching and researching culture* (2nd ed.). Edinburgh Gate, UK: Pearson Education Limited.

Hall, J. K. (2008). Language education and culture. In S. May and N. H. Hornberger (Eds), *Encyclopedia of Language and Education*, 2ⁿᵈ Ed., vol. 1: *Language Policy and Political Issues in Education* (pp. 45–55). New York, NY: Springer Science + Business Media.

Kramsch, C. (2012). Theorizing translingual/transcultural competence. In G. S. Levine & A. Phipps (Eds.), *Critical and intercultural theory and language pedagogy* (pp. 15–31). Boston, MA: Cengage Learning.

Ladson-Billings, G. (1995). But that's just good teaching! The case for culturally relevant pedagogy. *Theory into Practice, 43*, 159–165.

Ladson-Billings, G. (2006). "Yes, but how do we do it?" Practicing culturally relevant pedagogy. In J. G. Landsman & C. W. Lewis (Eds.), *White teachers diverse class- rooms: Creating inclusive schools, building on students' diversity, and providing true educational equity* (33–46). Sterling, VA: Stylus.

Milner IV, H. R. (2010). *Start where you are, but don't stay there*. Cambridge, MA: Harvard Education press.

Modern Language Association (MLA) Ad Hoc Committee on Foreign Languages. (2007). *Foreign languages and higher education: New structures for a changed world*. New York: Author. Retrieved from http://www.mla.org/flreport

National Standards in Foreign Language Education Project. (2015). *World-Readiness standards for learning languages*. Alexandria, VA: Author.

Oberg, K. (1960). Culture shock: adjustment to new cultural environments. *Practical Anthropology, 7,* 177–182.

Reagan, T., & Osborne, T. (2002). *The foreign language educator in society toward a critical pedagogy*. Mahwah, NJ: Lawrence Erlbaum Associates.

Schulz, R. A. (2007). The challenge of assessing cultural understanding in the context of foreign language instruction. *Foreign Language Annals, 40*, 9–26.

West, M., & Donato, R. (1995). Stories and stances: Cross-cultural encounters with African folk tales. *Foreign Language Annals, 28*(3), 392–405.

Appendix A

External Mediational Tool #5a:
The IMAGE Model for Exploring Cultural Perspectives

PLANNING STAGE: PREPARING FOR THE LESSON

A. <u>Who are the students?</u>

For what course is your culture lesson designed? What year/semester of study is this course? What is the time frame for the lesson—A single class? Divided across several days? A week?

B. <u>What is the cultural content of lesson?</u>

State the cultural product and/or practice you will show in the lesson and its/their relationship to a cultural perspective (that is, a value, belief, or meaning). What perspective(s) might your students explore? What images will you use?

Product/Practice [Note: It is best to begin with a single product and/or practice; however, others may emanate in the lesson]:

Perspective(s):

Images:

Set 1: _____

Set 2: _____

C. <u>What vocabulary do students need to participate in the lesson?</u>

List any **specific vocabulary** that students will need in this culture lesson. That is, what are the **essential vocabulary words** that are needed to understand your lesson? List this vocabulary. NOTE: Students will learn new vocabulary through your talk-in-interaction.

What **formulaic phrases** will you give to students to allow them to express opinions during a discussion? For example: "In my opinion," "I think that…," "I believe that…," "My opinion is…," "In general…" (for more examples, search on-line for *language for expressing opinions*).

D. <u>What grammar structures do students need to participate in the lesson?</u>

Are there any **specific grammatical structures** that will occur often in this lesson? **Be specific**, e.g., if students need *to describe*, what kind of **adjectives** or **adjectival phrases** will they use to achieve this function? If students need *to compare*, what **comparative forms** will be used in the lesson?

External Mediational Tool #5b:
The IMAGE Model for Exploring Cultural Perspectives

ENACTING THE CULTURAL IMAGES LESSON

Step 1: **I**mages and **M**aking Observations

Begin the lesson by asking students to describe **the product** and/or **practice** that they see in the first set of images. Ask **FACT questions in the TL** (*What do you see?*). Write **THREE to FIVE FACT questions** here for each image. (*Space provided for three images but it is up to you to decide how many. Use as many or as few images as you like for this step*).

Image 1 is a picture of _____

Fact questions:

Image 2 is a picture of _____

Fact questions:

Image 3 is a picture of _____

Fact questions:

Step 2: **A**nalyzing Additional Information about the Product and/or Practice:

At this point in the lesson, what **additional information** will you provide in the form of **TEXT** or **DATA in the TL** on the cultural product or practice? What will you ask students to do with this information? This information should help students to **BEGIN TO THINK ABOUT PERSPECTIVES**. (*Space provided for two sources of information but it is up to you to decide how many*).

Informational source #1 is _____

With this information, I will ask students to _____

_____

_____

Informational source #2 is _____

With this information, I will ask students to _____

_____

_____

Step 3: <u>G</u>enerating <u>H</u>ypotheses about <u>C</u>ultural <u>P</u>erspectives

Now show the second set of image(s) that prompt hypotheses about possible perspectives conveyed by the product and/or practice. Ask students to begin to **REFLECT** on perspectives. Ask **THREE to FIVE THOUGHT questions in the TL** (*What do you think?*). THOUGHT questions prompt students to think about possible **MEANINGS** of the product or practice. Since students are seeing the second set of images for the first time, you may begin this step with a few **FACT questions** to begin the interaction and encourage participation. (*Space provided for one image but it is up to you to decide how many. Use as many or as few images as you like for this step*).

Image #1 is a picture of _____

1. _____

2. _____

3. _____

4. _____

5. _____

<u>Option 1 for Intermediate- or higher-level language classes</u>:

Ask students to use the thought questions to hypothesize about and to state in their own words the *relationship of the product or practice to a cultural perspective*. This step should be carried out in pairs or small groups followed by a report back to class.

(a)   How you will carry out this part of the lesson?

(b)   What directions will you give to the students?

(c)   Can you anticipate any misinterpretations or cultural stereotyping that might occur? If yes, what might they be?

(d)   If misinterpretations occur or if students express cultural stereotypes, how will you respond?

<u>Option 2 for Elementary-level language classes</u>:

If you think your students will not be able to state a perspective in the target language on their own, provide a multiple-choice task. Write for the students *three possible perspective*s in the TL and ask students in pairs or small groups to (a) *select* one based on the images and information they have seen and analyzed and/or (b) *rank order* the three perspectives from the most to least important, obvious, comprehensive, interesting, etc. If possible, ask students to tell you WHY they selected or rank ordered the perspectives in this way.

Write the three perspectives for your images that you will give to students for their selection. Use comprehensible target language.

1. _____

2. _____

3. _____

Step 4: <u>**E**xploring Perspectives and Reflecting Further</u>

Ask students what they are *wondering* about the cultural product or practice. That is, what do they want to learn more about?

Students or student teams may be given *a homework assignment* or *project* to explore the cultural product, practice, and perspective(s) more deeply. Students may use Internet tools (e.g., websites, YouTube, blogs, Google images, texts) to expand their cultural knowledge and find additional cultural images and/or information related to the theme. Students bring the *findings* of their cultural exploration to class and present in the target language. Another option would be to engage students in making cultural comparisons between their own culture and the culture(s) of the target language users.

What homework assignment or project will you design to engage students in exploring in more depth the relationship of the cultural product and practice to the cultural perspective(s)?

Appendix B

RUBRIC: HLTP #5: Focusing on Cultural Products, Practices, and Perspectives in a Dialogic Context

	EXCEEDS EXPECTATIONS	MEETS EXPECTATIONS	DEVELOPING	UNACCEPTABLE
Cultural Content of Lesson	Lesson features a cultural product and/or practice that convey(s) a cultural perspective. Content is engaging, interesting, and relevant to learners.	Lesson features a cultural product and/or practice that convey(s) a cultural perspective. Content is relevant to learners.	Primary focus of lesson is on a cultural product or practice rather than on a cultural perspective. And/or content may lack interest and/or relevance to learners.	Lesson consists of discrete pieces of cultural information not presented within the 3P cultural paradigm.
Selection of Images	Images are culturally authentic and illustrate a cultural product and/or practice. Images provoke a reaction and stimulate interest and discussion.	Images are culturally authentic and illustrate a cultural product and/or practice. Images stimulate discussion.	Images are culturally authentic but do not illustrate an obvious cultural product and/or practice. Images might not stimulate either much interest or discussion.	Images are not authentic and may be taken from a textbook. Images either promote cultural stereotyping or do not illustrate an authentic cultural product or practice.
Target Language Scaffolded for Learners	Using talk-in-interaction, the teacher scaffolds vocabulary words, formulaic expressions, and grammar needed for students to participate in lesson. Teacher elicits and builds on students' previously learned language in the context of the lesson.	Using talk-in-interaction, the teacher scaffolds vocabulary words, formulaic expressions, and grammar needed for students to participate in lesson.	Teacher introduces vocabulary words, formulaic expressions, and grammar needed for students to participate in lesson through partial scaffolding and providing of lists of vocabulary and grammatical structures.	Teacher either provides a list of vocabulary, formulaic expressions, and grammatical structures in the absence of a context OR makes little attempt to scaffold new language for learners.

(continued on next page)

RUBRIC: HLTP #5 (*continued*)

	EXCEEDS EXPECTATIONS	MEETS EXPECTATIONS	DEVELOPING	UNACCEPTABLE
Guiding Learners to Cultural Perspective(s)	Teacher asks questions sequenced from fact questions to open-ended thought questions. Learner discussion, interaction, and hypothesizing about cultural perspectives are central to the lesson.	Teacher asks questions sequenced from fact questions to open-ended thought questions. Provides some opportunities for learners to discuss questions, interact with one another, and hypothesize about cultural perspectives.	Teacher asks fact and thought questions although fact questions may be more prevalent. Provides opportunities for learners to discuss questions but opportunities to interact and hypothesize about cultural perspectives with peers are limited.	Teacher asks only fact questions in a teacher-centered fashion. Learners are given information regarding cultural perspectives in the absence of hypothesizing with their peers.
Use of TL in Lesson	Target language is used exclusively in the lesson and is supported by comprehensible input and interactions with learners.	Target language is used at least 90% of the time in the lesson and is supported by comprehensible input and interactions with learners.	Target language is used at least 50% of the time in the lesson and is supported by comprehensible input and interactions with learners. OR target language is used 90% of the time but is only partially comprehensible to learners.	English is used for the majority of the lesson OR target language used is not comprehensible to learners.

CHAPTER 6

HLTP #6: Providing Oral Corrective Feedback to Improve Learner Performance

"The most effective teachers are likely to be those who are willing and able to orchestrate, in accordance with their students' language abilities and content familiarity, a wide range of CF [corrective feedback] types that fit the instructional context."
—Lyster, Saito, & Sato, 2013, p. 30

The HLTPs presented in previous chapters of this text have emphasized the importance of TL interaction within meaningful contexts with the goal of developing a discourse community and promoting L2 learning and development. As discussed earlier, the teacher plays a pivotal role in setting the stage for how interactions will occur in the classroom, i.e., whether talk will be scripted with a primary focus on grammatical accuracy or whether interpersonal communication will be fostered so that it unfolds naturally with a primary focus on meaning-making. A key issue that has been explored extensively in research in second-language acquisition and L2 teaching and learning is the place of teacher feedback, either provided to call learners' attention to errors in their speech or to respond to the content of a learner utterance. While there is evidence to indicate that extensive focus on error correction by the teacher can undermine L2 performance and demotivate learners, the research also shows that learners benefit from attention to form, which can serve as a meaning-making resource (see Chapter 4). Further, studies have revealed that learners prefer to receive feedback as opposed to having their errors ignored (A. Brown, 2009; Schulz, 1996). It is not surprising that novice language teachers are faced with a daunting task when it comes to deciding what types of feedback they should provide to learners and under which circumstances—when they should call attention to learners' errors in their speech and how they could do so in ways that assist learners to improve their performance. It should be noted that these decisions are critical in building a discourse community, in mediating language learning, and in supporting learner performance in the TL. For this reason, an important high-leverage teaching practice for novice teachers is providing oral corrective feedback—that is, feedback provided by the teacher in oral interactions (either between the teacher and learner or between learners)—to improve learner performance.

Two critical points are in order as a prelude to the discussion of this HLTP. First, the teacher's expectations during oral interaction should never be error-free performance by learners. As discussed in Chapter 4, errors are a natural part of language acquisition and can provide evidence that learners are progressing in their language development (Lightbown & Spada, 2013). For this reason, a teacher's approach to oral interaction that is focused on calling learners' attention to and correcting every single error has no place within a language program that prioritizes meaning-making and communicative interaction.

Secondly, it should be noted that the term **corrective feedback (CF)** has been defined as "a teacher's reactive move that invites learners to attend to the grammatical accuracy of their utterances" (Sheen, 2007, as cited in Rassaei, 2014, p. 417). However, the contemporary view of CF goes beyond the traditional notion of correcting grammatical errors inasmuch as CF can also be used as a tool for mediating language learning and development, as will be explained in the next section (Shrum & Glisan, 2016). Using CF as a mediational tool depends on the goal of the feedback, how it is delivered, and whether the CF is responsive to where students are in terms of their actual and potential levels of development (see Chapter 4).

ACTFL/CAEP Standards addressed: #3a, 3b; #5a, 5b

Research and Theory Supporting the Practice

A body of research has confirmed the effectiveness of corrective feedback in supporting language learning and development (see, for example, Li, 2010; Lyster & Saito, 2010; Rassaei, 2014). The critically important role of oral CF as a mediational tool is supported from two perspectives (1) a cognitive view that accounts for ways in which learners use the feedback they receive from the teacher to either repair some part of an inaccurate utterance or not, and (2) a sociocultural view that focuses on how corrective assistance from the teacher can enable learners to go beyond their current level of language development in performing tasks that they are unable to complete on their own.

Within a cognitive perspective, different types of feedback can be more or less useful in leading to what is called **uptake,** how learners use the oral feedback offered by the teacher to repair their error or not (Lyster & Ranta, 1997). For example, learners could immediately insert the correct form suggested by the teacher into their utterance, they could self-correct based on clues given by the teacher, they could incorporate correction provided by a peer, or they might even recall and use the correct form at a later point in time when producing a similar utterance. Of course, what learners do with the feedback that they receive is related to whether or not they *notice* the feedback as being corrective (see later discussion) (Long, 1996). The common types of teacher feedback in oral interactions were identified in Lyster & Ranta's (1997) seminal study, and their effectiveness continues to be examined in research on CF:

1. **Explicit correction**, in which the teacher provides the correct form or indicates that what the learner said was incorrect: *Oh, you mean…; You should say….*

2. **Recasts**, in which the teacher responds to the learner and rephrases part of the student's utterance so as to correct it, but in a more implicit way without directly saying that the form was incorrect: *S: I'm *interesting in seeing the movie. T: Oh, you're interested in seeing the movie.*

3. **Clarification request**, in which the teacher indicates that there is a problem in comprehensibility or accuracy or both and that a reformulation is required: *Excuse me? What do you mean?*

4. **Metalinguistic feedback**, in which the teacher indicates that there is an error by asking questions about what the student said and/or providing grammatical metalanguage that points out the nature of the error: *Are you referring to present or past?; You need a past-tense verb.*

5. **Elicitation**, in which the teacher elicits the correct form by repeating exactly what the learner said up to the point of the error: *S: I will go to the concert this night. T: I will go*

to the concert...? Teachers could also ask questions to elicit the form, as in: *How do we say X in French?*

6. **Repetition**, in which the teacher repeats the learner's incorrect utterance with rising intonation to highlight the error: *S: I goed to the gym this morning. T: I goed?* (Lyster & Ranta, 1997, pp. 46-48 [adapted]).

It bears mentioning that many of these types of CF can be used to provide conversational feedback instead of to call attention to linguistic errors. For example, the clarification request, "Huh?" can serve to question the meaning of what the speaker said and not necessarily a grammatical or lexical problem. Similarly, recasting what the learner said in another way can be used in conversation as a confirmation check of what the speaker said and as a way to move the interaction forward. In this case, the recast serves to show interest in what was said, to show alignment with the speaker, and/or to confirm that the listener indeed understood the meaning of the utterance accurately:

> **S:** I got up this morning at 5:00.
>
> **T:** Wow, you got up early! [Teacher recast of learner's utterance to show surprise]

Further, instead of using a linguistic utterance, the teacher could also use a ***paralinguistic signal*** to non-verbally elicit a self-correction from the learner—e.g., a quizzical look or nodding of the head (Lyster, Saito, & Sato, 2013).

These 6 types of feedback can also be considered from two other standpoints. The first is whether the teacher elicits a correction from learners or simply provides the correct form in anticipation that the learner will recognize it. To this end, Ranta and Lyster (2007) classified the CF types into two categories: (1) **reformulations**, which provide learners with corrected restatements of their utterances, consist of recasts and explicit correction, and (2) **prompt**s, which elicit self-repair from learners, consist of elicitation, clarification requests, metalinguistic feedback, and repetition. Reformulations are, in essence, paraphrases that are used to clarify meaning and make talk-in-interaction comprehensible, as discussed in Chapter 1. Although in this chapter we will explore reformulations from the standpoint of the corrective potential they hold, it should be noted that they are used often and extensively in the form of conversational reformulations that are used to move the interaction forward (see earlier example of the conversational recast) rather than to correct an inaccurate form or utterance.

The second standpoint from which these feedback types can be viewed is the degree to which the teacher makes obvious the error and the correction. For example, elicitation is considered to be ***explicit*** given that the learner knows exactly where the error occurred (i.e., right after the teacher pauses), whereas a recast is considered ***implicit*** because the learner must notice what had been corrected in the teacher's reformulated utterance. Perhaps it has become obvious at this point that the types of CF progress on a continuum from implicit to explicit and encompass the two categories of prompts (requiring learner output) and reformulations (providing a model of the accurate utterance) (Lyster, Saito, & Sato, 2013; Sheen & Ellis, 2011). For instance, feedback in the form of "Excuse me? What did you mean to say?" is on the implicit side of the continuum inasmuch as the learner must figure out what was wrong with his or her utterance, and it is also a prompt since the learner is expected to respond to the question. On the other hand, providing explicit correction is, of course, on the explicit side of the continuum and is a reformulation since the learner is not required to produce a response. Figure 6.1 illustrates the range of the most common CF types grouped according to these four classifications (reformulations, prompts, implicit, explicit) in quadrants.

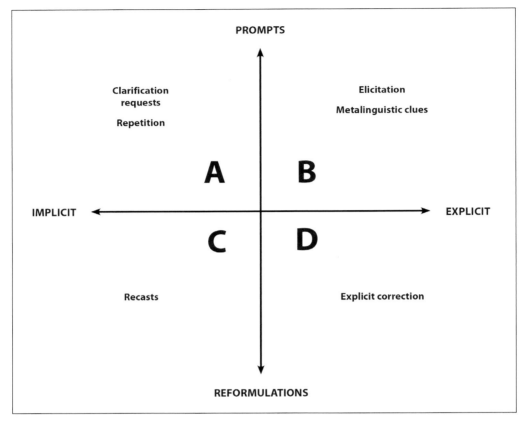

Figure 6.1. Range of Common CF Types
(based on work of Lyster, Saito, & Sato, 2013)

The explanation above may help explain the finding in the research that, although recasts tend to be the CF type used most by teachers, they have generally been found to be less likely to lead to uptake by learners in comparison to other strategies such as elicitation and clarification requests. The benefit of recasts appears to be in calling learners' attention to form without disrupting communication and meaning-making (Loewen & Philp, 2006). However, since recasts are often implicit in nature and do not necessarily prompt a learner response, learners may not notice the correction in the teacher's feedback as they would in the case of elicitation, for example. However, the issue is even more complex. Research has suggested that, even though learners might attend to explicit CF more easily, "the effects of implicit CF might be more robust (i.e., longer lasting) than those of explicit CF, which might be more effective in the short term" (Lyster, Saito, & Sato, 2013, p. 5). This finding could be the result of implicit CF prompting learners to access L2 knowledge and problem-solving as they work to notice the error, correct it, and perhaps produce a response. However, as stated earlier, learners often do not attend to implicit forms of corrective feedback. Therefore, the long-term effects of implicit feedback only apply in cases where learners' are motivated to attend to the teacher's reformulated part of the utterance and process for themselves what they heard and noticed.

While the discussion above presents a cognitive view of CF types and their role on internal learner processes such as noticing, uptake, and performance, a second perspective reflects a sociocultural view of CF and can be explained within the concept of the Zone of Proximal Development (ZPD) (Vygotsky, 1978, 1986) and scaffolding (Gibbons, 2015; Walqui & Van Lier, 2010) (see Chapter 4). According to sociocultural theory, language development "occurs *in* rather than *as a result of* interaction" (Ellis, 2009, p. 12). In this vein, learners perform beyond their current abilities through **scaffolding**, "a collaborative process through which a teacher or a more proficient learner provides support or guidance to assist a less proficient learner" (Rassaei, 2014, p. 420). Aljaafreh and Lantolf (1994) describe three characteristics of teacher feedback that is tailored to learners' ZPDs: (1) **graduated**, with no more help than is needed, (2) **contingent**, removed when the learner shows the capacity to function independently, and (3) **dialogic**, with both learners and teachers collaborating to solve the problem (as cited in Rassaei, 2014, p. 421). As an example, within an oral interaction, the teacher might first offer implicit CF to a learner who is experiencing linguistic difficulty, and if the learner is unable to repair the problem, then proceed to increasingly more explicit CF in a graduated and dialogic fashion:

S: I am talking to my friend this night about our plans.

T: What?

S: I am talking to my friend this night about our plans.

T: When are you talking to her?

S: This night.

T: Did you talk to her last night or are you going to talk to her tonight?

S: Oh, I'm talking to her tonight.

It should be noted that this example begins with an implicit, *less specific* type of CF—What?—which native speakers tend to use initially in a naturally occurring interaction when meaning is unclear (Schegloff, Jefferson, & Sacks, 1977). The teacher gradually provides more specific and explicit CF to assist the learner in noticing the feedback and repairing the problem. In the case above, after several turns the learner recognized the reformulated word 'tonight' and incorporated the word into her utterance. If this student's self-repair had not occurred what might be expected is that the teacher would move to greater degrees of explicitness and provide metalinguistic feedback, such as "what you should say is 'tonight', not 'this night'."

In sum, within a sociocultural perspective, CF is better understood as a mediational tool whose purpose is to assist learners in resolving their linguistic difficulties in a collaborative and supportive manner rather than expecting that a single correction of learners' utterances or that providing metalinguistic information is all that is needed for language learning and development. Further, this type of collaborative and assisted performance takes on a role beyond that of simply supporting communication in the classroom but also serves the form-oriented goal of error correction (Rassaei, 2014).

Considerations about Providing Corrective Feedback

(1) *Should I discuss the role of feedback with my learners?* Yes! Language learners benefit greatly from understanding how the teacher's feedback can help them learn and improve their performance, especially given that learning a language is so different from the learning that takes place in their other classes. To this end, at the beginning of

the academic year or semester, the teacher should engage in explicit discussion about CF with learners to accomplish two goals:

- To find out how learners feel about receiving CF. Do they welcome feedback at times? Are they anxious about it? In what ways can the teacher make them feel comfortable about receiving feedback? This will enable the teacher to acquire important information about the attitudes that learners have regarding CF—information that the teacher will use in making decisions about providing CF (see discussion in 2 below).

- To help learners understand how CF can help them progress in their language learning and improve their performance. The teacher might illustrate some of the frequently used strategies that will be used in providing CF (e.g., clarification requests, elicitation) as well as explain how sometimes the learner will be prompted to self-correct while at other times the learner should attend to how the teacher reformulates or rephrases the learner utterance (e.g., recasts). Learners should also discuss the role of peer assistance in offering CF in cases where the learner is provided enough time to self-correct but is unable to do so without help. It is important that learners recognize that peer assistance is not only effective but is a feature of a discourse community in which learners support and help one another, as discussed in Chapter 2. Finally, the teacher should help learners understand why sometimes their errors are not identified or corrected at all by the teacher and how that decision is based upon principles of language learning and development (i.e., when learners are engaged in conversation and the teacher does not want to interrupt their flow of thought and/or frustrate them).

(2) *How do I determine when I should provide corrective feedback?* The decisions that teachers make regarding when to provide CF are complex and dependent on one's unique instructional context. In a recent study examining the nature of instructors' CF decisions, Gurzynski-Weiss (2016) found that the factors that most impacted moment-to-moment CF decisions were those related to the specific learner and/or classroom context. An interesting finding was that the teachers who had completed one or more courses in second-language acquisition (SLA) were those who reported paying attention to learner factors such as developmental readiness, stage of learners' interlanguage (i.e., the language of the learner at a particular point in time), anxiety, and willingness to communicate; and/or to contextual factors such as task and course goal, error type, and course level (p. 266). Clearly, teachers' understanding of how language develops, of their students, and of the various contexts of particular classroom tasks will affect their decision-making regarding the types of CF to provide and the kind of assistance to offer to support learners' language learning and development.

Therefore, an approach to making the decision regarding CF would be for teachers to first consider CONTEXTUAL FACTORS:

- Does the error interfere with the learner's intended meaning?

- Is the error the linguistic target of the lesson, e.g., made during the focus on form lesson (see Chapter 4)?

- Is the error one that is being made frequently by many learners in the class?

Consequently, if the answer to any of the questions is "yes," then the teacher should probably consider providing CF. On the contrary, the teacher would be unlikely to offer CF if the error does not impact meaning (e.g., a definite article that is used in the incorrect gender), particularly if the activity involves a discussion or other interpersonal task in which communication and the negotiation of meaning are the focus. In these situations, the teacher should take note of common errors and defer discussion of them to another time when focus on form would be more appropriate and would not disrupt the flow of communication. Of critical importance is that, within a sociocultural perspective, corrective feedback should be approached in such a way as to serve meaning-making and interaction.

Once the contextual factors indicate that CF might be useful, teachers could then consider LEARNER FACTORS:

- Would the learner benefit from receiving CF—would the feedback enable the learner to perform with assistance in his/her ZPD? Another way to think about this is: Is the learner developmentally ready for the CF?

- Is the individual learner open to receiving CF (or does the learner tend to demonstrate anxiety when confronted with CF?)?

- Does the learner appear to be confused and in need of CF to make meaning and/or clear up misunderstanding?

- Does the learner appear to want CF assistance from the teacher?

If the answer to any of these four categories of questions is "yes," then the teacher would be justified in providing CF.

(3) *How do I know whether to use implicit or explicit CF strategies?* To discover the learner's ZPD and to be able to provide appropriate feedback within the ZPD, teachers should offer graduated assistance that begins with more implicit CF and gradually continues with more explicit strategies, depending on the level of help the learner requires (see the work on **dynamic assessment**: Davin, 2013; Lantolf & Poehner, 2011a, 2011b; Poehner, 2007). The decision to begin with implicit CF is to allow the teacher to observe what the learner can do with the least amount of assistance in order to identify where the learner is in his or her actual developmental level and where he or she might be able to go with help, i.e., what we mean by teaching in the learner's ZPD. Providing too much assistance initially would not allow for a clear picture of the learner's individual capabilities and may underestimate the learner's level of language development. By beginning with implicit forms of assistance, the teacher can then make informed decisions about the subsequent forms of CF needed and the appropriate level of challenge that the learner can realistically handle without frustration or resistance to participation, discussed in more detail below.

It should be noted that this process of offering graduated assistance is the basis of a dialogic approach to feedback, as discussed in Chapter 4, and enables the teacher and the learner to make use of CF as a tool to mediate language learning. It bears reiterating that the purpose of CF within the sociocultural framework is not to correct errors in a vacuum. As Rassaei has proposed, "ZPD-oriented feedback helps learners move from dependence on the teacher to independence and autonomous performance" (2014, p. 428). In this regard, the teacher could begin with a more implicit strategy such as a clarification request or a paralinguistic signal (see earlier discussion of these strategies), and then proceed to more explicit strategies if necessary, such as elicitation or a metalinguistic clue (see earlier explanation of these strategies). On the other hand, the teacher could decide to use only an explicit strategy, such as elicitation, given the nature of assistance that the individual learner may need to operate within his or her ZPD. That is, the teacher may know that a particular learner would not notice implicit CF for a specific type of error and, in this case, would opt to make the feedback more explicit. Elicitation, in which the teacher repeats what the learner says but pauses right before the error, has been found to be a highly effective type of CF inasmuch as in Lyster and Ranta's (1997) study, this strategy led to uptake by learners 100% of the time. It should be noted that more advanced language learners tend to prefer to deal with implicit CF and engage in self-correction to work out linguistic difficulties more on their own (N. A. Brown, 2009). In sum, teachers who wish to use CF as a mediational tool within a sociocultural approach would ideally use CF on a continuum from implicit to explicit as needed, recognizing that individual learners may sometimes require more explicit CF strategies.

(4) *On what basis should I decide to use prompts vs. reformulations in providing CF?* The decision to use prompts or reformulations depends on whether the teacher desires further output from learners following the CF. To this end, prompts elicit output and reformulations offer input without signaling a need to respond further (Sheen & Ellis, 2011). For example, clarification requests *(What do you mean by that?)* and elicitation *(He went to the library...[pause before error]?)* are prompts inasmuch as they seek further response from the learner. In the case of prompts, it is important that teachers create *space* following the CF for learners to process and *uptake* the correction (Ellis, 2009). Some evidence indicates that prompts may benefit younger learners more than reformulations given the potential challenge in their noticing the correction when assistance is not provided by the teacher (Lyster & Saito, 2010).

On the other hand, reformulations provide a reworked (i.e., corrected) response but no request for further interaction. Examples are recasts *(Oh, you went to the movies last night)* and explicit correction *(You should say...)* As indicated earlier in the case of recasts, there is no guarantee that the learner notices the input, particularly because they are also implicit in nature. However, as also mentioned, for learners who are attentive to the reformulations present in the teacher's utterances, the effects of implicit CF might be longer lasting. In this case, reformulations will prompt learners to notice the difference between what they said and what they heard which then may serve to mediate their L2 learning in the current interaction and in interactions in the future (Li, 2010; Lyster, Saito, & Sato, 2013).

Given these considerations, novice teachers might choose to use prompts with the goal of assisting learners in their individual ZPDs. In this case, the teacher provides assistance that begins with implicit CF and progresses to explicit CF; learners are signaled to self-correct in a dialogic manner with scaffolded assistance from the teacher. Teachers might choose reformulations to move the interaction forward, especially in the case of conversational recasts, or to provide a reformulated response when learners do not have the language to do so, or even to foreshadow linguistic structures that will become a focus in the future (e.g., the teacher uses third person of the past tense although learners have not yet focused on this form).

(5) *What if my learners experience anxiety when I provide CF?* Traditional explicit correction that is used as the teacher's primary agenda, whether expressed or implied, is the strategy that can potentially lead to frustration, anxiety, and even embarrassment. Oral CF should be given within the context of the classroom discourse community, the

members of which have developed a respect for and trust in one another over time (see Chapter 2). When viewed as a mediational tool and used in a variety of forms depending on contextual and learner factors, CF should not cause anxious feelings on the part of learners. Teachers should be advised, nonetheless, that they must know their learners for undoubtedly some individuals may be more sensitive than others to any form of what they may consider criticism. Hence, knowledge of one's learners is an important variable in making decisions about whether to provide CF and what type of CF to select.

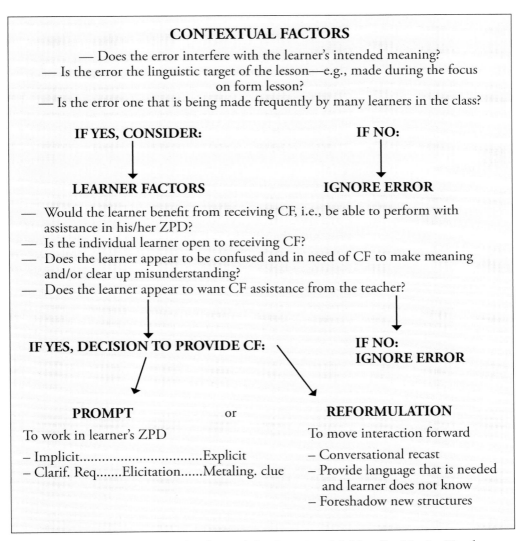

Figure 6.2. **A Hierarchy of Informed CF Decision-Making for Novice Teachers**

(Glisan & Donato, based in part on Gurzynski-Weiss, 2016)

Deconstructing the Practice

The steps for enacting this practice are depicted in visual form in Figure 6.2. The key to carrying out this practice is the decision-making that must take place in a moment-to-moment fashion as the lesson unfolds in the classroom. While this HLTP cannot be planned in advance as is the case with the majority of the other practices presented in this text, novice teachers can become skilled in (1) recognizing the conditions under which CF would best contribute to language learning and performance, and (2) selecting the specific CF strategy that would be most appropriate given contextual and learner factors. You may find Figure 6.1 to be useful for reference as you read further about these types of feedback and how they unfold in the classroom. The following are the specific steps to enact this practice:

1. In the face of an incorrect utterance spoken by a learner, consider first contextual factors by answering the three questions listed in Figure 6.2 (and reviewed earlier). If the error does not interfere with meaning, or is not the linguistic focus of the lesson, or is not one that is being made frequently by learners in the class, then ignore it. In this regard, keep in mind the role of errors in the language acquisition process (see earlier discussion and Chapter 4). If, on the other hand, the contextual factors support the giving of CF, then proceed to the second step.

2. Consider next the factors pertaining to the learner by responding to the four questions listed in the figure. If the answer to any of these questions is "yes," you should provide CF, as it would help mediate the learner's language learning and performance.

3. The next decision pertains to whether or not the teacher wants the student to attempt to repair the utterance and respond to the CF. The two choices, prompt or reformulation, involve the following rationale:

    -   **Prompt:** A prompt would give you an opportunity to work within the learner's ZPD on a concept/structure that the learner could repair with scaffolded assistance from the teacher. Provide as many of the following graduated prompts as needed, progressing from more implicit to more explicit:

    (1) Begin with an implicit prompt first as a *clarification request*; examples: *What?; What do you mean by X?; Could you clarify X?;* or any question to request a specific clarification based on what the learner said.

    (2) If the learner still requires assistance, provide a more explicit prompt such as *elicitation*, in which you repeat exactly what the learner said and pause right before the error, which signals to the learner where the problem is. Example:

    > **S:** If I had more time, I will travel around the world.

    > **T:** If I had more time, I .....?

    (3) If the learner is still experiencing difficulty, you could provide a final explicit prompt in the form of a *metalinguistic clue*, or some grammatical hints. Example: "You need the conditional tense, not the future." Metalinguistic clues can also be effective in combination with a teachable moment when it would be helpful to remind students to use structures that they have studied in the past. For example, in an advanced-level literature or culture class in which an authentic text is being discussed in Spanish, students would need to express hypotheses using the imperfect subjunctive in the if-clause and the conditional tense in the main clause. If students began to use the simple present tense,

the teacher could have a brief teachable moment in which students are reminded, via metalinguistic clues, that they need to use verb forms other than the present tense: Sample metalinguistic clues: *Do you mean to use present tense? Do you remember how we express hypotheses in Spanish? In which part of the sentence is the imperfect subjunctive used?* [9]

Remember to provide the learner with sufficient space to reflect on the CF and formulate a subsequent utterance. As discussed in Chapter 2, avoid relying on the IRE interactional pattern to confirm learner's repaired utterances, but rather respond to the content of the message to indicate that the misunderstanding in the original message has been resolved by means of the repair. For example, if the student is able to self-correct in the example provided above, the teacher might then respond to the content of the message:

S: [repaired utterance]: If I had more time, I would travel around the world.

T: I would love to travel also! What places would you most like to see?

- **Reformulation:** A reformulation is best when the learner would not be able to repair the utterance, even with teacher assistance, but a reformulated reply is necessary in the following contexts:

(1) To move the interaction or discussion forward, especially when learners are experiencing difficulty. You might provide a recast by responding to the learner utterance and repairing the error, which some call a *didactic recast*, as in:

S: If I had more time, I will travel around the world.

T: Oh, if you had more time, you would travel around the world.

However, remember that recasts can be purely *conversational recasts* and not provided to correct an utterance:

S: If I had more time, I would travel around the world.

T: Interesting! That would sure take a lot of time and money!

(2) To provide language that the learner does not know but needs to continue the interaction (i.e., particularly in the case of vocabulary/expressions):

S: I don't agree with that. The issue is... well, it has a lot of parts.. not sure how to say it...

T: You mean it's complex?

S: Yes! It's complex, so I think that...

(3) To ***foreshadow*** new structures. For example, in a beginning-level class that has been speaking only in the present tense, you could begin to use some past tense verbs in recasts when this time frame would be the most appropriate to use but learners have not studied it yet. The desired outcome would be that learners would begin to notice the new form so that whenever they focus on the form, it will already be somewhat familiar to them:

---

[9] A body of research has revealed that instructors of advanced-level literature classes often miss opportunities to integrate advanced-level grammatical forms appropriately when they are needed given the context of text-based discussions (Donato & Brooks, 2004; Mantero, 2006; Polio & Zyzik, 2009). These classes offer an effective context for teachable moments when students could be reminded about using a form that they learned earlier, but now in more of an authentic context where it serves meaning-making and self-expression (e.g., the imperfect subjunctive and conditional tense in Spanish for expressing hypotheses within an argument).

S: I wake up at 5:00 every morning.

T: Every morning? That's early! Did you wake up at 5:00 this morning?

In the context of foreshadowing grammar, teachers should remember that (1) learners can understand more than they can say, (2) new structures and vocabulary can be made comprehensible in the context of prior knowledge, and (3) introducing new forms in a meaningful context before turning attention to grammatical analysis is consistent with the approach advocated in the text—a contextualized approach to language teaching and to grammar instruction (see Chapter 4).

Rehearsing the Practice (See this chapter's Appendix A, External Mediational Tools #6a, #6b, #6c)

The following tasks provide novice teachers with practice in making decisions about when and how to provide CF in the classroom.

1. Below are four different scenarios that could occur in your language classroom. For each, decide whether you would or would not provide CF, and if you would provide it, which CF strategy you would implement and why. Justify your decision and choice of strategy. Use Figure 6.2 to mediate your decision-making.

   a. The class is engaged in a follow-up task to a pair activity in which they are reporting back the results. A learner is confused about indirect discourse (i.e., reporting what someone said) and asks for assistance from the teacher. This structure is one on which the class has focused before.

   b. The class is participating in a lively discussion about an authentic text. A learner is making errors with some verbs in past tense, although none of them impact meaning of the message. The errors do not seem to be widespread among the other learners.

   c. The class is sharing what happened to them over the weekend. A learner needs some vocabulary that he or she does not know to express intended meaning and solicits help from the teacher.

   d. The class is engaged in a discussion about a current event or an event that happened at school. A learner has expressed an opinion and there is a long lull in the discussion—no one else has volunteered to contribute an idea.

2. Select two of the scenarios above for which you selected CF, and for each, script out a possible interaction that could exemplify the situation. The interaction should occur in the target language that you teach or are preparing to teach in the future. Include what both the teacher and student(s) say in the exchange. Then role play your interaction with peers or colleagues. If you are enrolled in a practicum course, your instructor might provide some coaching during the role play to refine your CF moves and then ask you to revise your performance of the CF interaction.

3. Now practice making decisions about CF and implementing CF in a lesson that you are teaching, either as an in-service teacher, a student teacher or intern, or a teacher candidate practicing with peers in a practicum course. If possible, either record the lesson or ask a colleague or peer to observe it. Later, discuss effectiveness of the CF you provided (or decisions you made regarding CF) with your colleague or peer. If you

could teach this lesson again, what changes would you make your CF decision-making and why?

Assessing the Practice

Use Rubric #6 in this chapter's Appendix B to self-assess your use of CF. As an alternative, you could ask a colleague to observe your integration of CF into a lesson and provide feedback using the rubric.

Putting the Practice into a Larger Context: Instructional Goals and Challenges

In this chapter, the HLTP of providing oral corrective feedback to improve learner performance has been deconstructed. Providing feedback within a sociocultural approach is critical to mediating language learning, development, and performance, given that

- learners themselves report wanting to have feedback and assistance regarding the errors they make;

- within the sociocultural framework (see discussions in earlier chapters), our linguistic, cognitive, and social development are constructed through interaction with mediational tools and with others; and

- providing feedback within a dialogic approach contributes to the building of a discourse community in which the teacher and learners collaborate to make meaning and improve performance (see Chapter 2).

Beyond mediating learners' language, this HLTP supports contemporary views regarding the role of assessment and learning as well as addressing larger teaching challenges. First, current approaches to assessment stress

- the need to integrate instruction and assessment in a "seamless fashion" so that assessment informs learning and instruction (Adair-Hauck, Glisan, & Troyan, 2013; Wiggins, 1998; Wiggins & McTighe, 2005);

- the critical role of modeling and feedback in a learning culture (Hattie & Timperley, 2007; Shepard, 2000); and

- the role of teacher as a joint problem solver/mediator with the learner instead of as an external assessor of learner performance (Poehner, 2007).

Providing oral CF in a dialogic fashion integrates learning and informal assessment in an integrated fashion in which teacher feedback and scaffolding serve to enhance student learning and performance, in a similar way to that of co-construction of form, as presented in Chapter 4. Hence, this HLTP, in addition to the other practices presented earlier, all of which involve teacher feedback and scaffolding in some way, reflects the current view regarding the pivotal role of modeling, feedback, scaffolding, and informal assessment within the teaching and learning process.

Secondly, offering oral CF prompts teachers to work within their learners' ZPDs, a process that is critical to mediating student learning within a sociocultural approach, as has been suggested throughout the practices presented in this text. As Lantolf (2000) explains, "the ZPD is not a physical place situated in time and space" (p. 17), nor is it a one-way transmission of knowledge from the teacher to learners. Rather, this concept helps explain how social interaction and guided assistance mediate learners' language learning and development (refer back to Chapter 4). To provide oral CF, the teacher must observe and listen to the utterances of learners as they interact in oral tasks and discussions with the other members of the classroom discourse community. These consistent opportunities provide valuable evidence to the teacher that can be used as he or she makes decisions regarding the types of CF that would be most effective in enhancing learning and performance.

Thirdly, this HLTP also addresses larger teaching challenges, some of which have been presented in earlier chapters. Providing oral CF enlists student participation since it is given within a dialogic framework, as opposed to the absence of participation in an approach to feedback that is one-way (i.e., teacher to learner). Dialogic feedback prompts learners to actively think about what they are learning and saying, to understand underlying relationships between content and skills, and remember the concepts or skills about which they are actively thinking (Kennedy, 2016; Willingham, 2009). Further, this HLTP exposes student thinking by involving learners in dialogue and co-construction of meaning as they work to make their performance more meaningful and accurate (Kennedy, 2016).

Finally, this HLTP also prompts teachers to engage in constant self-reflection as they pay attention to student performance and find ways to improve it through CF and dialogic interaction with learners.

For Further Reading

Adair-Hauck, B., Glisan, E. W., & Troyan, F. J. (2013). *Implementing Integrated Performance Assessment.* Alexandria, VA: American Council on the Teaching of Foreign Languages.

Aljaafreh, A., & Lantolf, J. P. (1994). Negative feedback as regulation and second language learning in the Zone of Proximal Development. *The Modern Language Journal, 78,* 465–483.

Brown, A. (2009). Students' and teachers' perspectives of effective foreign language teaching: A comparison of ideals. *The Modern Language Journal, 93,* 46–60. doi: 10.1111/j.1540-4781.2009.00827.x

Brown, N. A. (2009). Argumentation and debate in foreign language instruction: A case for the traditional classroom facilitating advanced-level language uptake. *The Modern Language Journal, 92,* 534–549.

Davin, K.J. (2013). Integration of dynamic assessment and instructional conversations to promote development and improve assessment in the language classroom. *Language Teaching Research 17*(3), 303–322.

Donato, R., & Brooks, F. B. (2004). Literary discussions and advanced speaking functions: Researching the (dis)connection. *Foreign Language Annals, 37,* 183–199.

Ellis, R. (2009). Corrective feedback and teacher development. *L2 Journal, 1,* 3–18.

Gibbons, P. (2015). *Scaffolding language, scaffolding learning* (2nd ed.). Portsmouth, NH: Heinemann.

Gurzynski-Weiss, L. (2016). Factors influencing Spanish instructors' in-class feedback decisions. *The Modern Language Journal, 100,* 255–275.

Hattie, J., & Timperley, H. (2007). The power of feedback. *Review of Educational Research, 77,* 81–112.

Kennedy, M. (2016). Parsing the practice of teaching. *Journal of Teacher Education, 67*(1), 6–17.

Lantolf, J. P. (2000). Introducing sociocultural theory. In J. P. Lantolf (Ed.), *Sociocultural theory and second language learning* (pp. 1–26). Oxford, UK: Oxford University Press.

Lantolf, J. P., & Poehner, M. E. (2011a). Dynamic assessment in the classroom: Vygotskian praxis for second language development: Bringing the past into the future. *Language Teaching Research, 15*, 323–340. doi: 10.1177/1362168810383328

Lantolf, J. P., & Poehner, M. E. (2011b). *Dynamic assessment in the foreign language classroom: A teacher's guide* (2nd ed.). University Park, PA: CALPER Publications.

Li, S. (2010). The effectiveness of corrective feedback in SLA: A meta-analysis. *Language Learning, 60,* 309–365.

Lightbown, P., & Spada, N. (2013). *How languages are learned* (4th ed.). New York: Oxford University Press.

Loewen, S., & Philp, J. (2006). Recasts in the adult English L2 classroom: Characteristics, explicitness, and effectiveness. *The Modern Language Journal, 90,* 536–556.

Long, M. H. (1996). The role of the linguistic environment in second language acquisition. In W. Ritchie & T. Bhatia (Eds.), *Handbook of Second Language Acquisition* (pp. 413–468). New York: Academic Press.

Lyster, R., & Ranta, L. (1997). Corrective feedback and learner uptake. *Studies in Second Language Acquisition, 19,* 37–61.

Lyster, R., & Saito, K. (2010). Oral feedback in classroom SLA: A meta-analysis. *Studies in Second Language Acquisition, 32,* 265–302.

Lyster, R., Saito, K., & Sato, M. (2013). Oral corrective feedback in second language classrooms. *Language Teaching, 46,* pp. 1–40. doi: 10.1017/S0261444812000365

Mantero, M. (2006). Applied literacy in second language education: (Re)Framing discourse in literature-based classrooms. *Foreign Language Annals, 39,* 99–114.

National Standards in Foreign Language Education Project (NSFLEP). (2015). *World-Readiness standards for learning languages.* Alexandria, VA: Author.

Poehner, M. E. (2007). Beyond the test: L2 dynamic assessment and the transcendence of mediated learning. *The Modern Language Journal, 91,* 323–340.

Polio, C., & Zyzik, E. (2009). Don Quixote meets *ser* and *estar*: Multiple perspectives on language learning in Spanish literature classes. *The Modern Language Journal, 93,* 550–569.

Ranta, L., & Lyster, R. (2007). A cognitive approach to improving immersion students' oral language abilities: The Awareness–Practice–Feedback sequence. In R. DeKeyser (Ed.), *Practice in a second language: Perspectives from applied linguistics and cognitive psychology* (pp. 141–160). Cambridge, UK: Cambridge University Press.

Rassaei, E. (2014). Scaffolded feedback, recasts, and L2 development: A sociocultural perspective. *The Modern Language Journal, 98,* 417–431.

Schegloff, E. A., Jefferson, G., & Sacks, H. (1977). The preference for self-correction in the organization of repair in conversation. *Language, 53,* 361–382.

Schulz, R. (1996). Focus on form in the foreign language classroom: Students' and teachers' views on error correction and the role of grammar. *Foreign Language Annals, 29,* 343–364. doi:10.1111/j.1944-9720.1996.tb01247.x

Sheen, Y. (2007). The effect of focused written corrective feedback and language aptitude on ESL learners' acquisition of articles. *TESOL Quarterly, 41,* 255–283.

Sheen, Y., & Ellis, R. (2011). Corrective feedback in language teaching. In E. Hinkel (Ed.), *Handbook of research in second language teaching and learning: Volume II* (pp. 593–610). New York: Routledge.

Shepard, L. A. (2000). The role of assessment in a learning culture. *Educational Researcher, 29*(7), 4–14.

Shrum, J. L., & Glisan, E. W. (2016). *Teacher's handbook: Contextualized language instruction.* 5th ed. Cengage Learning: Boston, MA.

Vygotsky, L. S. (1978). *Mind in society: The development of higher psychological processes.* Cambridge, MA: Harvard University Press.

Vygotsky, L. S. (1986). *Thought and language.* Cambridge, MA: MIT Press.

Walqui, A. & Van Lier, L. (2010). *Scaffolding the academic success of adolescent English language learners.* San Francisco, CA: WestEd.

Wiggins, G. (1998). *Educative assessment.* San Francisco: Jossey-Bass.

Wiggins, G., & McTighe, J. (2005). *Understanding by design.* Alexandria, VA: Association for Supervision and Curriculum Development.

Willingham, D. T. (2009). *Why don't students like school? A cognitive scientist answers questions about how the mind works and what it means for the classroom.* San Francisco, CA: Jossey-Bass.

Appendix A

External Mediational Tool #6a: Providing Oral Corrective Feedback to Improve Learner Performance: Types of Teacher Feedback in Oral Interactions

1. *Explicit correction:* Teacher provides the correct form or indicates that what the learner said was incorrect: *Oh, you mean...; You should say...*

2. *Recasts:* Teacher responds to the learner and rephrases part of the student's utterance so as to correct it, but in a more implicit way without directly saying that the form was incorrect: *S: I'm *interesting to see the movie. T: Oh, you're interested in seeing the movie.*

3. *Clarification request:* Teacher indicates that there is a problem in comprehensibility or accuracy or both and that a reformulation is required: *Excuse me? What do you mean?*

4. *Metalinguistic feedback*: Teacher indicates that there is an error by asking questions about what the student said and/or providing grammatical metalanguage that points out the nature of the error: *Are you referring to present or past?; You need a past-tense verb.*

5. *Elicitation:* Teacher elicits the correct form by repeating exactly what the learner said up to the point of the error: *S: I will go to the concert this night. T: I will go to the concert...?* Teachers could also ask questions to elicit the form, as in: *How do we say X in French?*

6. *Repetition:* Teacher repeats the learner's incorrect utterance with rising intonation to highlight the error: *S: I goed to the gym this morning. T: I goed?*

External Mediational Tool #6b: Range of Common CF Types

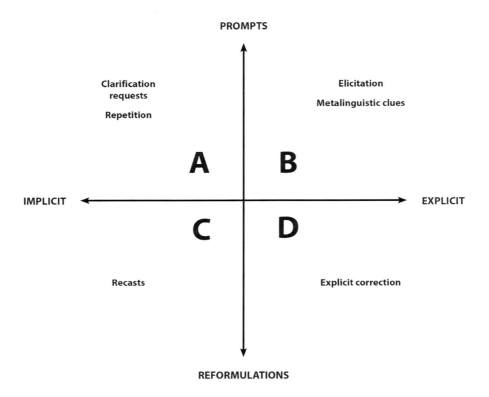

External Mediational Tool #6c: Providing Oral Corrective Feedback to Improve Learner Performance: CF Decision-Making

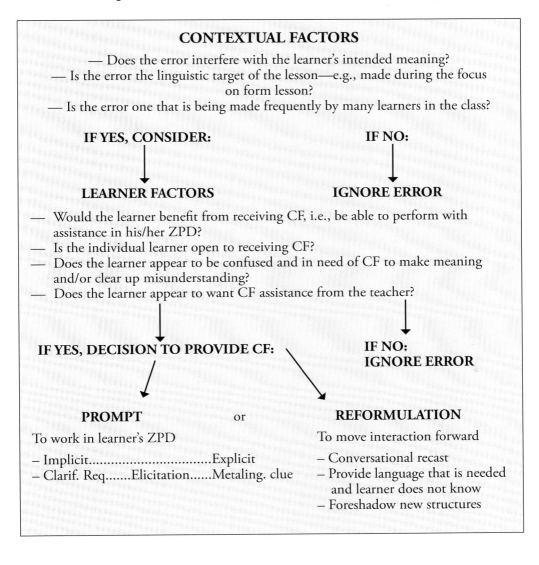

CONTEXTUAL FACTORS

— Does the error interfere with the learner's intended meaning?
— Is the error the linguistic target of the lesson—e.g., made during the focus on form lesson?
— Is the error one that is being made frequently by many learners in the class?

IF YES, CONSIDER: **IF NO:**

LEARNER FACTORS   **IGNORE ERROR**

— Would the learner benefit from receiving CF, i.e., be able to perform with assistance in his/her ZPD?
— Is the individual learner open to receiving CF?
— Does the learner appear to be confused and in need of CF to make meaning and/or clear up misunderstanding?
— Does the learner appear to want CF assistance from the teacher?

IF YES, DECISION TO PROVIDE CF: **IF NO:**
                                                        IGNORE ERROR

PROMPT   or   **REFORMULATION**
To work in learner's ZPD   To move interaction forward

– Implicit................................Explicit   – Conversational recast
– Clarif. Req.......Elicitation......Metaling. clue   – Provide language that is needed and learner does not know
                                                        – Foreshadow new structures

Appendix B

RUBRIC: HLTP #6: Providing Oral Corrective Feedback to Improve Learner Performance

	EXCEEDS EXPECTATIONS	MEETS EXPECTATIONS	DEVELOPING	UNACCEPTABLE
Use of Contextual Factors in Making CF Decision	Teacher focuses on whether error interferes with meaning, on whether error is the linguistic target of lesson, and on whether error is made frequently by learners.	Teacher focuses on whether error interferes with meaning and on whether error is the linguistic target of lesson.	Teacher focuses on whether error is the linguistic target of lesson.	Teacher disregards contextual factors in making decisions about CF.
Use of Learner Factors in Making CF Decision	Teacher focuses on whether learner would benefit from CF, is open to receiving CF, wants to receive CF, and whether learner is confused.	Teacher focuses on whether learner would benefit from CF and whether learner is confused.	Teacher focuses on whether learner is confused.	Teacher disregards learner factors in making decisions about CF.
Use of Implicit vs. Explicit CF	Teacher provides graduated assistance beginning with implicit and proceeding to explicit as necessary.	Teacher provides a balance of implicit and explicit CF but not in a graduated fashion.	Teacher provides some implicit CF but primarily explicit CF and not in a graduated fashion.	Teacher provides only explicit CF and/or provides excessive amounts of CF.
Use of Prompts vs. Reformulations	Teacher uses a balance of prompts and reformulations as necessary to mediate learning and performance within learners' ZPDs.	Teacher uses more prompts than reformulations to mediate learning and performance within learners' ZPDs.	Teacher uses more reformulations than prompts. Learners may not notice the correction in all cases.	Teacher tends to use either prompts or reformulations but not both; selection of one or the other does not appear to have a justification.

	EXCEEDS EXPECTATIONS	MEETS EXPECTATIONS	DEVELOPING	UNACCEPTABLE
Affective Factors	Learners seek out CF from teacher and participate in the dialogic approach to CF. No evidence of anxiety in classroom community.	Majority of learners participate in the dialogic approach to CF. No evidence of anxiety in classroom community.	Only half of the class participates in the dialogic approach to CF. A few individuals may demonstrate some anxiety.	Learners demonstrate anxiety when given CF and/ or hesitate to speak unless their utterances are totally error free.

CHAPTER 7

Putting HLTPs into Practice: A Cycle of Enactment

"Rehearsal...addresses the dual challenge of preparing beginning teachers to actually be able to do teaching when they get into classrooms, and preparing them to do teaching that is more socially and intellectually ambitious than the current norm."
—Lampert, Franke, Kazemi, Ghousseini, Turrou, Beasley, Cunard, & Crowe, 2013

Throughout this text, six high-leverage teaching practices have been examined in light of current research and theory, deconstructed into instructional moves to make them visible to novice teachers, and put into practice through rehearsal and self-assessment. Further, they have been placed into a larger educational context that prompts teachers to reflect on how these practices address instructional goals, issues, and challenges. The purpose of this final chapter is to present an instructional model that can be implemented in a cyclical fashion to learn how to enact each of the HLTPs presented in this text. This **cycle of enactment** leads teachers through six specific phases of instruction that are used in an iterative fashion to deconstruct, observe, analyze, plan, and rehearse the practices, in preparation for ultimately enacting and assessing the practices with their own classes. Although the HLTP literature addresses almost exclusively ways in which novice teachers (i.e., teacher candidates enrolled in a teacher preparation program) learn to enact the practices, the cycle presented in this text accounts for ways in which both novice teachers and in-service teachers can learn to enact them. Accordingly, it acknowledges that skill in enacting specific HLTPs might occur in the professional development of a teacher once he or she assumes total responsibility for language learners in a classroom rather than only taking place in the university teacher preparation program.

This chapter presents a discussion of the model for enacting the HLTPs and establishes the role of the various partners in this collaborative cycle:

- *Novice teacher (NT)*, defined as either:

    (1) a teacher candidate in a university program of teacher preparation who is learning HLTPs in the teaching or field experience course and who is not yet employed in a PK-16 classroom, e.g., an undergraduate or post-baccalaureate student working toward teacher certification; or

    (2) a teacher who is employed in a PK-16 language classroom and who is learning HLTPs in a teaching course, e.g., a student with a teaching position and who is also enrolled in a Master's degree program.

- *In-service teacher (IST),* defined as a teacher in a PK-16 language classroom who is not enrolled in a university teaching course but is learning about HLTPs through another avenue such as a professional development workshop or self-directed learning (reading about the practices either alone or with colleagues).

- *Teacher educator (TE)*, defined as an instructor of a teaching course or field experience as part of the university teacher preparation program, who is presenting HLTPs to students enrolled in one of these courses/experiences. TEs guide planning, coach rehearsal, facilitate enactment, and assess the performance of teachers as they learn to do the work of teaching as exemplified through the practices.

- *Mentor teacher (MT)*, defined as a PK-16 language teacher who is supervising the NT in a field experience such as pre-student teaching, student teaching, or an internship experience. This individual may also be called a *cooperating teacher*. MTs demonstrate these practices in their classes and support the learning of these practices by novice teachers.

- PK-16 students who perform cognitively demanding tasks.

- Peers of novice teachers and colleagues of in-service teachers who provide feedback to each another and learn about HLTPs together.

Situating HLTPs within Practice

A practice-based approach to teacher preparation is based on the notion that novice teachers need opportunities to rehearse and experiment, with coaching and support, the complex moves that make up HLTPs. The literature on practice-based teacher education stresses the need to ground HLTPs in specific **instructional activities (IAs)** that limit the context of the practice so that novices can draw upon specific knowledge and moves as they make judgments about how to interact with their students within the construct of the high-leverage practice (Lampert, Franke, Kazemi, Ghousseini, Turrou, Beasley, Cunard, & Crowe, 2013; Lampert & Graziani, 2009). Novices typically learn these IAs first in the teaching course and then transfer them to enactment in the actual school setting with real students. Troyan, Davin, and Donato (2013) found that IAs that pre-service teachers selected themselves were not always the appropriate context for the HLTP being practiced, that teacher educators needed to provide scaffolding in this regard, and that over time pre-service teachers were able to decide on their own which practice or groups of practices are relevant to specific types of IAs. Figure 7.1 depicts sample IAs in which the HLTPs presented in this text might be situated.

In practice-based teacher preparation, teaching practices—principles that guide teachers' judgment in the use of these practices (e.g., designing clear instructional goals, knowing learners as individuals), and knowledge of the content area (e.g., target language, cultural knowledge, pragmatics)—are used in an interrelated fashion and in relationships among the teacher, students, and the content/skills to be learned (Lampert, 2001). Further, improving teaching performance requires a "back and forth between applying routine procedures and learning *how* to use those procedures appropriately in different situations" (Hatano & Inagaki, 1986; c.f. Lampert, et al., 2013, p. 228). Through a cycle of **deliberate practice**, novice teachers receive both instruction and practice in the company of others (e.g., peers, more accomplished teachers, teacher educators), which helps them "develop an organized system for knowing when, why, and how aspects of their competency are relevant to any particular situation" (Lampert, et al., 2013, p. 228). In this "cycle of enactment and investigation," novice teachers experience iterative rounds of investigating teaching and enacting it within the context of the instructional activities (see earlier discussion) (Grossman & McDonald, 2008; Lampert, et al., 2013; Lampert & Graziani, 2009).

HLTP	Instructional Activities (IAs)
Facilitating Target Language Comprehensibility	• Telling a story by making it comprehensible and actively involving learners • Introducing new vocabulary or grammatical structures within an engaging context
Building a Classroom Discourse Community	• Facilitating a whole-class discussion based on a shared context such as an important school or local community event, popular media, or an important social issue.
Guiding Learners to Interpret and Discuss Authentic Texts	• Guiding learners through an authentic reading by means of a series of tasks that elicit literal comprehension followed by interpretation of the text • Leading a class discussion based on an authentic text
Focusing on Form in a Dialogic Context through PACE	• Presenting an authentic story from the target language culture(s) that features a grammatical structure occurring naturally within a meaningful context • Guiding learners in dialoguing about and co-constructing grammatical form based on its meaning and function in a story leading to the development of a conceptual understanding of the form beyond a grammatical rule
Focusing on Cultural Products, Practices, and Perspectives in a Dialogic Context	• Making use of engaging images of a cultural product or practice as a launching point for identification and hypotheses about cultural perspectives • Making use of informational texts or data of various kinds for reflecting on the cultural meanings of products and/or practices
Providing Oral Corrective Feedback to Improve Learner Performance	• Facilitating a whole-class discussion in which oral teacher feedback plays a role to support student speaking and to move the conversation forward • Conducting an oral extension activity in which learners use a grammatical structure to make meaning and are guided by teacher feedback

Figure 7.1. **HLTPs Situated within IAs**

Cyclical Model for Enacting HLTPs

The model proposed here is based on the work of Lampert and colleagues (2013) and Troyan, Davin, and Donato (2013). The cycle of enactment features the following 6 phases that occur in an iterative fashion:

1. Deconstruction of the HLTP

2. Observation and analysis of the HLTP

3. Planning to enact the practice

4. Rehearsal and coaching

5. Enactment of practice in the PK-16 classroom

6. Assessment of enactment by one or more of the collaborative partners, including self-assessment and reflection.

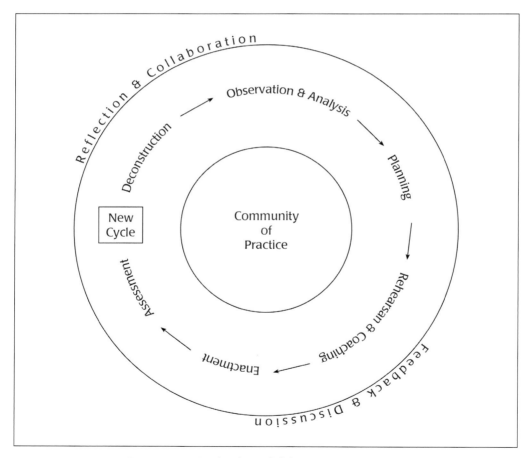

Figure 7.2. Cyclical Model for Enacting HLTPs

It is essential to recognize that, although this cyclical model features 6 phases that are carried out in a particular order, the cycle is *iterative*—that is, teachers can go back and forth between phases before proceeding to the next one. For example, if NTs or ISTs are finding it challenging to analyze the HLTP moves they observe in the observation and analysis phase, they may need to return to the deconstruction phase for further reflection, discussion, and, if needed, direct instruction. Similarly, if teachers experience difficulty in the rehearsal phase, they may need to return to planning the IA and make changes to enable the rehearsal and ultimate enactment of the practice to be more successful, before they continue to the next phase. Thus, the phases do not occur in a static linear manner but reflect back-and-forth movement as learning is mediated and leads to successful enactment of the HLTP. Further, this iterative feature of the cycle aids teachers in developing flexibility in the use of the practices to fit the unique PK-16 instructional contexts in which they operate.

This cycle stands in sharp contrast to traditional teacher training in which NTs learn about teaching in a university preparation program largely through transmission of information. Instead, this model positions the teacher's interactions within the social and cultural contexts as being central in learning the work of teaching (McDonald, Kazemi, & Kavanagh, 2013; Troyan & Peercy, 2016). It should be noted that the cycle can be implemented with both NTs and ISTs, as illustrated in Figure 7.3, which depicts the avenues through which each phase can be undertaken depending on whether or not

	Novice Teachers	**In-service Teachers**
Deconstruction	• Teaching class: analyze transcripts of lessons and/or video recorded lessons	• Literature about HLTP • In collaboration with colleague • PD workshop
Observation & Analysis	• School site or teaching class • Video recorded lessons	• School site
Planning	• With peers in teaching class	• With colleagues at school site • With peers in PD workshop
Rehearsal & Coaching	• Teaching class, coached by TE	• School site, coached by more experienced colleague • PD workshop, coached by workshop leader, department chairperson, or mentor
Enactment	• School site • Teaching class, if only option	• School site
Assessment	• By TE, mentor teacher, peers, self	• By colleagues, self, PD workshop leader, if possible

Figure 7.3. **Enactment Cycle for Novice and In-service Teachers**

teachers are learning HLTPs in a university methodology course or as a professional development endeavor.

Phase One: Deconstructing the Practice

In the first phase, teachers deconstruct the practice as demonstrated in each HLTP presented in this text so that the individual instructional moves are made visible to them. NTs engage in this activity in a teaching class or field experience class as part of their teacher preparation program. ISTs might complete this first phase as they read about the practice (i.e., in a text such as this one), perhaps in collaboration with a colleague, and/or by participating in a professional development workshop in which this deconstruction would occur. As part of the deconstruction, both NTs and ISTs could also analyze transcripts and rate video recorded exemplars of the HLTP, as in the Troyan, Davin, and Donato (2013) study. The rubrics included with each HLTP could also be used by teachers in deconstructing the practice as they consider the criteria that contribute to making each practice effective.

Phase Two: Observing and Analyzing the Practice

In the second phase, after deconstruction of the practice, teachers observe the HLTP in action in an instructional activity. Ideally, this would occur at the school site in a language class taught by an MT. However, if this is not possible, the teacher educator, as the instructor of the teaching or practicum class, could demonstrate the practice in the class of NTs. If videotaping the class is possible, the TE could model the HLTP to the entire class who act as students and later review the video with the class, focusing on the pedagogical moves of the HLTP. In this way, students' attention is not divided by being required to act simultaneously as students and as reflective practitioners.

ISTs could either observe the HLTP in the class of a more experienced colleague or watch video recorded exemplars of it. Whether or not NTs observe the HLTP at a school site, TEs may find it advantageous to demonstrate the practice in the teaching class so that the group of NTs can engage in discussion about it together. In this case, as suggested by Troyan, Davin, and Donato (2013), NTs should not be required to play the role of PK-16 students so that they can focus on observing, analyzing, and recalling the specific instructional moves illustrated in the model lesson. It has been found that when NTs are called upon to play the role of students, their attention shifts from analysis of the complex practice to a focus on their feelings and experiences as students. What can be done if the practice is demonstrated in a practicum class is to select a few NTs to act as students as needed in the lesson while the majority of the class observes and analyzes the various moves of the practice. In this way, student observers are not required to divide their attention and simultaneously process the model lesson as a student and teacher. If possible and the appropriate clearances are secured, inviting a few language students to the class to participate in lessons is also a way to free the NTs of the burden of assuming two roles—student and observer. As depicted in Figure 7.2, the first two phases feature *reflection* and *collaboration* as the teachers, their peers or colleagues, TEs, and MTs work together to form an understanding of the instructional moves involved in each practice.

Phases Three and Four: Planning and Rehearsing the Practice

Phases three and four involve teachers preparing to teach the practice within a specific and clearly identified instructional activity and then rehearsing it in a class of their peers. As indicated earlier, novices have greater success if they receive guidance regarding the type of IA to design that would be most appropriate for the enactment of the HLTP. Novices can work together to decide upon an IA that will support the particular HLTP being learned during which time they receive guidance, feedback, and final approval from the TE. Rather than invent a freestanding IA, a preferable way to select an IA is to consult the curriculum of the class and decide what objectives and tasks require the enactment of a particular HLTP (or, in some cases, a combination of HLTPs). They then rehearse their lesson with the class of their peers. The rehearsal phase is critical in enabling NTs to practice the HLTP in "a controlled environment that provides time for reflection and careful deliberation" (Troyan & Peercy, 2016, p. 5; see also Ball & Forzani, 2009; Grossman & McDonald, 2008). From a sociocultural perspective, rehearsals are thought to be a venue for **dialogic mediation**, a form of social interaction that facilitates understanding of concepts (Johnson, 2009; Troyan & Peercy, 2016; Vygotsky, 1978). As Troyan and Davin (2015) have found, novices may be able to state what a specific HLTP is by providing an academic definition but may be unable to enact that practice with real students in PK-16 classrooms. The interactive dialogue afforded by rehearsals serves as a tool for mediating the learning of teachers, i.e., enabling them to develop a deep understanding of how to enact the high-leverage complex practice (Troyan & Peercy, 2016).[10] Hence it is of the utmost importance that TEs assist novices in understanding the role of rehearsal in shaping their development of deep conceptual knowledge about the HLTP and its enactment with learners.

According to Lampert and colleagues (2013), the way in which rehearsal is accomplished is different from the microteaching that is often done with peers in the teaching class. The TE serves as coach by (1) stopping the lesson to coach the novice teacher in the moves used to respond to student action, (2) asking the NT to revise and re-teach a segment of the practice based on coaching, and (3) leading a discussion among the novice teachers to consider the effectiveness of the various instructional moves. What is important is that the NTs understand that peer teaching is not a finalized performance to be observed, as if it were a theatrical production, but a site for mediation, coaching, and discussion. From this perspective, the rehearsal is a place for immediate intervention and ongoing feedback in a community of practice that provides a venue for exploring the work of ambitious teaching. Accordingly, "as a member of this community of practice, the novice develops his or her identity as a teacher with ambitious goals for all students" (Lampert, et al., 2013, p. 230). ISTs might engage in rehearsal with a group of colleagues, particularly if at least one of them is familiar with the HLTP and can offer coaching and guidance. Subsequent to the feedback and discussion, teachers would then revise their lessons to prepare them for the enactment in the next phase.

Phases Five and Six: Enacting and Assessing the Practice

In the fifth and sixth phases, teachers enact the practice with learners in an actual PK-16 language class in terms of the IA that they have planned and rehearsed and their

---

[10] There are other tools that mediate learning of the HLTPs, such as the External Mediational Tools included in this text. See Troyan and Davin (2015) for a discussion of additional types of mediational tools useful in the enactment cycle.

performance is then assessed. Teachers could use the EMTs provided in each chapter to mediate their enactment of each HLTP—these could be used as note cards or "short-cut" reminders of key aspects of the practices to remember as they enact them. Ideally the TE would observe this lesson and assess the NT's performance using the rubrics that accompany each practice presented in this text. Additionally, NTs could self-assess using the rubrics, and could then engage in feedback and discussion with their TEs and even with their peers if the lesson is recorded. In-service teachers would enact the practice with learners in their own classes and could either record the lesson and/or invite a colleague to observe it, after which assessment, feedback, and discussion could occur. As illustrated in Figure 7.2, the planning, rehearsal and coaching, enactment, and assessment phases are supported within feedback and discussion through which teachers receive scaffolding, have opportunities to rehearse multiple times, and engage in meaningful dialogue with their collaborative partners.

Challenges of Implementing the Enactment Cycle

Two challenges of implementing the enactment cycle have been documented in the literature (Troyan, Davin, & Donato, 2013) and alluded to above. First, NTs often have preconceived ideas of what peer teaching involves and are not prepared for the emotions associated with being coached during a public performance of an HLTP, in particular being interrupted or stopped at particular points in the rehearsal. NTs will often complain and even sometimes get angry at being interrupted by the TE, thinking that assessment of performance is given only at the end of a presentation rather than during it. NTs need to be told that moment-to-moment coaching is involved in all types of professional practice, such as in developing athletic ability, playing a musical instrument, or working in a theater company with a director. Additionally, NTs need to understand that coaching during the enactment of professional practice is commonplace in many professional communities, for example, learning to be a physician, a pilot, or a clinical counselor, and is a necessary part of what it means to develop professional expertise. If students understand this orientation to the rehearsal, they will be more willing to engage in coaching experiences and will be open to direction and requests for revisions.

A second challenge, discussed above, is the need for NTs to situate the rehearsal of the specific HLTP in a relevant instructional activity (IA) that would be used in real classrooms with real students. HLTPs only make sense in instructional activities that engage students in purposeful, meaningful, and contextualized tasks. The HTLP and the IA work, therefore, in unison. The HLTP supports the enactment of the IA and the IA provides the context for the meaningful use of the HLTP. For example, a teacher cannot work on providing feedback for students' oral interaction if the topic of discussion does not prompt students to express and elaborate upon their ideas, opinions, or feelings. Increasing comprehensible target language use and interaction during instruction cannot be carried out if the learners are uninterested in what is being said or in what they are being asked to express. For this reason, care must be taken to select an IA that provides instructional authenticity and motivation for the enactment of the IA.

The two suggestions described above involve the need for NTs to learn to become contributing members of a community of practice in the way it has been described within the HLTP enactment cycle, and further, how to feel increasingly more comfortable in this role. In this regard, prior to beginning the rehearsal phase, TEs should have a discussion with NTs regarding how they will need time to become accustomed to this type of coaching model in which they may be interrupted or asked to start over again. NTs would benefit from being reassured that, as in any type of theatrical production, there are natural interruptions and multiple starts to improve performance. Undoubtedly NTs are likely to not be familiar with this approach to microteaching and will need support to gain more confidence in functioning in this type of professional community. See Chapter 2 for ideas on how to develop a discourse community; many of these strategies also apply to developing a professional community of learners as depicted in this enactment model.

Final Thoughts

This text has brought foreign language education into the national educational dialogue on practice-based teaching by

- identifying 6 high-leverage teaching practices that are fundamental to advancing language learning and performance;

- situating the practices within research and theoretical considerations;

- addressing commonly asked questions that language teachers often raise about various aspects of teaching practice;

- deconstructing each HLTP in detail to make the instructional moves visible to novice and in-service language teachers;

- suggesting specific ways to rehearse and enact the practices;

- providing tools for mediating the learning of HLTPs (e.g., EMTs) and for assessing and self-assessing the enactment of the practices (e.g., assessment rubrics for each HLTP);

- proposing a cyclical model for enacting HLTPs that highlights the roles of various collaborative partners who engage in dialogic mediation and together form a community of practice, and

- situating the HLTPs within larger educational challenges, goals and contexts that educators face in today's classrooms.

Practice-based teaching has much potential to move language teaching and learning forward in the coming decades. Undoubtedly there is much to be learned about HLTPs for foreign languages, HLTP mediational tools, and the enactment cycle as the approach presented in this text is put into action and investigated. These ideas will hopefully serve as the catalyst for on-going discussion about the value of HLTPs in the field of language education and direction for the future of practice-based teacher education.

For Further Reading

Ball, D. L., & Forzani, F. M. (2009). The work of teaching and the challenge for teacher education. *Journal of Teacher Education, 60*(5), 497–511.

Grossman, P., & McDonald, M. (2008). Redefining teaching, re-imagining teacher education. *Teachers and Teaching: Theory and practice, 15*(2), 273–289.

Hatano, G., & Inagaki, K. (1986). Two courses of expertise. In H. Stevenson, H. Azuma, & K. Hakuta (Eds.), *Child development and education in Japan* (pp. 262–272). New York, NY: Freeman.

Johnson, K. E. (2009). *Second language teacher education: A sociocultural perspective.* New York: Routledge.

Lampert, M. (2001). *Teaching problems and the problems of teaching*. New Haven, CT: Yale University Press.

Lampert, M., Franke, M. L., Kazemi, E., Ghousseini, H., Turrou, A. C., Beasley, H., Cunard, A., & Crowe, K. (2013). Keeping it complex: Using rehearsals to support novice teacher learning of ambitious teaching. *Journal of Teacher Education, 64*(3), 226–243.

Lampert, M., & Graziani, F. (2009). Instructional activities as a tool for teachers' and teacher educators' learning. *Elementary School Journal, 109*(5), 491–509.

McDonald, M., Kazemi, E., & Kavanagh, S. S. (2013). Core practices and pedagogies of teacher education: A call for a common language and collective activity. *Journal of Teacher Education, 64,* 378–386. doi: 10.1177/0022487113493807

Troyan, F. J., & Davin, K. J. (2015, June). *Pre-service L2 teachers' appropriation of praxis tools: Windows into concept development.* Paper presentation at the second annual Thinking, Doing, and Learning Conference. University of Groningen. Groningen, The Netherlands.

Troyan, F., J., Davin, K. J., & Donato, R. (2013) . Exploring a practice-based approach to foreign language teacher preparation: Work in progress. *The Canadian Modern Language Review, 69,* 154–180.

Troyan, F. J., & Peercy, M. M. (2016). Novice teachers' perspectives on learning in lesson rehearsal in second language teacher preparation. *International Multilingual Research Journal*. Advance online publication. doi: 10.1080/19313152.2016.1185908

Vygotsky, L. (1978) *Mind in society.* Cambridge, MA: Harvard University Press.